Leon Hunt is Senior Lecturer in Film
His books include *Kung Fu Cult Maste*
(2003) and *Cult British TV Comedy*
Cinemas: Exploring Transnational Cor

Sharon L is Senior Lecturer in Sociology and Communications at Brunel Uni . She is editor of *Reading Little Britain: Comedy Matters on Contempor elevision* (2010). She is also co-editor (with Michael Pickering) of *Beyond ke: The Limits of Humour* (2005, 2009) and (with Feona Attwood, Campbell and I. Q. Hunter) of *Controversial Images: Media Represent n the Edge* (2013).

Milly Wil n is Senior Lecturer in Film and TV Studies at Brunel University is the author of *The Lure of the Vampire: Gender, Fiction and Fandom fr am Stoker to Buffy* (2005) and *Celebrity: The Making of Fame* (forthcomi

SCREENING THE UNDEAD

VAMPIRES AND ZOMBIES IN FILM AND TELEVISION

EDITED BY LEON HUNT, SHARON LOCKYER AND MILLY WILLIAMSON

I.B. TAURIS

LONDON · NEW YORK

Published in 2014 by I.B.Tauris & Co Ltd
6 Salem Road, London W2 4BU
175 Fifth Avenue, New York NY 10010
www.ibtauris.com

Distributed in the United States and Canada Exclusively by Palgrave Macmillan
175 Fifth Avenue, New York NY 10010

ISBN: 978 1 84885 924 1

A full CIP record for this book is available from the British Library
A full CIP record is available from the Library of Congress

Library of Congress Catalog Card Number: available

Printed and bound in Great Britain by Page Bros, Norwich

CONTENTS

Part 2
Rewriting the Living Dead – The Zombie in Popular Culture

Part 3
Hybrid Bloodlines

ILLUSTRATIONS

CONTRIBUTORS

Stacey Abbott is Reader in Film and Television Studies at Roehampton University. She is the author of *Celluloid Vampires* (2007), *Angel: TV Milestone* (2009) and *TV Horror: Investigating the Darker Side of the Small Screen* (with Lorna Jowett, 2013), and has written on a wide range of vampire TV series, including *Dark Shadows*, *True Blood*, *Ultraviolet*, *Being Human* and *Buffy the Vampire Slayer.* She is also the editor of *The Cult TV Book* (2010) and series editor of I.B.Tauris's *Investigating Cult TV* series.

Costas Constandinides is Assistant Professor of Film Studies in the Department of Communications at the University of Nicosia, Cyprus. He is the author of *From Film Adaptation to Post-celluloid Adaptation: Rethinking the Transition of Popular Narratives and Characters across Old and New Media* (2010) and a member of the artistic committee of Cyprus Film Days International Film Festival.

Ian Cooper is an author and screenwriter. His publications include *Devil's Advocates: Witchfinder General* (2011) and *Bring Me the Head of Alfredo Garcia* (*Cultographies* series, 2011). His screenplay *Red Claw Way* is in pre-production and he has two features in development. He is currently writing a book on British horror films.

Emma Dyson is Associate Senior Lecturer in Film and Media at the University of Portsmouth, with research interests in horror and popular culture. Her 2010 doctoral thesis is entitled 'A Strange Body of Work: The Cinematic Zombie', and her published work and conference papers focus on horror film in general and zombie culture specifically.

Darren Elliott-Smith is Lecturer in Film at the University of Hertfordshire. He is currently completing his PhD thesis on New Queer Horror at Royal Holloway and has published 'Queering the Cult of Carrie: Appropriations of a Horror Icon in Charles Lum's *Indelible*' in *Scope* and '"Go be Gay for that Poor Dead Intern": Gay Conversional Fantasies in *Supernatural*' in *TV Goes to Hell: An Unofficial Road Map of Supernatural*, edited by Stacey Abbot and David Lavery (2011).

Leon Hunt is Senior Lecturer in Film and TV Studies at Brunel University. He is the author of *British Low Culture: From Safari Suits to Sexploitation* (1998), *Kung Fu Cult Masters: From Bruce Lee to Crouching Tiger* (2003), *BFI TV Classics: The League of Gentlemen* (2008) and *Cult British TV Comedy: From Reeves and Mortimer to Psychoville* (2013), and co-editor of *East Asian Cinemas: Exploring Transnational Connections on Film* (2008).

Russ Hunter is Lecturer in Film and Television in the Department of Arts at Northumbria University. He has published on a variety of aspects of Italian horror and genre cinema and is the author of *An Introduction to European Horror Cinema* (2013).

Peter Hutchings is Professor of Film Studies at Northumbria University. His books include *Hammer and Beyond: The British Horror Film* (1993), *Terence Fisher* (2002), *Dracula* (*British Film Guide* series, 2003), *The Horror Film* (*Inside Films* series, 2005) and *Historical Dictionary of Horror Cinema* (2008). He has also published on science fiction and the thriller in film and television.

Sharon Lockyer is Senior Lecturer in Sociology and Communications at Brunel University. She researches in the sociology of mediated culture, critical comedy studies and the politics of popular culture. She is editor of *Reading Little Britain: Comedy Matters on Contemporary Television* (2010), co-editor (with Michael Pickering) of *Beyond a Joke: The Limits of Humour* (2005, 2009) and co-editor (with Feona Attwood, Vincent Campbell and I. Q. Hunter) of *Controversial Images: Media*

Representations on the Edge (2013). She has published in a range of academic journals, including *Comedy Studies*; *Discourse & Society*; *Ethical Journalism Studies*; *International Journal of Social Research Methodology: Theory & Practice*; *Participations: International Journal of Audience and Reception Studies*; *Popular Communication: The International Journal of Media and Culture*; *Social Semiotics*; and *Space: The International Journal of Communication Ethics*.

Steven Rawle is Lecturer in Film Studies at York St John University, and the author of *Performance in the Cinema of Hal Hartley* (2011). His previously published work on Miike's films has appeared in *The Journal of Japanese and Korean Cinema* and *Asian Cinema*, and he has also published in *Film Criticism*. In addition, he has published book chapters about the *Ring* films, *Battlestar Galactica*, *Eternal Sunshine of the Spotless Mind* and Martin Donovan. He is also one of the co-authors of *Basics Film-Making 04: The Language of Film*.

Jeffrey Sconce is Associate Professor in Screen Cultures at Northwestern University. He is the author of *Haunted Media: Electronic Presence from Telegraphy to Television* (2000) and editor of *Sleaze Artists: Cinema at the Margins of Taste, Style, and Politics* (2007). His work on cult cinema has appeared in *Screen*, *Cineaste* and numerous anthologies.

Milly Williamson is Senior Lecturer in Film and TV Studies at Brunel University. She is the author of *The Lure of the Vampire: Gender, Fiction and Fandom from Bram Stoker to Buffy* (2005) and *Celebrity: The Making of Fame* (forthcoming). She has written a number of articles on vampire fiction and has co-edited journals on the topic.

Andy Willis is Reader in Film Studies at the University of Salford. He is the co-author of *The Cinema of Alex de la Iglesia* (2007, with Peter Buse and Nuria Triana Toribo), editor of *Film Stars: Hollywood and Beyond* (2004) and co-editor of *Defining Cult Movies: The Cultural Politics of Oppositional Taste* (2003, with Mark Jancovich, Antonio Lázaro Reboll and Julian Stringer) and *Spanish Popular Cinema* (2004, with Antonio Lázaro Reboll).

Nicola Woodham is an artist and film writer based in London. She regularly contributes to *Electric Sheep* magazine. In her written and moving image practice, she explores the dark undercurrent that exists in modern social experiences that are often framed as the everyday. Nicola is particularly interested in economies of energy and the way these are manifest in occult belief systems.

INTRODUCTION

Sometimes They Come Back – The Vampire and Zombie on Screen

Leon Hunt, Sharon Lockyer and Milly Williamson

This book examines the undead in film and television, focusing mainly on its two most prolific incarnations – the vampire and the zombie – as well as hybrids that combine characteristics of both. It evolved out of Brunel University's annual Cine-Excess conference devoted to the examination of global cult media. Cine-Excess III, held in 2009 at the Odeon Covent Garden, examined representations of, theoretical approaches to, and different cultural traditions surrounding the undead. Of the main undead archetypes, vampires have the longest history in popular fiction and the media, but at the same time, they have rarely been more current. The vampire was given a new lease of life by the success of the cult TV series *Buffy the Vampire Slayer* (US, 1997–2003), which spawned an academic industry of its own. Since *Buffy*, the vampire remains central to cult and mainstream popular culture, from the 'paranormal romance' of *Twilight* (novels, 2005–08; films, 2008–) and Charlaine Harris' 'Sookie Stackhouse' novels (2002–), adapted into the TV series *True Blood* (US, 2008–), to British cult TV shows like *Being Human* (BBC 3, 2008–), proliferation and invasion narratives such as the *Underworld* film series (US, 2003–), and those situated in remote locations such as *30 Days of Night* (US, 2007), set in a far-flung Alaskan town, *Frostbite* (Sweden, 2006), in a bleak anonymous Scandanavian town, and the critically celebrated film *Let the Right One In* (Sweden, 2008), in a grim outlying suburb of Stockholm. Its recent English language remake, *Let Me In* (US, 2010) – a production of the revived Hammer films – is set in New Mexico in the bleak winter.

The particular type of zombie discussed in this book – a mindless carnivorous walking corpse – is a much more recent creation, a hybrid of ghoul, vampire and the traditional zombie. Most modern versions of the zombie take their inspiration not from the voodoo mythology that informed early zombie cinema, but rather from George Romero's *Night of the Living Dead* (US, 1968), which established the shambling cannibalistic undead as horror cinema's prime harbinger of apocalyptic social breakdown. Romero's influence is visible in three films that seemed to renew the zombie's currency in recent horror: Danny Boyle's *28 Days Later* (UK, 2002); Zack Snyder's remake of Romero's 1978 *Dawn of the Dead* (US, 2004); and the British 'rom-zom-com' (Romantic Zombie Comedy), *Shaun of the Dead* (UK, 2004). While seemingly less available to radical reinvention than the vampire, zombies show no sign of losing their rotting grip on the popular imagination, whether as lovably mindless figures of fun or as genuine source of terror – they proliferate in literary mash-ups with Jane Austen and others and comprise the apocalyptic backdrop to the comic-turned-TV-series *The Walking Dead* (US, 2010–). *The Walking Dead* refers to its undead as 'Walkers', but as Russ Hunter reminds us in his chapter, zombies were running as early as Umberto Lenzi's *Nightmare City* (1980) – and it has recently become more common for them to be disconcertingly fast on their feet. The zombie lends itself to metaphors of the masses, standing in for consumerism (Romero's *Dawn of the Dead*), or the audience for reality TV (besieging the *Big Brother* house in Charlie Brooker's TV series *Dead Set*, Channel 4, 2008). Its recent resurgence has been seen by some as a reaction to global recession or to ongoing anxieties about global terrorism – Gregory Waller calls zombies 'un-terrorists', a telling counterpoint to fears of 'single-minded true believers able to infiltrate and wreak havoc on the everyday'.[1]

When selecting papers for this collection, it was not our intention to exclude the nearest undead rival to the vampire and zombie, the mummy. Nevertheless, it is worth saying something about why 'the beat of the cloth-wrapped feet' (as the poster for Hammer's *The Mummy's Shroud* puts it) doesn't seem to have sustained either popular or scholarly attention to the same degree. Confined to mostly repetitive studio cycles (Universal and Hammer) and some intriguing one-offs (*Blood from the Mummy's Tomb*), the bandaged undead more recently seems to have been extracted from the horror genre altogether to be

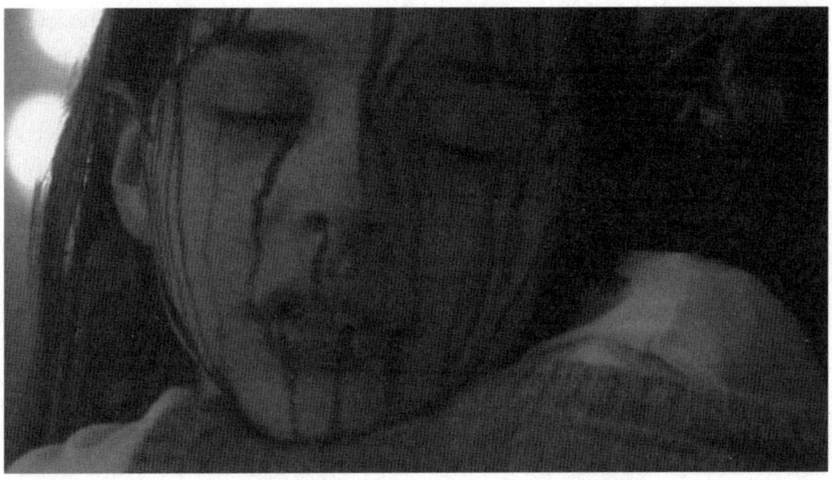

1. Hammer films return to the vampire film: *Let Me In*.

the supernatural heavy in an action-adventure-fantasy franchise.[2] The mummy, says David Flint dismissively, is 'little more than an Egyptian zombie',[3] but one might equally see it as a vampire who has aged less well and whose appetites are less clearly defined. Like the zombie, the most iconic mummies are decaying bodies that shuffle towards their victims (lacking the zombie's strength of numbers, as Flint observes), but like the vampire, the mummy is ancient and a person of social status in their lifetime (a prince or princess, a high priest), frequently motivated by desire rather than simple hunger. But given that the zombie didn't rival the vampire in popularity until it started to feed on the living, it might be that it is this 'unnatural' hunger for human flesh and/or blood that is as much the key to their popular longevity as it is to their survival onscreen. Not all vampires are necessarily 'undead'. There are 'historical' vampires like the 'Bloody Countess' Erzsebet Bathory and Peter Kurten, the 'Vampire of Dusseldorf'. George Romero's *Martin* (US, 1977) is encouraged to believe himself undead but ultimately the film appears to invite us to see his blood-drinking (aided by razor blades and syringes) as driven by a mixture of psychological disturbance and his oppressively superstitious family. In films like *Nightmare City* and *28 Days Later* (or at least in discussions of them), the category of 'zombie' seems to have been extended to mindless infected hordes who aren't technically undead. But all of the 'undead' in this book are united by their 'unnatural' hunger, whether draining a victim by classic vampiric means or tearing entrails from the living like dogs fighting over a bone.

The zombie and vampire share three interconnected proclivities: they *feed* on humanity, they *infect* humanity, and by these means they also *proliferate* (at a particularly alarming rate in the case of the zombie, whereas vampires are often given the option of draining victims to the point of actual death or feeding sparingly, thus leaving the person comparatively unharmed). But this convergence is a comparatively recent one. The pre-Romero zombie, created by voodoo, is more mindless slave than 'a vampire with a lobotomy'.[4] In *White Zombie* (US, 1932), *I Walked with a Zombie* (US, 1943) and *Plague of the Zombies* (UK, 1965) – arguably the three most highly-regarded voodoo-themed zombie films – the undead are variously unpaid labour in a mill (*White Zombie*) or tin mine (*Plague*), the imposing but seemingly harmless giant Carrefour and the unfaithful wife cursed with a 'living death' (*I Walked with a Zombie*). In other words, the pre-Romero zombie genre is one of supernatural enslavement rather than flesh-hungry besiegement (see Jeffrey Sconce in this book for a discussion of the latter motif). *Plague of the Zombies*, a characteristically full-blooded Hammer film, now seems to look ahead to the rampaging ghouls to come as well as conforming to the theme of undead labour controlled by a voodoo master (here a Cornish squire). A sickly-hued dream sequence has the decaying dead claw their way out of their graves and surround the terrified hero – these are the grotesque nightmarish figures that will resurface in the modern zombie films of Romero, Lucio Fulci and others. But when the hero's zombified wife, played by cult actress Jacqueline Pearce, rises from her coffin in the preceding scene (which is not a dream), her deathly white beauty is closer to the undead glamour of the Hammer vampire. There is a hunger in her eyes, even though the zombie is not yet given to feeding on the living – her destruction (beheaded with a shovel) may even put us in mind of Van Helsing's decapitation of Lucy in Stoker's *Dracula*.

Two closely connected texts – Richard Matheson's novel, *I am Legend* (1954), and Romero's *Night of the Living Dead* (US, 1968) – bring our two undead archetypes closer together. On the DVD sleeve for *The Last Man on Earth* (Italy/US, 1964), the first of three adaptations of Matheson's novel, the infected creatures are described as both 'vampire-like' and as zombies, while the film is identified as a 'primary influence'

2. The zombie as pale vampiric beauty: *Plague of the Zombies*.

on Romero's film. They are destroyed by wooden stakes, by a hero who also makes defensive use of garlic. At one point, reading and then casting Stoker's novel aside, hero Robert Neville calls time on the supernatural vampire – 'Begone, Van Helsing and Mina and Jonathan and blood-eyed Count and all!'[5] But as well as 'modernising' the vampire myth, the novel is widely credited with inadvertently leading to the modern zombie genre in its influence on Romero. While the 'vampires' have a leader of sorts, they are primarily a horde – we are in an apocalyptic world of houses under siege, boarded up windows, a hero who must be stealthy in tackling the sheer numbers that face him. If vampires are an aristocratic minority, zombies always seem to be in the process of becoming the majority.

In *The Vampire Cinema*, David Pirie approaches *Night of the Living Dead* as a vampire film on the basis that it is about the dead feeding on the living – he calls it 'probably the only truly modernist reading of the vampire myth'.[6] In the era of *The Walking Dead*, videogames like *Resident Evil*,[7] and zombie flash-mobs, this probably now seems like an eccentric designation for the movie widely seen as the first modern zombie film. However, there are two reasons why Pirie's classification makes more sense than might first appear. First, *Night of the Living Dead*'s initial influence was primarily on the vampire film – both Pirie (in *Vampire Cinema*) and Ian Cooper (in this book) observe the shambling vampire

3. Vampire plague, zombie besiegement: *The Last Man on Earth.*

women and downbeat endings in 1970s vampire films like *Count Yorga, Vampire* (1970). Second, while Romero-influenced zombie films *were* made in the 1970s – *Children Shouldn't Play with Dead Things* (US, 1972) and *The Living Dead at the Manchester Morgue* (Italy/Spain, 1974), for example[8] – it wasn't until his later sequel, *Dawn of the Dead* (US, 1978), that a full-blown cycle followed. In particular, it led to an explosion of Italian zombie films, spearheaded by Lucio Fulci's *Zombie Flesh Eaters* (Italy, 1979), promoted in Italy as a sequel to Romero's film but very different in style. While the modern zombie is primarily the creation of scientific catastrophe or biological mutation, viruses, radiation and toxic chemicals, it can also (like the classic vampire) be a product of metaphysical 'evil'. While it's Romero's secular *Dawn of the Dead* that includes the line 'When there's no more room in hell, the dead will walk the earth', it was Fulci who took such portents of biblical apocalypse more literally – Stephen Thrower has suggested that Italian horror's particular take on the physical corruption of the zombie was driven by the legacy of Catholicism.[9]

The vampire is predominantly intelligent (dangerously so in its 'evil' incarnation) and profoundly individualistic – it suggests, as Milly Williamson argues, 'an attractive outsiderdom ... in a culture where a dominant experience for the self is predominantly marginalisation and outsiderdom'.[10] This individualism has taken a multiplicity of forms: hyper-masculine King Vampire, Fatal Woman (often a lesbian or bisexual succubus), romantic bohemian, tortured addict, monstrous child,[11] human psychopath, punk rock rebel, ass-kicking action heroine, preternatural aristo-fascist preoccupied by the purity of the 'race' or vampires' superiority to humans. Zombies are even more diverse in appearance, but the signs of social identity – a zombie Hari Krishna or cheerleader, say – are merely a cruel reminder of the individuality that they have lost. In contrast, the sympathetic vampire, whose interior experience of suffering and pain (as well as of sensuousness, as Stacey Abbott points out in this book) is a significant modern generic convention, represents a dramatisation of distinctiveness, individuality and significance at a cultural moment marked by anomie and social dislocation. The vampire's individuality and claims to meaning are shaped for different markets of the genre (which supports its range of meanings), from the restrained artiness of *Let the Right One In* and its equally arty remake *Let Me In*, to the blockbuster *Twilight Saga*. The differing sympathy-inducing performances of the sympathetic vampire make it a figure of empathy for diverse audiences.

The zombie's lack of sentience seems to render it less available to identification, but there are ways of activating sympathy for the 'walker'. One of these is to allow them to retain their intellectual faculties. *Return of the Living Dead 3* (US, 1993) gives us a zombie protagonist whose surviving intelligence invests her with vampiric tragedy as she wrestles with her monstrous hunger. But even brain dead 'walkers' have been granted moments of pathos since at least the original *Dawn of the Dead*. In Romero's zombie-verse, there are disturbing reminders (already hinted at in *Night of the Living Dead*'s overzealous posse) that a sub-species that can be tormented and exterminated – or sexually abused, as in *Deadgirl* (US, 2008) – without consequence or recrimination creates a licence for human behaviour that might make us, at least some of the time, side with the zombies. Notwithstanding their recent ability to move at Olympic velocity, zombies are the most conspicuously disabled of horror movie monsters – malfunctioning motor skills, missing limbs (or in extreme cases, entire lower torsos) and severely damaged brains characterise the zombified body. In *Night of the Living Dead*'s celebrated opening scene, we are presented with a zombie who seems to have been mistaken for someone who is either drunk or suffering from some form of mental disability – the lone undead who staggers towards and then attacks Barbara and Johnny in the graveyard. Barbara seems as embarrassed as afraid because Johnny's taunts of 'They're coming to get you, Barbara!' could prove to be deeply inappropriate (as opposed to unwittingly prophetic) – 'You're *ignorant!*' she scolds him. As Sconce notes in his chapter, a lone zombie usually poses little threat (although tell that to Johnny!); more than that, they may even seem cruelly vulnerable. The no-budget British film *Colin* (2008) explores this vulnerability by focusing on a lone undead protagonist who never quite becomes part of the horde that might provide zombie empowerment. In one scene, he is preyed on for his trainers by opportunistic youths, and the cumulative effect of the film is to make us fear for his survival. But Colin also seems to exhibit some residual humanity, constantly returning to his former home as if trying to fathom who he is (or was). Growing zombie sentience is a theme in the Romero cycle, starting with Bub in *Day of the Dead* (1985) and reaching particular resonance with black working-class zombie Big Daddy in *Land of the Dead* (2005), intelligent enough to lead the undead army and target those most oppressive towards them. As Romero's series progresses, survival can no longer rely on simply destroying the undead (a logistical impossibility anyway) – it requires one to show them some respect, to possibly even recognise (as seems to be the case at the end of *Land*) that such a powerful group might have some rights. Anne Billson offers an intriguing explanation for the sympathetic zombie – that our attitude towards the anarchic mob is likely to change in a period where the dominant order has shown itself to be the greater danger to our survival:

> [W]hereas zombies might once have been a metaphor for the dreaded underclass, the recession is a reminder that we are that underclass, those faceless masses that need to be contained lest they take bites out of the bankers and politicians.[12]

In this respect, perhaps the rampaging zombie is closer to its earlier enslaved incarnation than first appears.

4. The pathos and vulnerability of the lone zombie: *Colin.*

* * *

Screening the Undead opens with 'The Mark of the Vampire – Race, Place, Gender and Identity in the Modern Vampire Film'. This section provides a wide-ranging discussion of the modern vampire – a cinematic figure located in urban settings and addressing contemporaneous concerns of social upheaval, location and cultural dislocation, anomie and liberation. Each chapter in this section examines the different ways that the modern vampire is set in its moment and place, moving on from the traditional signifiers of the vampire associated with Hammer and Universal, often with a knowing irreverence. Ian Cooper demonstrates this in his examination of a significant group of 1970s vampire films that were 'fiercely contemporary' and influential: *Count Yorga, Vampire* (Bob Kelljan, 1970), *The Velvet Vampire* (Stephanie Rothman, 1971), *The Return of Count Yorga* (Kelljan, 1972), *Blacula* (William Crain, 1972), *Deathmaster* (Ray Danton, 1972) and *Scream Blacula Scream* (Kelljan, 1973). Cooper argues that these films were both marked by the modernity of the counterculture of their time and left a mark on the genre, influencing vampire films and horror in the 1980s and beyond with their cynicism and generic reflexivity. But while these vampires were transplanted from 'old' Europe onto modern American soil, this was not simply a site of hip language, groovy outfits and flower-power children; it was also a 'sun-bleached, acid-frazzled place' where the more disturbing side of the counterculture, such as drug addiction and the Manson Family murders, were represented (*Deathmaster* and *The Return of Count Yorga*). Prevalent issues of racism and the black power response are also present in this group of films, particularly in the blaxploitation films *Blacula* and *Scream Blacula Scream*, while *The Velvet Vampire* evokes the atmosphere of sexual liberation with fascination and dread. Locating the vampire in the reality of the time reinvigorated the genre and enabled the figure to dramatise contemporary concerns and issues and to reorient horror in tune with the more cynical and irreverent decades to come.

Stacey Abbott and Peter Hutchings are also concerned with how the vampire moves in a contemporary location and how it traverses boundaries. For Abbott, the cityscape is the significant location of the modern vampire. In the city, the males of the species are afforded agency and moral ambiguity denied to female vampires in mainstream film. Part of the male vampire's agency is an articulation of the freedom and pleasure in the sensations of his embodied vampire experience as he wanders through the city with a flaneurial gaze. Abbott argues that while the freedom of the city is denied to the female vampire in mainstream film, when she crosses another border – from mainstream into independent film – she also walks out into the city night. Abbott has identified a group of independent films – Michael Almereyda's *Nadja* (1994), Abel Ferrara's *The Addiction* (1995) and Larry Fessenden's *Habit* (1995) – which 'all reimagine the female vampire as a *flâneuse*' at home in New York City. Through a close analysis of *Nadja*, Abbott demonstrates that it is the use of indie film techniques and aesthetics which enables Almereyda to visualise Nadja's point of view and her subjective experience, including the vampires' heightened sensual experience of the city at night. This adds new contours and complexity to the presentation of the female vampire's subjectivity and again reinvigorates generic conventions.

Peter Hutchings examines the snow-filled locations of two Swedish vampire films, *Frostbite* (Anders Banke, 2006) and *Let the Right One*

In (Tomas Alfredson, 2008), to question the image of the vampire as an agent of globalisation. While the vampire seems able to appear anywhere and traverse national boundaries, Hutchings wonders why it tends to appear in specific national locations. He argues that there is a creative tension between the distinctiveness of the Swedish vampires and their connection to international developments in the vampire cinema, including the cult associations of specific European traditions of horror and their markets. Through a detailed analysis of these two films, Hutchings demonstrates that the films' ambitions to be nationally distinctive can be placed in a wider pattern of generic development. This results in a vampire cinema that draws sustenance from national locations and distinctiveness in order to send the reworked conventions back out into international markets.

Milly Williamson is interested in the critical location of the modern vampire, and issues of interpretation. She is concerned with the genre's ability to traverse the borders between mainstream and independent film and examines how this is critically received and generationally dependent. Her chapter compares three films, *The Hunger* (Tony Scott, 1983), *Twilight* (Katherine Hardwicke, 2008) and *Let the Right One In*, to explore differing interpretations of each film and to ask questions about the celebration of the independent film and the vilification of the mainstream one. Williamson argues, for instance, that the critics' disparagement of *Twilight* depends on the twin process of cultural distinction and the feminisation of the mainstream. Instead, she asks us to consider an interpretation of *Twilight* that both recognises its similarity to other alternative vampire films, such *as Let the Right One In*, and which addresses, and takes as seriously as discussions of independent film, the possible pleasures of the films intended young female audience.

The second section of *Screening the Undead*, 'Rewriting the Living Dead – The Zombie in Popular Culture', examines the socio-political role of the zombie in contemporary society. Jeffrey Sconce considers the defining features of the contemporary zombie genre in order to understand how modern zombies can be interpreted. Sconce counters the Freudian interpretation of zombies as he argues that zombies are 'ungothic, un-Freudian, un-uncanny' and that the modern zombie is a creature of the 'post-uncanny-social'. He maintains that the zombie genre centres on 'two bodies in decay', on the one hand the individual corpse(s) of the undead, and on the other, the whole social body. A number of other interesting features of the zombie genre are considered, including the importance of the 'tactics of invasion' in the zombie narrative, the role of comedy in zombie films such as *Dawn of the Dead* and *Shaun of the Dead*, and the role of the 'social death drive'. Sconce also evaluates recent developments in the zombie genre and the zombie's increasing presence and integration in twenty-first-century popular culture. A number of examples are focused on, including literary 'mash ups' such as *Pride and Prejudice and Zombies* (Seth Grahame-Smith and Jane Austen); self-help manuals, including *The Zombie Survival Guide* (Max Brooks); organised zombie pub crawls; 'Zombie on Ice' events; 'Run for Your Lives' charity events; and traffic signs warning 'zombies ahead'.

Russ Hunter examines the ways in which zombie films can be used as vehicles through which scientific and technological (or 'human-made') developments can be scrutinised and critiqued. Hunter argues that although there are numerous films that focus on the scientific and technological implications of human action on the environment (e.g., *Frankenstein*, James Whale, 1931), there has been a comparative lack of academic discussion focusing on late 1970s/early 1980s Italian cinema which sought to connect the undead with environmental disaster and devastation. Hunter unpacks the complex, innovative and literal ways in which Italian zombie (or the 'infected') films, such as *Nightmare City* and *The Living Dead at Manchester Morgue*, function as interesting and timely texts for examining the deep, wide-ranging (and often unexpected) consequences of experiments, creations and actions of human begins on the environment. Whilst the analysis highlights how such narratives are deeply embedded in their socio-historical context and contributed to the national environmental discourses circulating in Italy in the 1970s and 1980s, it simultaneously counters the popular perception that late 1970s/early 1980s Italian horror cinema can simply be dismissed as 'trash' cinema.

Continuing with images of disaster and devastation and the link between zombie narratives and their socio-historic, political and global context, Emma Dyson examines two key characteristics of zombie films from the 1990s onwards: the concept of global infections as one of the main narratives running through the films; and the use of news media reportage of protests and disasters within the narratives. Dyson reflects on the production factors that have facilitated the use of mediated news reports in the construction of the film's narrative and assesses the impact of such usage on the aesthetic, thematic and ideological features of contemporary zombie films. Topics discussed include the increasing representation of the body within zombie films as the 'diseased individual body', connections between film narratives and national and global problems and the narrative shifts towards large-scale destruction. Dyson argues that films such as *28 Days Later* and the *Masters of Horror* episode 'Homecoming' (Joe Dante, 2005) draw on the familiar media tropes and techniques used in global news media to facilitate the film's narrative, whilst simultaneously critiquing such media techniques, mass media manipulation and the domination of global communication.

To date, the homosexual zombie figure has received scant attention in film and television narratives and academic analysis. Darren Elliott-Smith rectifies this imbalance by firming placing the homosexual zombie on the film analysis map through consideration of how the zombie can be used in metaphorical terms for homosexuality. Elliott-Smith examines the opportunities provided by 'the zombie' for queer meanings and readings before moving on to survey the representation of the gay zombie in contemporary queer horror, including *Creatures of the Pink Lagoon* (Chris Diani, 2006) and *The Nature of Nicholas* (Jeff Erbach, 2002). A range of interesting representational patterns are identified, including the gay zombie as a body that is explicitly penetrable/penetrating; the gay zombie being used, in some cases, to celebrate heterogeneity in sexual desire whilst concurrently criticising the homogeneity within homosexual subcultures; links being made between homosexuality and cannibalism; a preoccupation with the zombie's sexuality and the risks its poses to itself and others; repressed homosexual desire; and the implications of heteronormativity. Such discussions contextualise and frame the remaining analysis in the chapter – the gay zombie from Bruce LaBruce's *Otto; or, Up With Dead People* (2008).

The final section of the book, 'Hybrid Bloodlines', looks at hybridisation in two broad senses. The first is a product of the globalisation of the undead (a theme that surfaces elsewhere in the book, in discussions of Swedish vampires and Italian zombies): the undead proliferate across national and cultural boundaries, local traditions merge with dominant and already successful generic conventions. Hybrid variants emerge, such as the hopping undead of 1980s Hong Kong cinema, a combination of the Chinese *jiangshi* (a cadaver retaining an 'extra breath') and the Western vampire[13] – one of its earliest cinematic outings is in a co-production between the British Hammer films and Hong Kong's Shaw Brothers Studios, *The Legend of the Seven Golden Vampires* (UK/HK, 1974). Undead films have been made in Britain, the US, Japan, Hong Kong, Italy, Spain, Mexico, the Philippines, Sweden, France, Nigeria, South Korea, amongst other places – cycles that vary in size and longevity, that are often the result of co-productions and the targeting of multiple markets as well as influences from one another. The second form of hybridity complicates the clear demarcation of undead archetypes – produces other variants and blurs the line between existing ones. As we have suggested, the modern zombie is already an undead hybrid, its bloodline mixed with the vampire and the ghoul (which eats flesh but is not undead).

Both forms of hybridity feature prominently in Costas Constandinides' analysis of the undead films of Guillermo Del Toro. On the one hand, Del Toro is a 'disobedient', border-crossing *auteur* with careers in Hollywood and Spanish-language cinema – Constandinides contrasts the reinvention of the undead in *Cronos* with the more franchise-friendly vampires of *Blade 2*, but finds in both the same interest in 'impure' vampirism, the product of genetic engineering and biological engineering. Jesus, the undead protagonist of *Cronos*, is not a vampire in the traditional sense – his need for blood is also connected to the bio-mechanical 'Cronos device' that keeps him alive after death. Constandinides finds the character rooted in biological transformation, fairy tale and magical realism. The film offers not the charismatic, seductive, all-powerful vampire but a protective grandfather, a figure sometimes rendered clownish, frail or abject, as in the signature sequence where he licks blood from a toilet floor, the aftermath of a nosebleed. Nicola Woodham explores a comparatively undocumented area of vampire/undead cinema – the video film industry of Nigeria, or 'Nollywood'. Where the Western vampire is increasingly secular, the Nollywood vampire seems to belong to a tradition of evangelical Nigerian horror. But Woodham also discerns anti-colonial themes in the films, as well as a culturally-specific take on the idea of the vampire as economic predator. Vampire tales, she explains, are already rooted in anti-colonial sentiments, circulating rumours of blood stolen and sold. In these films, the vampire is associated with 419 culture (economic crime) and bloodsucking neo-liberal capitalism.

When is a 'zombie musical' not a zombie musical? Steve Rawle examines the way in which a single set piece – a zombie musical number in Miike Takashi's cult film *The Happiness of the Katakuris* – came to define it in Western promotional material and critical and fan reception. A Japanese remake of a South Korean comedy, a combination of family comedy, horror film and musical (just to list three of the generic labels Rawle suggests could be legitimately attached to it), *Katakuris* is as hybrid as they come. But to reduce it to that one (admittedly attention-grabbing) component, he argues, risks selling short the extent of that hybridity as well as conforming to the neo-Orientalist 'only in Japan' rhetoric of 'extreme' Asian cinema as a promotional category.

The 'Blind Dead' series – dealing with undead Knights Templar riding undead horses – is one of the most unique hybrid manifestations of the living dead: zombie-like in their decay and inexorable movement, but manifestly evil and given to drinking blood. Andy Willis discusses this quartet of films much beloved by cult horror fans, and draws attention to the problems of analysing films at once so seemingly 'Spanish' in their concerns and at the same time designed for international distribution (in this case, often in 'stronger' versions). How, he asks, should we read the Templars – as a critique of Francoist 'National Catholicism' or as agents of its implementation, punishing the permissive and the perverse? While violent and sexual imagery in Spanish cinema is often read as subversive of Franco-era politics, Willis argues that a close reading of the films makes such an interpretation harder to sustain.

Encompassing films from the UK and the US, Spain, Nigeria, Mexico, Italy, Japan and Sweden; vampires who range from the romantic to the countercultural; zombies who shamble, run, ride horses and even dance, *Screening the Undead* offers a broad-ranging examination of the manifestations and meanings of the walking dead. Our contributors come not to stake them or shoot them in the head but to see what they have to tell us.

Notes

1 Gregory A. Waller, *The Living and the Undead: Slaying Vampires, Exterminating Zombies* (Urbana, Chicago and Springfield: University of Illinois Press, 2010), p. xii.
2 *The Mummy* (US, 1999) generated two sequels and a spin-off series focusing on 'The Scorpion King'.
3 David Flint, *Zombie Apocalypse: How the Living Dead Devoured Pop Culture* (London: Plexus, 2009), p. 41.
4 James Twitchell, *Dreadful Pleasures: An Anatomy of Modern Horror* (New York and Oxford: Oxford University Press, 1985), p. 266.
5 Richard Matheson, *I am Legend* (London: Corgi, 1956), p. 21.
6 David Pirie, *The Vampire Cinema* (London: Hamlyn, 1977), p. 141.
7 The revival in the zombie's popularity might also be because they make better videogame antagonists than almost any other monster, testing the player's skill in evasion as well as the deployment and management of ammunition.
8 See Russ Hunter's Chapter 6 for a discussion of *The Living Dead at the Manchester Morgue*.
9 Stephen Thrower, 'Zombies', in K. Newman (ed.), *The BFI Companion to Horror* (London: BFI/Cassell, 1996), p. 351.
10 Milly Williamson, *The Lure of the Vampire: Gender, Fiction and Fandom from Bram Stoker to Buffy* (London and New York: Routledge, 2005), pp. 35–36.
11 Vampire children feature in the 'Wurdalak' episode of Mario Bava's *Black Sabbath/I Tre Volti della Paura* (Italy, 1963) and Stephen King's *Salem's Lot* (novel, 1975; TV adaptations in 1979 and 2004), but they are newly-sired child vampires. *Interview with the Vampire* (novel, 1976; film, US, 1994) and *Let the Right One In* present older vampires still inhabiting the bodies of the children they were when they were sired.
12 Anne Billson, 'March of the Zombie', *Guardian*, 1 June 2009; http://www.guardian.co.uk/film/2009/jun/01/zombie-horror-film-doghouse (accessed 23 February 2012).
13 See Stephen Teo, *Hong Kong Cinema: The Extra Dimension* (London: BFI, 1997), p. 224.

Part 1

THE MARK OF THE VAMPIRE – RACE, PLACE, GENDER AND IDENTITY IN THE MODERN VAMPIRE FILM

1

MANSON, DRUGS AND BLACK POWER

The Countercultural Vampire

Ian Cooper

In the early 1970s, North America offered an array of screen vampires. On television, there was the Gothic soap *Dark Shadows* (1966–71) and the stylish TV movies *The Night Stalker* (Moxey, 1972) and *The Night Strangler* (Curtis, 1973), which spawned the short-lived TV show *Kolchak The Night Stalker* (1974). Independent/exploitation filmmakers of the early 1970s produced a number of strikingly unusual contributions to the vampire mythos. This disparate collection of films includes *Let's Scare Jessica to Death* (Hancock, 1971), *Lemora: A Child's Tale of the Supernatural* (Blackburn, 1973), *Ganja and Hess* (Gunn, 1973), *Grave of the Vampire* (Hayes, 1974) and *Dead of Night* aka *Deathdream* (Clark, 1974). The focus of this chapter is a loose collection of six such films that sought to revitalise the vampire myth, melding generic Gothic traditions with contemporary social concerns. *Count Yorga, Vampire* (Bob Kelljan, 1970), *The Velvet Vampire* (Stephanie Rothman, 1971), *The Return of Count Yorga* (Kelljan, 1972), *Blacula* (William Crain, 1972), *Deathmaster* (Ray Danton, 1972) and *Scream Blacula Scream* (Kelljan, 1973) not only share some important thematic and stylistic concerns but also a number of key creative personnel. They use graphic gore and a hip irreverence, which at times borders on the reflexive, to breathe life into a fusty sub-genre that elsewhere was descending into camp and soft-core sex fantasies. This kind of vampire, savage and satirical, stylish and fiercely contemporary, would prove influential. A number of the more offbeat and unusual vampire films made since would seem to owe something to these films, their faded bite-marks visible on the angsty, alienated *Martin* (Romero, 1977), the undead, motel-dwelling drifters of *Near*

Dark (Bigelow, 1987) and the gloomy strung-out blood-drinkers that populate Abel Ferrara's *The Addiction* (1995).

Three of the films were directed by Bob Kelljan and three starred Robert Quarry. *The Velvet Vampire* and *Scream Blacula Scream* were co-written by Maurice Jules while the *Yorga* films and *Deathmaster* were shot by Bill Butler (who would go on to much bigger things including *The Conversation* (Coppola, 1974) and *Jaws* (Spielberg, 1975)). Kelljan and Rothman were Roger Corman *protégés* (although this latter connection was far from uncommon in the independent sector at this time) and all six films were produced by the exploitation specialists, American International Pictures. To add to this blurring, both the *Yorga* sequel and the re-released original used the term 'deathmaster' in their publicity campaigns, with the trailer for *The Return of Count Yorga* actually containing the line 'beware the return of the Deathmaster'.

Corman, Romero, Polanski

The influence of Corman looms large over these films, in particular his patented trick of making genre films that dealt with contemporary social issues. Tony Rayns has written of 'the secret kinship between his [Corman's] Gothic genre movies and the mood of the counter-culture'.[1] Corman's LSD film, *The Trip* (1968), would serve to bridge the gap between his studio-bound Poe adaptations and the hippie milieu, locating the irrational and the Gothic in the modern West Coast.

Two films from 1968 also had an important influence on this collection of films. Roman Polanski's stylish adaptation of Ira Levin's *Rosemary's Baby* (1968) was a big commercial success and offered a hip, witty makeover of a hoary Gothic tale (in this case, of demonic possession) taking place in an all-too familiar urban setting; as one critic put it, 'the film's style is deliberately naturalistic, using familiar everyday locations (telephone boxes, kitchens) as its tools of terror'.[2] In contrast, George Romero's ultra low-budget *Night of the Living Dead* (1968) refashioned elements of vampire lore, presenting undead flesh-eaters spawned (it is suggested) by science rather than supernatural blood-drinkers. Although the stark black-and-white *faux*-newsreel approach used by Romero is far from Polanski's use of a luxurious brightly-lit Manhattan apartment building, both films have the same irreverent tone, a revisionist approach to their genre and a sour cynicism that would become commonplace in the horror of the 1970s.

The Dream is Over

It has been commonly observed that vampire fictions often appear at times of social upheaval. Bram Stoker's novel *Dracula* was published in 1897, during the shift from the Victorian era of empire to the uncertainties of the twentieth century. In 1922, an unstable post-war Germany produced *Nosferatu* (Murnau). Hammer's *Dracula* (Fisher, 1958) was a product of a 1950s Britain dealing with the humiliation of Suez. Anne Rice's *Interview with the Vampire* (1976) was published as the US was struggling to recover from the twin humiliations of Vietnam and Watergate. It's no surprise, then, that the social upheaval and cultural changes of the late 1960s would spawn a new wave of vampires.

The term counterculture often conjures up images of Haight-Ashbury, the Beatles, paisley shirts and long-haired teens giving flowers to cops. But the flip-side to all this love and acid invokes a set of images just as, if not more, firmly imprinted on the public imagination, such as the killing of Meredith Hunter at a free Rolling Stones concert at the Altamont racetrack in California, violent anti-war demonstrations and the shootings at Kent State. By 1970, John Lennon was singing that 'the dream is over', as the mind-expanding psychedelic Summer of Love was swiftly followed by a harsh comedown best symbolised by the Manson murders. As Joan Didion put it in an oft-repeated quote, the 1960s 'ended abruptly on August 9th 1969',[3] the night of the first murders committed by the Family. It is perhaps no coincidence that the setting for these six films is California, the sun-bleached, acid-frazzled place where the hippie dream both began and ended. These films manage to meld traditional vampire lore and some very familiar generic tropes to a low-budget aesthetic and such zeitgeisty issues as the women's movement and the drug culture, free love and black power, the end of the blissed-out 1960s and the coming of the cynical 1970s.

Dracula's Soul Brother

In many ways, the *Blacula* films are typical blaxploitation entries, offering up a conventional genre item distinguished only by the presence of black actors in the main roles. Although *Blacula* was directed by William Crain, one of the few African-Americans making blaxploitation pictures, in many ways the subject of race is dealt with superficially; a play on the phrase 'black arts', the publicity that describes the title character as 'Dracula's soul brother' and the mooted sequel title, 'Blacula is Beautiful', suggest the kind of word-play that also gave us *Blackenstein* (Levey, 1973) and *Dr. Black, Mr. Hyde* (Crain, 1976).[4] As one would also expect from a blaxploitation film, there is popular music (in a lengthy night-club sequence), a smattering of contemporary references (with mentions of police brutality and the Black Panthers) and some of the most eye-catching costumes seen in the genre. Indeed, there is a nice comment on this obsession with sartorial style in *Scream Blacula Scream*, where a newly-vamped hipster reacts badly to the discovery that he can no longer pose in front of the mirror, protesting, 'Hey, look man, I don't mind being a vampire and all that shit but this really ain't hip.' When he does accept his fate, he dons the traditional cape, but matches it to crotch-hugging flares, sunglasses and a red fedora.

But beyond the groovy sounds and outrageous fashions, the films touch on more resonant issues, such as the explicit connection made between slavery and vampirism. In the prologue to *Blacula*, we see how the African Prince Mamuwalde is bitten after a (somewhat credibility-stretching) journey to Transylvania in an attempt to persuade Count Dracula to join his anti-slavery campaign. Mamuwalde, dubbed Blacula by the racist Count, is brought to America by two outrageously stereotyped gay antique dealers. Harry Benshoff is very generous in noting how the portrayal of an interracial gay relationship is 'ahead of its time' but also suggests that the characters are in the film solely to be dispatched in an attempt to make the title character more sympathetic.[5] In addition, I would argue that these cartoonish characters also serve to emphasise Blacula's hyper-masculinity. He may wear evening dress, possess an unfashionable courtly manner and put the bite on a couple of flamboyant gay men, but the viewer can be reassured as to his propensity for violence. It is surely no coincidence how similar images of effeminate, pathetic and/or grotesque gays turn up in a number of films from this period when long-haired, flashily-dressed males were becoming the norm. Consider the hitchhikers in *Vanishing Point* (Sarafian, 1971), Ken Sinclair's squealing Sammy in *Mean Streets* (Scorsese, 1973), and more than one of the characters in *A Clockwork Orange* (Kubrick, 1971); as with Crain's film, they all seem to act as what Robin Wood called 'a disclaimer'.[6]

Four years before the publication of Alex Haley's celebrated *Roots: The Saga of an American Family* (1976), *Blacula* has its African central character displaced in the ghettoes of LA after being 'enslaved' (as Mamuwalde himself puts it) by a racist white European. As one anonymous reviewer quoted by Benshoff put it, 'I have ... chosen to look upon the entire film as an effort by those responsible to show satirically the black man's plight as a victim of white vampirism.'[7] This notion of enslavement is developed and further complicated in *Scream Blacula Scream*, as Blacula dispatches a couple of pimps after telling them they have 'made a slave of your sisters and you're still slaves imitating your slavemasters'. These references to slavery seem to have been added to *Blacula* only when Crain and Marshall came on board. The script by Raymond Koenig and Joan Torres was originally titled *Count Brown Comes to Town* and the title character was plain Andrew Brown. By the time of the sequel, Afrocentrism has become an issue, as Mamuwalde visits a show of African antiquities and converses in a Nigerian dialect before telling Pam Grier's voodoo priestess of his stated desire to go back to his homeland if she can only cure him.

Mamuwalde is portrayed in both films as a tragic figure, whether pining for his dead wife or desperately seeking to be cured. This impression is reinforced by William Marshall's air of gloomy theatricality and the rich, resonant way this trained opera singer delivers his lines. As David Pirie writes, 'William Marshall plays Blacula in the tradition of black nobility associated with Othello.'[8] However, the scenes where he attacks his victims, sprouting excessive facial hair, emphasise his monstrousness and his status as an anti-hero, albeit a sympathetic one. This is not only a familiar role for a vampire to occupy, it's also par for the course for the blaxploitation cycle (such as the drug-dealing title character of *Superfly* (Parks Jr, 1972)). The climactic scene in *Blacula*, as a grieving Mamuwalde walks into the sunshine, is clearly supposed to be tragic, but it's entirely in keeping with the flip, ironic tone of these films that we see a prominently-placed 'No Smoking' sign just before the character is immolated.

As well as the issue of slavery, the trailer for the film vividly depicts another topic that was as relevant then as it is now, containing a number of scenes showing the black protagonist beating up or killing white cops. The same trailer even goes so far as to describe the title character as 'the black avenger'. These scenes of Mamuwalde evening the score with the forces of white America would no doubt appeal to the target audience, but the emphasis placed on them is misleading, given that the closest thing the film has to a savant, Dr George Thomas (played by the splendidly-named Thalmus Rasulala), works closely with a not-unsympathetic cop. This kind of relationship is carried over to the sequel, when we discover that the white cop in charge of the case (who admits to being 'a little prejudiced') used to be a colleague of one of the main characters, an ex-cop turned dealer in African antiquities. That's not, however, to deny the crowd-pleasing spectacle of Mamuwalde picking up a cop and throwing him across the room after he threatens to arrest his 'uppity black ass'.

Dope

The subject of hard drugs also leaves its (track) mark on a number of these films, in much the same way as another blood-borne contagion, AIDS, would find its way into the vampire cinema of the 1980s. The imagery of addiction and hard drug use can be found in a number of vampire films made since the late 1960s and the emergence of a visible drug culture. There is the puking, blood-starved Count in *Blood for Dracula* aka *Andy Warhol's Dracula* (Morrissey, 1974); pale, wasted Udo Kier resembling the junkies who inhabit earlier Warhol films; and the eponymous hero of *Martin*, a syringe for extracting blood held between his teeth. The film which best embodies the notion of vampire as junkie is the aforementioned, emblematically-titled *The Addiction*, which, as the critic Hal Hinson suggests, 'manages to connect vampirism to AIDS, drug addiction and all sorts of worldly evils'.[9]

This drug imagery can clearly be seen in the presentation of Yorga's brides. In the first film they silently glide around the castle in evening gowns, glassy-eyed and piranha-mouthed. By the time of the sequel, they are considerably more monstrous, straggly-haired, desiccated ghouls with ulcerated, discoloured faces. They are far from the seductive sirens seen in Hammer's Karnstein Trilogy (1970–72) and the work of Jean Rollin, although they can still turn on the charm, as in the creepy scene where the newly-vampirised Erica attempts to seduce her boyfriend while her face is still smeared with the blood of her half-eaten cat. In the *Blacula* films, the black vampires are also given a (fairly-unconvincing) greenish complexion and heavy-lidded eyes. In *Scream Blacula Scream*, they are shown as a gang of shambling cop-killing zombies who wander the corridors of Mamuwalde's mansion. This portrayal of the vampire as a kind of ghoul also reflects the pervasive influence of *Night of the Living Dead*, with the same kind of zombie-esque blood-drinkers turning up in the likes of *Let's Scare Jessica to Death*, *Messiah of Evil* (Huyck, Katz, 1973), *Dead of Night* and *Lemora*. The opening of *The Return of Count Yorga* seems particularly indebted to Romero's film, as a boy plays in a rural cemetery at dusk while reanimated corpses emerge from the ground.

Healter (sic) Skelter

Of course, for a 1970s audience, a harem of dead-eyed, lank-haired women doing the bidding of a charismatic killer in California would seem eerily familiar. The murders committed by the Manson Family had an enormous impact in the US and elsewhere, not least in the way they helped to transform the image of flower children from sweet-natured, docile college kids to bloodthirsty, knife-wielding killers. It's not surprising, given Manson's status as icon of evil, that he both inspired and influenced a number of horror films. Some dealt explicitly with The Family, such as the weirdo cheapie *The Other Side of Madness* aka *The Helter-Skelter Murders* (Howard, 1970), with Manson songs on the soundtrack; the Oscar-nominated documentary *Manson* (Hendrickson, Merrick, 1973); and the TV mini-series *Helter Skelter* (Gries, 1976). But there were other films which used Manson Family imagery, as in the crazed cults and assorted freaks in the likes of *I Drink Your Blood* (Durston, 1970), *Blood on Satan's Claw* (Haggard, 1971) and *The Night God Screamed* (Madden, 1973). Even films made before Manson was caught were rebranded with The Family touch: Robert

Thom's tale of Hollywood excess, *Angel, Angel, Down We Go* (1969), was re-released in 1971 with the new title *Cult of the Damned*.[10]

While any Manson references in *Count Yorga, Vampire* are coincidental (the film opened a few days before the trial of The Family members began), both the sequel and the nakedly-opportunistic *Deathmaster* make the connection explicit. In the former film, Yorga sends out his zombie brides to attack a house full of people in a frightening sequence that consciously echoes the Tate–LaBianca murders, the carpets of this middle-class suburban home spattered with blood, furniture overturned and broken glass and corpses littering the floor. The power of the scene is heightened by the lack of music; the only sounds the whistling Santa Ana winds and the screams of the victims. The use of Yorga's blank-faced, straggly-haired brides, acting as one, underlines the Manson connection: with one exception, all those who took part in the attack on the Tate–Polanski house were women. In *Deathmaster*, Robert Quarry plays Khorda, a long-haired, bearded undead guru who falls in with a group of impressionable hippies ('Wow, that cat is something else'). The film was something of a labour of love for the actor, who also helped produce it. 'I had an idea,' Quarry said in 2004. 'This was at the time of the Manson murders so I thought just make Charles Manson a vampire – that's logical.'[11]

Promoted with the tagline 'He offered them peace, love and misunderstanding', *Deathmaster* opens with the striking image (albeit one cribbed from the Lon Chaney Jr vehicle *Son of Dracula* (Siodmak, 1943)) of a coffin floating on the waves and washed up on a deserted beach. Directed by a former actor, Ray Danton, the film contains a bewildering variety of then-voguish exploitation elements: some insipid folk songs, soft drugs, deeply unscary bikers and poorly-staged kung fu fight scenes. The 'hip' dialogue is awful and must have seemed terribly dated in 1972, while the song lyrics aren't much better ('a man without a vision, is a man without a dream, a man without a dream is like a willow floating on a stream'). It is also, given the potentially wild subject matter, very tame. The acid-fuelled orgies that The Family were fond of are here replaced by some freaky dancing, a solitary bong and a topless woman painting ('Man, who's the chick?' / 'Wow, I dunno'). There is also none of the leavening, knowing humour which appears in the other films discussed. The tone of Danton's film is uncharacteristically solemn and consequently invites laughter at it, not with it. Wearing a long embroidered white robe and a bad wig, Quarry has none of the icy charm he displays as Count Yorga, as he swans around delivering a series of homilies that are part Lugosi's Dracula, part Manson: 'Would you be willing to exchange the little passions of your life for the ecstasy of eternity?' and 'The nights of our lives are filled with meaningless screams.'

He is accompanied by a devoted Renfield-esque companion, Barbado, an Afro-ed mute who plays frenzied bongos while the newly-vampirised hippies perform strange dance moves to a sitar soundtrack. Manson, an inveterate self-mythologiser, was fond of invoking such iconic figures as Hitler, the Beatles and Christ (although he claims he never gave his name upon arrest as 'Charles Manson aka Jesus Christ', as often reported, he did admit in a radio interview with KALX in 1985 to staging crucifixion scenes with his Family). Khorda is the literal embodiment of this idea, having apparently spent time in Babylon and Caesar's Rome and knowing Attila the Hun, Hitler and Stalin personally.

Climax after Climax of Terror and Desire

In contrast to the muted, murky photography of the Yorga films, *The Velvet Vampire* stands out for a number of reasons, including its visual style. Although clearly a low-budget offering, there is a striking use of colour and some surreal dream sequences, which owe more to Corman than Cocteau. The emphasis on psychedelic visuals (such as the undulating patterns of the opening credit sequence) put it at odds with the hand-held Gothic *vérité* seen in the Kelljan films. It also benefits from a haunting, atmospheric score by Clancy B. Grass III and Roger Dollarhide. These elements combine to create a film more memorable for its lurry, mildly kinky atmosphere than for its generic script and often terrible performances.

The title character seems to embody contemporary counterculture values, being both liberated and uninhibited, unlike the sullen, savage vampires dwelling in ghettoes and dungeons elsewhere. Like a latter-day Norma Desmond, the bisexual Diane LeFanu (surely named after Sheridan Le Fanu, author of the prototype lesbian vampire story *Carmilla* (1872)) swans around her desert hideaway in a variety of extravagant costumes and driving a dune-buggy, sheltering from the sun under a selection of wide-brimmed hats. The film plays fast-and-loose with vampire lore, showing Diane cowering from crosses and ultimately killed by the sun while at the same time having her up and about in the day and scrutinising her reflection in a compact mirror. There is also an unexpected twist in the scene where she uses her blood-drinking skills to preserve life rather than take it away, when she sucks out the venom after a woman is bitten by a rattlesnake. Like Delphine Seyrig in *Daughters of Darkness* (Kumel, 1971), Diane (Celeste Yarnall) is a very glamorous creature, lounging on the sofa in a striking pink dress, wolfing down raw liver. Like the earlier *Incense for the Damned* (Hartford-Davis, 1970) and the later *Martin*, the film suggests that Diane may not actually be a vampire at all in the supernatural sense. Rather, we are told she suffers from a rare blood disorder.

The director was Stephanie Rothman, the first woman to be awarded a Fellowship from the Directors Guild of America. Rothman has a cult following as a result of a handful of exploitation films made in the early 1970s, such as *Group Marriage* (1973) and *Terminal Island* (1973), although *The Velvet Vampire* remains her best-known work. After meeting a couple, Lee and Suzy, at the (again, pointedly-named) Stoker Gallery, Diane invites them to stay at her isolated desert dwelling. She quickly loses interest in the boorish, boneheaded Lee after they have sex and she then turns her attentions to his uptight wife, attempting to seduce her by paraphrasing Germaine Greer's *The Female Eunuch* (1970), saying of men, 'in their secret hearts they hate us'.

When she is attacked by a would-be rapist, Diane turns the tables and it's her attacker who is violently penetrated when she stabs him. Given such events, the statement in *The Aurum Encylopedia of Horror*, that 'despite the film's reputation, it is difficult to perceive any particularly feminist slant on the proceedings', is baffling.[12] The desert setting of the film means that Rothman can largely do away with the usual Gothic trappings (with the exception of the scenes in an old cemetery). The locations here are familiar not from horror films but from the Western: a ghost town, the Mojave Desert, a deserted mine. The desert, complete with double bed and ornate mirror, is also the setting for the frequent, dissolve-heavy dream sequences. We see Suzy and Lee in bed, interrupted by Diane, wearing a flowing scarlet dress. She drags Lee from his wife's arms and they embrace, only to have her swiftly abandon him and join Suzy between the sheets, where she cuts the not-unwilling woman's

5. Dream sequence in *The Velvet Vampire.*

breast with her knife and laps at the blood. As with the rest of *The Velvet Vampire*, what matters here is not the content of the dream/s (basically a re-emphasis of the love triangle plot which we are seeing elsewhere) but the drawn-out wooziness of the scenes.

Despite this desert setting, the most undeniably effective moments in Rothman's film come towards the end, where Diane follows Suzy to LA. Everyday locations become menacing as the vampire traps her would-be victim in a phone box and chases her through the crowded bus station and out into streets thronged with people. Suzy ends up being rescued by a bunch of cross-wielding hippies, a long-haired, bell-bottomed version of the torch-bearing villagers of the Universal Gothic horrors.

This ending is an ambivalent one: while this bunch of Jesus Freaks manage to rescue the heroine, they are also a creepy, amorphous mob and frighteningly eager to harass Diane, waving crosses, repeatedly crying out 'Get her' as they surround her and strip off her clothing as she writhes in agony.

Rothman and her co-writers, producer Charles S. Swartz and the aforementioned Maurice Jules, manage to evoke the would-be swinging lifestyle of the period: after Lee confesses to his wife that he had sex with Diane ('Ok, I got laid last night'), he placates her with 'Diane doesn't turn me on. She's a desert freak and I'm a Suzy freak.' The events of the film can be read as a sardonic comment on the death of the 1960s dream of free love: the square Suzy, married and possessive, uses Christianity to kill the swinging, polymorphously perverse Diane. This is a hippieish spin on the lesbian vampire films produced by Hammer with their string of wild and sexy female protagonists dispatched by old men with stakes and swords.

The sexual aspects of *The Velvet Vampire* may be emphasised (indeed overemphasised) by the tag-line 'She's waiting to love you to death ... climax after climax of terror and desire', but in contrast to European vampire films of the period, explicit sex is largely absent from the other counterculture vampire films. Instead, both *Blacula* and the *The Return of Count Yorga* offer up some Gothic romance as the vampires moon over mortal women. The *Blacula* films recycle a couple of hoary plot-lines from the Universal monster films, with Mamulwalde falling for the reincarnation of his dead wife, an idea Kim Newman calls 'the most tiresome of monster motivations',[13] that goes as far back as *The Mummy* (Freund, 1932) and which was still being recycled as recently as *Bram Stoker's Dracula* (Coppola, 1992). In the sequel, the vampire is seeking a cure for his affliction, as does *The Wolf Man* (Wagner, 1941) and the eponymous vampire of *House of Dracula* (Kenton, 1944). Even the scenes that could be played for titillation are undercut, as when two of Yorga's brides make out in a coffin while he watches with a joyless, jaded expression. The scene where one of the Count's victims caresses herself as he approaches may leave no doubt that the appeal of vampirism is sexual, but it pales next to the soft-core writhings of Hammer's lesbian vampire pictures or the genuinely perverse erotic charge of *Daughters of Darkness*.

Count Iorga

In the case of the Yorga film, the lack of nudity is particularly ironic. Kelljan and producer/actor Michael Macready had previously co-directed an incest-themed soft-porn picture, *Flesh of My Flesh* (1969), and *Count Yorga, Vampire* was conceived as a skin-flick with a bloodsucking theme, sporting the unwieldy title *The Loves of Count Iorga*. In fact, the print used for the MGM DVD still has this title but is followed by a separate card that reads *Vampire*. If the project hadn't been transformed into a horror film at the behest of Robert Quarry, it would have been the first vampire porno, anticipating the likes of *The Case of the Full Moon Murders* (Cunningham, 1973), *Spermula* (Matton, 1976), *Dracula Sucks* (Marshak, 1980) and *Cathula* (Barry, 2001).

One of Yorga's undead brides is played by the well-known soft-core performer Marsha Jordan, who had starred in the likes of *Her Odd Tastes* (Davis, 1969) and *Marsha the Erotic Housewife* (Davis, 1970). It's also notable how attractive young women appear in a number of scenes in roles so minor as to be almost funny: the mini-skirted doctor's assistant who we are told 'speaks no English' and the same doctor's bedmate, who provides a little comic relief before delivering a creepy story about a blood-drained baby. Both of these performers stand out for their poor line delivery, but that's perhaps understandable when one considers they were there for soft-core scenes that were shot, to be added later if the project needed spicing up.

The lack of the kind of seductive vamping that became a staple of vampire films since Christopher Lee became a virile, sexy Dracula is conspicuous by its almost total absence (although the scene where Yorga seduces Erica is strikingly shot like a traditional love scene). Rather, the trademark vampire attack in these films is a slow-motion, animalistic charge. Often these sequences provide genuine scares, with blaring, discordant sounds and grotesque make-up: the straggly-haired undead female cabbie who attacks Elisha Cook Jr in a morgue in *Blacula* or the corpse-like red-eyed Yorga jumping out on intruders. Indeed, in 1976, when the TV cops *Starsky and Hutch* encountered a disabled ballet teacher turned bloodsucker (played by John Saxon), in an uncharacteristically supernatural episode directed by the ubiquitous Kelljan, it was just such a vampire, arms outstretched, charging in slow-motion.

The form of these films, with their location shooting, hand-held cameras, often-amateurish performances, terrible make-up and grainy cinematography, is also striking, offering up a kind of *vérité* vampirism far removed from the sumptuous settings of European Gothic fantasies. The porno origins of *Count Yorga, Vampire* are again significant here, as the occasional wooden performance, post-sync sound and sleazy aesthetic are reminiscent of 1970s skinflicks. The *Blacula* and *Yorga* films use some obvious day-for-night photography and the lighting is variable. The cinematography is often very murky, presumably to hide the sparseness of the set decoration. The locations in the *Blacula* films are either papery sets (Castle Dracula) or anonymous interiors. Sometimes this aesthetic is used effectively to bring new life to a familiar image, as when a caped Yorga is filmed gliding down the winding staircase in his mansion with a shaky hand-held camera.

Both *Yorga* films feature long scenes where characters are seen in long shot walking around the city (in the first film, LA; the second, San Francisco) while dubbed dialogue plays on the soundtrack. Although clearly used for budgetary reasons (the use of long shots meaning the characters faces can't be seen, so there is no need to match up the sound post-production), these sequences help to further locate their horrors in a naturalistic setting.

The slipshod qualities of *Count Yorga, Vampire* could be put down to Kelljan's inexperience as a director and it's undeniable that *The Return of Count Yorga* is a more accomplished piece of work. But even with some brilliantly-staged sequences (such as Yorga filmed from under water as he strangles a man) and the confident, deliberate pacing, many of the same stylistic elements of the first film are carried over. There is a lot of hand-held camera work, particularly when the vampire women stage their home invasion. There are also a number of effective expressive devices used in both films, such as slow-motion, choppy editing, rapid zooms into the sun and/or moon and, in the sequel, pink-tinted flashbacks.

Unhappy Endings

Also noteworthy are the then-fashionable downer-endings to these films and the way they resist the restoration of order seen in traditional genre fare. The *Blacula* films end with the destruction of the vampire but with a distinct lack of the triumphalism one might expect. In the first film, Mamuwalde kills himself while the sequel ends with his voodoo doll being pierced with a wooden arrow. However, rather than the usual melting scene, we get a high-angle shot of the contorted vampire as the image freezes. The credits play out over a red-tinted image of an anguished Mamuwalde, while the upbeat disco sounds of the song 'Torment', by Marilyn Lovell and Bill Marx, are undercut by lyrics about 'living alone in endless empty space, so alone, so empty'.

The Yorga films pinch their closing scenes outright from *Dance of the Vampires* (Polanski, 1967), as would-be rescuers are bitten by their newly-transformed loved ones. In much the same way, the heroine of *The Velvet Vampire* finds out too late that her friend has been infected by the titular bloodsucker, the eerie score reappearing on the soundtrack. *Deathmaster* ends with the protagonist's girlfriend crumbling to dust in his arms before the film image itself appears to shatter. These endings are devoid of the draining nihilism seen in *Night of the Living Dead* and *Witchfinder General* (Reeves, 1968), both of which evoke a real and very timely sense of despair. Rather, this parade of crumbling bodies and fanged mouths lurching towards the camera comes over as one last good scare for the cinema audience, a series of 'flip/cynical evil-lives-on endings'.[14] It is entirely fitting given this sardonic viewpoint that unlike the many screen adaptations of Dracula, where the vampire is pitted against his charismatic and experienced nemesis Van Helsing, in these films there is no real hero figure. Both *Yorga* films feature the same actor (Roger Perry) playing different (seemingly-unrelated) doctors who take on the vampire, only to end up dead or undead. In an ironic twist, the first time we see Perry's character, Dr David Baldwin, in *The Return of Count Yorga*, he is attending a costume party dressed as Sherlock Holmes.

Where are Your Fangs?

Perhaps the main appeal of this group of films is the way they manage to successfully juxtapose the generic and the Gothic alongside the contemporary and the everyday. This idea is baldly spelt out by the narrator of *Count Yorga, Vampire*, when he says of the undead, 'I seem to be making use of the past tense. Perhaps the present would be more precise.'

Indeed, decades before the bloody post-modern hi-jinks of Wes Craven's *Scream* series (1996–2011), the counterculture vampire consciously highlights the absurdity of an undead monster in contemporary California. Pirie refers to this aspect as '"Vampires, you've got to be kidding" etc.'[15] A good example of this can be seen in *Count Yorga, Vampire*, when one character (no doubt speaking for the audience) says, 'I can't accept that vampires exist today,' only to be answered with a triumphant 'Today! Then you can concede they could have at one time.' There are numerous other examples of this as characters give a voice to the knowing viewers who are all-too-familiar with the genre. The gay antique dealer in *Blacula* who describes Dracula as 'the absolute creme de la creme of camp' or the incredulous response of one character in *The Return of Count Yorga* to the mention of vampires, 'Twentieth century man on the moon!'

Straight after Yorga's shock first appearance in the sequel, white-faced and baring his fangs, we cut to a fancy dress party and a character in a very unconvincing Dracula costume. When Yorga arrives, unaware of the party theme, he is greeted as 'another vampire' and asked 'Where are your fangs?' He spits back, 'Where are your manners?' This kind of waspish wit is a Yorga trademark. When asked by a long-haired youth playing a piano, 'Do you like this kind of music?', the Count replies 'Only when it's played well.' Dracula goes on to win the prize for best costume, apologising to Yorga as he accepts it.

The closest thing to a Van Helsing character we get in *The Return of Count Yorga* is Professor Rightstat, who is described as an authority on the undead. Rather than being a dynamic hero in the Peter Cushing mould, however, the Professor is portrayed by George Macready (the narrator of the first film) as a buffoon, a Ken Russell-lookalike wearing fringed buckskin, who answers a question about Yorga with a rambling speech about yoga, including the detail that he once got stuck in a locust (sic) position. Rightstat underlines the idea that anyone who believes in vampires in this contemporary milieu can only be regarded as an eccentric windbag.

There is also a strange scene where we see Yorga in his mansion, relaxing by watching Hammer's *The Vampire Lovers* (Baker, 1970) on TV, dubbed into Spanish.[16] The extract we see was no doubt chosen to add a further referential layer, as the screaming victim of Ingrid Pitt's vampire is played by Ferdy Mayne, who himself played a vampire Count in *Dance of the Vampires*.

These kinds of scenes, where familiar generic conventions and imagery are reimagined, occur throughout the six films: Mamuwalde transformed into a bat, flying through the streets of contemporary LA; Diane LeFanu,

6. A victim of Yorga feeds on her pet cat – *Count Yorga, Vampire.*

sitting at the back of a greyhound bus or slowly descending on a bus terminal escalator; an unfortunate Yorga victim, shambling though her chic, airy apartment eating her pet cat; a surfer dude who comes across Khorda's coffin on the beach; the creepy credit sequence of *The Return of Count Yorga*; the empty rooms and silent corridors of the grand mansion far from the cobweb-draped ruined castle of *Dracula* (Browning, 1931); the flashily-dressed pimps who admire Mamuwalde's cape, taking it as a sign not that he is a vampire but that he has money and is therefore worth mugging. Perhaps the emblematic scene for this cycle is the one which is used with little variation in three of the films. In the opening scene of *Count Yorga, Vampire*, we see a coffin on the back of a truck driving through the city. There is an almost identical scene in *Blacula* where we follow the coffin containing the undead Mamuwalde off a ship and into the city, while in *Deathmaster*, Barbado loads a coffin containing the title character onto a flat-bed truck and drives it along rural backroads.

Just how well these films transplant their monsters into a modern milieu can be underlined by a comparison with Hammer's last two Dracula pictures, both inspired by the box-office success of *Count Yorga, Vampire.*[17] *Dracula AD 1972* (Gibson, 1972) places a listless Christopher Lee as the eponymous Count in a would-be swinging Chelsea of coffee bars and groovy parties. But the decision to keep Dracula confined to a derelict church renders the whole exercise fairly pointless; indeed, it's very telling that the opening scene set in Victorian London is by far the best sequence in the whole film. The following year's *Satanic Rites of Dracula* (Gibson) is a considerable improvement, accurately described by Kim Newman as 'a James Bondish superscience thriller'.[18] Casting the Count as a property-developer/supervillain is a neat idea, but again, Lee spends most of his time lurking indoors. Hammer didn't have their heart in these updates, being much more comfortable with the forests and castles of an imaginary mittel Europa or the drawing rooms of Victorian England. The generational clashes of the late 1960s and early 1970s were dealt with in a much more resonant style in period Hammers such as *Taste the Blood of Dracula* (Sasdy, 1969) and *Demons of the Mind* (Sykes, 1972) than in their slipshod Dracula updates.

Everything Old is New Again

Although this device of locating the supernatural within a recognisable reality may seem startling to those more familiar with the period films of Hammer and the soft-porn surrealism of Jean Rollin, they are actually a throwback to Bram Stoker's novel, the ur-text of vampire lore with its letters, diary entries recorded on phonographs and use of real locations such as Whitby and Hampstead Heath. Indeed, for all their Afros and sideburns, free love and VW camper vans, almost all of these films follow the template laid down by Stoker, with an aristocratic vampire travelling from the old world (be it Africa, Bulgaria, Europe) to the new. Only *The Velvet Vampire* offers an authentically American vampire. For contemporary audiences, this vampire-infested California would have been every bit as familiar as Dracula's London was to Stoker's Victorian readership. Thus, the counterculture vampire films offer something which tastes very like fresh blood simply by going back to the source.

Notes

1 Tony Rayns, 'What Might Have Been', in *1000 Films to Change Your Life* (London: Time Out, 2006), p. 179.

2 Anon., 'Rosemary's Baby', in P. Hardy (ed.), *The Aurum Encyclopedia of Horror* (London: Aurum Press, 1985a), p. 199.

3 London Bugliosi, 'The Manson Murders Forty Years On', *Newsweek*, 2009; http://www.newsweek.com/2009/07/31/the-manson-murders-at-40.html (accessed 1 May 2011).

4 The intriguingly titled *Black the Ripper* is mentioned in Kim Newman's *Nightmare Movies* (1988), but it's doubtful the film was ever made.

5 Henry Benshoff, 'Blaxploitation Horror Films: Generic Reappropriation or Reinscription', in E. Mathijs and X. Mendik (eds), *The Cult Film Reader* (New York: Open University Press, 2008), p. 219.

6 Robin Wood, 'From Buddies to Lovers', in *Hollywood from Vietnam to Reagan* (New York: Columbia University Press, 1986), p. 229.

7 In Benshoff, 'Blaxploitation', p. 219.

8 David Pirie, *The Vampire Cinema* (London: Galley Press, 1977), p. 138.

9 Hal Hinson, 'The Addiction', *Washington Post*, 1995; http://www.washingtonpost.com/wpsrv/style/longterm/movies/videos/theaddictionrhinson_c03419.htm (accessed 1 May 2011).

10 Manson Family imagery and references are still turning up in horror films 40 years after the Tate–LaBianca murders: *The Manson Family* (Van Bebber, 2003), *Snuff-Movie* (Rose, 2005) and *The Strangers* (Bertino, 2008).

11 Steve Biodrowski, 'Count Yorga Speaks!', Cinefantastique Online, 2004; http://cinefantastiqueonline.com/2008/05/interview-count-yorga-speaks/ (accessed 24 April 2011).

12 Anon., 'Velvet Vampire, The', in P. Hardy (ed.), *The Aurum Encyclopedia of Horror* (London: Aurum Press, 1985b), p. 244.

13 'Bloodlines', *Sight and Sound*, 3:1 (1993): 13.

14 Kim Newman, *Nightmare Movies* (New York: Harmony Books, 1988), p. 25.

15 Pirie, *Vampire Cinema*, p. 136.

16 The underrated British film *The Fiend* (Hartford-Davis, 1971) has a similar reference to Hammer's output, where the eponymous sex killer picks up a woman at a cinema showing a double-bill of *Scars of Dracula* (Baker, 1970) and *Horror of Frankenstein* (Sangster, 1970).

17 Wisely, Lee was absent for Hammer's last Dracula project, *The Legend of the Seven Golden Vampires* (Houghton, 1974), and his place was taken by the woeful John Forbes-Robertson.

18 Newman, *Nightmare Movies*, p. 18.

2

TAKING BACK THE NIGHT

Dracula's Daughter in New York

Stacey Abbott

In the 1897 novel *Dracula*, the eponymous Count informs the young solicitor Jonathan Harker that:

> I long to go through the crowded streets of your mighty London, to be in the midst of the whirl and rush of humanity, to share its life, its change, its death, and all that makes it what it is.[1]

With this statement, Bram Stoker's novel introduced a significant new element to the vampire story that over time has become a common trope of the genre in literature, film and television. The modern vampire has finally escaped the rural aristocratic castle associated with the pre-modern and the Gothic, and relocated to an urban setting. As I have argued elsewhere, from Dracula to Martin and from Lestat to Blade or Angel, the vampire has increasingly been represented as released from superstition and tradition, and part of this reconfiguration is his change of location.[2] These vampires regularly circulate around cities as diverse as London, Pittsburgh, New Orleans, Los Angeles, Paris, Prague, Toronto and Moscow, transforming the vampire from a pre-modern monster to an urban *flâneur*, increasingly at home in the night-time city.

The cinematic female vampire, however, has largely been denied this transformation, often relegated to the margins in favour of her male counterparts. Rarely has she been allowed to escape the image of the 'Fatal Woman' described by Christopher Frayling as the female alternative to the male 'Satanic Lord' immortalised in such stories as Polidori's *The Vampyre* (1819) and Stoker's *Dracula*. The 'Fatal

Woman' is a sexually aggressive and predatory woman that developed in nineteenth-century literature, such as Johann Ludwig Tiek's 'Wake Not the Dead' (1800) and Sheridan Le Fanu's *Carmilla* (1872).[3] This representation was reinforced within nineteenth- and early twentieth-century paintings such as Philip Burne-Jones' *The Vampire* (*c.* 1897), Félicièn Robs' *The Absinthe Drinker* (1890), Manuel Rose's *Interior of a Café* (*c.* 1914) and Edvard Munch's *Vampire* (*c.* 1895/1902). As Bram Dijkstra argues, 'the vampire had come to represent woman as the personification of everything negative that linked sex, ownership, and money ... creatures with unnatural, viraginous tendencies, polyandrous murderers, seed-hungry, blood lusting vampires'.[4] This perception of the female vampire is encapsulated in Dracula's three monstrous brides, who evoke in Jonathan Harker an uneasy sense of longing and dread, causing him to describe them as 'both thrilling and repulsive'.[5] This representation of the female vampire – both beautiful and monstrous – still holds as one of the most dominant images in vampire cinema, best exemplified in the recurring representation of the brides in Tod Browning's *Dracula* (1931), Terence Fisher's *Bride's of Dracula* (1960), Francis Ford Coppola's *Bram Stoker's Dracula* (1992), and Stephen Sommers' *Van Helsing* (2004).

In recent years, the genre has progressively privileged the male vampire's point of view in both mainstream and independent film (see *The Dracula Tape, Interview with the Vampire*, *Near Dark*, *Blade* and *Angel*), giving the vampire an increasingly morally ambiguous representation, while female vampires in mainstream film have been provided with less agency or ambivalence. Their voice and perspective are usually suppressed and they are rarely allowed to embrace and express the pain *and* exhilaration at being a vampire in the manner of Anne Rice's Lestat, let alone their experience of the 'whirl and rush' of the city. When they do, as when television vampires Darla and Drusilla go on both a shopping and murder spree in downtown Los Angeles,[6] they are presented as out of control and monstrous, eventually to be hunted down and torched by the 'good' vampire Angel.[7]

All of this tends to conform to beliefs that the night-time urban landscape is an inappropriate place for women – even vampiric ones. Meanwhile, the female vampire is depicted as simply the physical embodiment of voracious desire, lacking the restraint demonstrated by contemporary male vampires such as Gary Oldman's Dracula who chooses not to turn Mina into a vampire because he 'loves her too much to condemn' her – or Blade's resistance to the thirst. In the 1990s, however, a series of American independent films were made that challenged these notions. Michael Almereyda's *Nadja* (1994), Abel Ferrara's *The Addiction* (1995) and Larry Fessenden's *Habit* (1995) all reimagine the female vampire as a *flâneuse* at home in New York, the city that never sleeps.[8]

More significantly, as I will demonstrate through a close analysis of *Nadja*, the choice to make independent rather than mainstream films enabled the filmmakers to undermine the established conventions of the genre by offering an alternative representation of the female vampire, highlighting her emotional complexity and moral ambiguity. There are of course significant precursors to *Nadja*, such as the Universal sequel to Browning's *Dracula*, *Dracula's Daughter* (Lambert Hillyer, 1936), the European art-horror film *Daughters of Darkness* (Harry Kumel, 1971), Tony Scott's MTV-styled adaptation of Whitley Streiber's book, *The Hunger* (1983), and Kathryn Bigelow's indie action film, *Near Dark* (1987). To varying degrees, each of these films stand somewhat apart from mainstream cinema to offer a morally ambiguous and at times sympathetic representation of their lead vampires, Countess Zalenska, Elisabeth Bathory, Miriam Blaylock and Mae respectively. Each film suggests that the women enjoy a sensual and sensorial experience of the world as a result of their vampirism, but they do not, however, go so far as to provide their direct point of view, causing the women to remain dangerously enigmatic. Anna, in Fessenden's *Habit*, is equally enigmatic as the film is told from the male protagonist Sam's point of view. While Sam's perspective is, due to his drinking and a potential breakdown, not to be trusted, Anna still remains elusive. *The Addiction* is told from the female vampire Kathy's point of view but is so preoccupied with Kathy's philosophical debates about the nature of evil and addiction, that it offers little in the way of sensorial experience. In contrast, I will demonstrate that *Nadja* adopts an experimental aesthetic form that privileges the female vampire's point of view and subjective experience of the city, while also engaging in a dialogue with earlier vampire films as a means of offering an alternative reflection on the genre.

Indie Cinema

In beginning his discussion of independent American cinema, Michael Allen raises the question, 'What, exactly, is an independent American film?' Allen quite rightly points out that there is not one way of understanding this term. It can range from 'small, personal, and personally financed films' to 'larger-budget productions ... intended for distribution by the major studios'.[9] The methods of identifying independent films can vary, but generally focus on financing, 'personal vision', approaches to narrative and aesthetics, and the 'presence or absence of well-known names, actors and stars'.[10] More specifically, Allen argues that notions of American independent and mainstream cinema are indelibly intertwined for 'each needs to identify the other as "Other"'.[11] In this respect, much of indie cinema is designed to present an alternative perspective or vision that is distinct from the mainstream. Indie vampire films like *Nadja* (and *The Addiction* and *Habit*), therefore, are a self-conscious response to the well-established vampire genre, offering a fresh approach, informed by the director's personal vision for the genre. While mainstream vampire films perpetuate the dominance of the male vampire, the indie vampire film responded with a re-examination of the representation of women in the genre.

Directing his first short in 1985, Michael Almereyda emerged as a filmmaker during a period of growth for indie cinema. As Allen points out, in 1985, 50 independent American films were released, but by 1998, this had risen to over 1,000. Jim Hillier argues that the phenomenal success of Steven Sodenbergh's *sex, lies and videotape* in 1989 was a landmark moment, as it demonstrated the artistic and financial potential for indie cinema. The 1990s was also a period in which there was an increase in local indie cinema produced out of New York due to a boycott on mainstream filmmaking by the East Coast Council of Movie-Trade Reps.[12] Almereyda became known at this time for his low-budget art-house films. Throughout his career he has hovered on the margins of the mainstream, making films like *Nadja* and *The Eternal* (1998), genre films with comic undercurrents and a quirky indie style and sensibility, while interspersing these feature productions with low-budget experimental shorts, such as *Another Girl, Another Planet* (1992) and *The Rocking Horse Winner* (1997), and documentaries, such as *At Sundance* (1995) and *This So-Called*

Disaster (2003). His work draws on significant influences from the avant-garde, particularly the experimental films of Sadie Benning, as well as European art cinema.[13]

Indie Aesthetics

Nadja's independent status stands out particularly at a time when the vampire genre was becoming increasingly big budget with films such as *Bram Stoker's Dracula* (Francis Ford Coppola, 1992), *Interview with the Vampire* (Neil Jordan, 1994) and *Blade* (Stephen Norrington, 1998), each featuring sumptuous production values, special effects, major stars (such as Anthony Hopkins, Tom Cruise and Wesley Snipes) and/or star directors. In contrast, *Nadja* uses minimal, if any, special effects and quite realistic mise-en-scene, foregoing traditional vampire fangs and monster make-up in favour of a more natural, human appearance. Its cast includes actors such as Elina Löwensohn, Martin Donavan, Galaxy Craze and Suzy Amis, largely associated with independent cinema; in particular, Donavan and Löwensohn have repeatedly appeared in the films of indie darling Hal Hartley. *Nadja* further showcases its roots in indie filmmaking by casting Peter Fonda, an icon of 1960s counterculture and star and writer of *Easy Rider* (Dennis Hopper, 1969), as a hippie Van Helsing.

The aesthetics of the film also emphasises its independent nature. *Nadja*, like *The Addiction,* was shot in black and white at the insistence of its director to draw links with the vampire genre's classic horror origins as well as to emphasise an association with the avant-garde. Black and white, while once an industry standard, is now largely the purview of pastiche or art cinema – here it is both. For instance when Van Helsing's nephew Jim is first told, by his wife Lucy, that his uncle has murdered a man by thrusting a stake through the heart, Jim repeats this statement, declaring, 'I just can't picture it.' This statement is followed by a close-up of a shadow of an arm with a hammer which cuts to a close-up of the hammer pounding the stake, accompanied by a loud clap of thunder. The sequence then cuts to Lucy responding, 'I can' – and of course so can the audience. The use of expressionist shadows and thunder in this sequence, as well as the grainy scratched-up film stock, is deliberately reminiscent of

7. Nadja's pale face and cloak, reminiscent of Countess Zaleska from *Dracula's Daughter*.

the classic black and white horror films that *Nadja* is both remaking and pastiching. This aesthetic association with Universal horror is reinforced by the use of a flickering close-up of Bela Lugosi (star of Browning's *Dracula*), providing a hypnotic stare (the shot is actually taken from *White Zombie* (Victor Halperin, 1932)), as Van Helsing recounts Dracula's history. While the extreme long shots of Dracula looming over a cliff-face seem to suggest the image of Christopher Lee as Dracula, this shot of Lugosi firmly locates *Nadja* within the Universal horror tradition. Also, the vampire Nadja herself, with her pale face, dark lips and hair, and propensity for wearing a long black cloak, is a conscious allusion to the expressionist image of Countess Zaleska from *Dracula's Daughter*.

The film's black and white cinematography, however, also contains within it echoes of art cinema, with a particular affinity with Carl Dreyer's *Vampyr* (1932). While Almereyda's film is a creative remake of *Dracula's Daughter* (as well as a loose adaptation of André Breton's surrealist novel *Nadja*), *Vampyr* is credited as being adapted from Sheridan Le Fanu's collection of novellas *In a Glass Darkly* which includes the iconic female vampire story *Carmilla*. This adaptation is, however, interpreted through the lens of impressionist cinematography and sound. David Rudkin argues that *Vampyr* is 'visually the most transgressive [film] in existence'.[14] Shot largely as a silent film, with the sound post-synchronised, Dreyer's film leads its protagonist Allan Gray through a haunted landscape populated by vampires, ghosts and shadows, created through his use of a roving camera, the disjunction between sound and image, and a series of unsettling compositions. The aesthetic approach to *Vampyr* produces a disturbing and dream-like atmosphere, in which the line between dream and reality is not blurred but invisible. *Nadja* similarly takes place in a disorienting, dream-like landscape as the film's protagonists – Jim, Lucy and Van Helsing – are lured into the surreal world of the vampire. The film's use of low-key lighting transforms Nadja's contemporary New York apartment into a Gothic enclave, where she can 'find comfort in shadows', but this Gothic atmosphere is rendered increasingly oneiric by the film's use of soft-focus, as well as a slow roving camera that seems to haunt every location. The sound in the film is often disjunctive, sometimes hypnotic and dreamy, other times grating and disjointed, calling to mind the work of American surrealist director David Lynch who produced *Nadja*.

The haunting surrealism of the film is particularly enhanced by Almereyda's use of pixelvision – the Fisher Price PXL2000 toy video camera that was favoured by experimental filmmakers in the 1990s and which Almereyda uses intermittently throughout the film. To Almereyda, this toy camera's pixelated imagery brings out both the poetry and the reality of its subject. Almereyda explains that with pixelvision 'you have the sense that you're watching something intensely fragile and secret, on the threshold of visibility'.[15] Its shimmering grainy quality calls to mind the imagery of *Vampyr*, which looks as if the majority of the film was shot through gauze. Where in *Vampyr* the style suggests that Gray has entered a dreamy netherworld in which among other things he encounters a vampire, the repeated transitions from 35mm footage into pixelvision throughout *Nadja* gives the impression that as they come under the vampire's influence, the characters become overwhelmed by her subjective experience and perception. This is a significant difference from both *Vampyr* and *Dracula's Daughter.* In *Vampyr*, the vampire Marguerite Chopin is a shadowy presence that haunts the periphery of the narrative, and while *Dracula's Daughter* may initially offer a more sympathetic portrayal of the Countess's desire to be free of the vampire curse, her point of view is still withheld from the audience so she remains mysterious.

Geoff King claims that the use of pixelvision in *Nadja* is less radical then in Almereyda's earlier film *Another Girl Another Planet,* as 'it is more clearly motivated' by the plot.[16] I would argue, however, that while the pixelvision is narratively motivated rather than experimental, it is precisely *because* of its narrative function that this aesthetic choice *is* radical in genre terms. It is an attempt to visually convey the perspective of the vampire, something that has largely been associated with the male vampire, but here the point of view is with the female vampire. In *Interview with the Vampire,* Louis explains that when he was transformed into a vampire, he began to see 'as a vampire', becoming transfixed by the beauty of all shapes and colours as if he had never seen them before.[17] Similarly, the vampire Lestat explains that with his transformation came a new sensual experience of the world, in which

> [e]ach change in the moving air was caressing. And when there came from the softly lighted city beyond a chorus of dim church bells ringing the hour, they did not mark the passage of mortal time. They were only the purest music, and I lay stunned, my mouth open, as I stared at the passing clouds.[18]

Through these passages, Rice suggests that the vampire's heightened senses enable him to take pleasure in every emotion and sensation. While many mainstream vampire films, like *Dracula* (John Badham, 1979) and *Bram Stoker's Dracula*, use an opulent mise-en-scene to convey the sensuality of the vampire, and others, such as *Blade* and *Underworld* (Len Wiseman, 2003), use fast paced editing, time-lapse photography and action choreography to convey their pleasure in violence, these films never traverse beneath the surface to capture the interiority of the vampire. *Near Dark* does *suggest* that for Mae the allure of being a vampire is *how* she experiences the night as she desperately tries to get love-interest Caleb to see and hear the night as she does:

> Caleb: Something you want to show me?
> Mae: The night.
> Caleb: What about it?
> Mae: It's dark.
> Caleb: I noticed.
> Mae: It's also bright. It'll blind you.

Caleb: I can't see.
Mae: Well, listen. Do you hear it?
Caleb: Listen? I don't hear nothing.
Mae: Well listen hard ... Do you hear it?
Caleb: Hear what?
Mae: The Night. It's deafening.

While Mae describes the night as both blinding and deafening, the film is, however, unable to convey what it is that she sees and hears. Her subjectivity remains elusive, as is her sensual experience of the night.

The stylistic choice to use pixelvision in *Nadja*, therefore, is an attempt to aesthetically convey the female vampire's sensual experience of her vampiric night-time existence. Nadja is alive to all stimuli as clearly expressed in her opening line in the film: 'Nights. Nights without sleep. Long nights in which the brain lights up like a big city.' This haunting narration is accompanied by a close-up of Nadja's face, over which the pixelated streaming lights of the city are superimposed. The dreaminess of the opening montage of urban images establishes an atmosphere of late night reverie for the urban vampire.

This is later reaffirmed during the love scene between Nadja and Lucy in which they laugh, dance, stare hypnotically at the shimmering light of sparklers before making love, all captured in the euphoric visual style of pixelvision. This sequence is playful and light-hearted, standing in contrast to Countess Zaleska's attempted seduction of a destitute model which ends with the girl's screams, or the graphic eroticism of *The Hunger* in which Miriam orchestrates an elaborate seduction of Sarah. The use of pixelvision in this scene conveys Nadja's happiness, and the seduction of Lucy is presented as impulsive and erotically fulfilling for both women.

The scene between Lucy and Nadja, as they play with sparklers, talk about Lucy's pet tarantula Bela, and snap polaroids, is a brief moment of tenderness and whimsy; most of the other characters in the film appear traumatised, unhappy or numb, shuffling through their daytime existence and described by Van Helsing as the Walking Dead. Lucy and her husband Jim are disconnected, alienated from each other and the world around them; Nadja's brother Edgar is in love with his nurse Cassandra but is unable to act because he is paralysed by self-loathing; and Cassandra describes herself as 'having

8. City lights superimposed over Nadja's face, whose 'brain lights up like a big city'.

a nervous breakdown'. In contrast, Nadja is alive to the sensations around her, and embraces positive and negative experiences. She tells Lucy that she is afraid of nothing and while she recognises that 'life is full of pain', her pain is 'the pain of fleeting joy' – the sorrow gained from the experience of happiness while also knowing it is ephemeral. The vampire, open to all sensations, feels both pain and joy simultaneously.

Furthermore, as I've argued elsewhere, the abstract use of superimposition and seamless dissolves in the opening montage sequences visually equates Nadja with the city itself.[19] Almereyda's Nadja, however, is not simply drawn to any city, but rather demonstrates a particular affinity with the New York experience as she explains, 'Here you feel so many things rushing together. It even gets more exciting after midnight.' For Nadja, New York has replaced the London depicted in Stoker's novel and in *Dracula's Daughter* and it is truly the city that never sleeps. In *Dracula's Daughter*, the vampire only appears on the street when she is hunting, and spends the rest of her time sequestered in her apartment in Russell Square as well as her Chelsea artist's studio. In *Daughters of Darkness*, Elisabeth Bathory describes herself as 'an outmoded character, nothing more ... The beautiful stranger, slightly sad, slightly mysterious, that haunts one place after another. Two weeks ago in Nice and Monte Carlo, two days ago in Brouage.' While the implication is that she circulates through these European cities, she is only shown haunting the empty and desolate hotel in Ostend, seemingly an echo of the past. Similarly, Miriam Blaylock may live in New York but in an Edwardian-styled townhouse. These vampires do not embrace the modern or the urban, but rather, like ghosts, haunt timeless environments in which they can secure themselves from the passage of time. While Mae in *Near Dark* is a far more modern vampire who seems to share Nadja's sensorial pleasures, she circulates within the more liminal border space between the city and the desert, hunting on highways, truck stops and roadside bars. She is denied entry into the centre of the city and therefore prohibited from the vampire experience that Nadja enjoys. In *Nadja*, the vampire is repeatedly represented in the city and recognises that the streets are crowded, offering stimulus, choice and a cloak of invisibility, all ideal for a vampire. Nadja may occasionally dream of peace and tranquillity, but it is the 'whirl and rush' of the city that, like Dracula, attracts and excites her.

Indie Storytelling

The indie vampire film not only provides access to the female vampire's subjectivity through its propensity for a more offbeat aesthetic style, but also utilises its 'relaxed ... decentred structure' to present the vampire as morally complex and ambiguous.[20] The female vampires in *The Addiction*, *Habit* and *Nadja* are dominant and sexually aggressive, but they cannot be reduced to the one-dimensional female sexual predators of *Bram Stoker's Dracula* and *Van Helsing*. They are either seemingly complex but unknowable as in *Habit*, or they are women who are struggling with their inherent good and evil. In *The Addiction*, Kathy, a philosophy doctoral student, is bitten by a vampire and, as Geoff King argues, the fact

> ... that Kathleen becomes a vampire in the literal sense is strongly suggested – she cannot eat or sleep, cannot bear strong sunlight, covers up her mirrors and possesses what appears to be superhuman strength – but the parallels drawn with both drug addiction and historical evils suggest that this

experience is not so easily separable from its more earthbound equivalents.[21]

In this film, Kathy both condemns and commits great evil, and continually struggles with what this means for her and humanity. As King suggests, it is the independent status of the film that enables it to integrate the vampire film with discourses inspired by Nietzsche, Sartre, Becket and Burroughs.[22]

In *Nadja*, Almereyda presents the vampire's struggle with her vampiric nature more ambiguously. While in *Dracula's Daughter*, Zaleska clearly searches for release from her vampiric condition, first through the death of Dracula and secondly through the promise of scientific help provided by Doctor Garth – both attempts fail. Realising that she is doomed to darkness, Zaleska, in vampiric fashion, looks for eternal companionship which eventually leads to her death. Nadja, in contrast, talks of being free of her 'bastard' father Count Dracula and is haunted by the loss of her human mother who died in childbirth, but what that freedom means for her is unclear. Zaleska initially celebrates the death of Dracula before realising that her curse has not been broken and that she must go out into London to hunt. Nadja goes out into the night by choice to celebrate Dracula's death. But this sojourn into the night is presented as both euphoric and melancholic, as shots of her dancing are intercut with her walking down the street, looking up into the sky as snow begins to fall and her smile turns to tears. From this point onward, Nadja is driven, but unlike Zaleska who is driven by her obsessive desire for release, Nadja is driven by love – love of Lucy, her brother Edgar and her experience of life. This ambiguity means that while she continues to be violent and manipulative (i.e., she still embraces being a vampire), she is not reduced to a stereotype like her monstrous sisters in *Blade* and *Bram Stoker's Dracula*. Instead, she is shown to be capable of great tenderness and love.

In many mainstream vampire films, following the classic Hollywood model, the female vampire must be destroyed in order to facilitate a return to normality, so Blade must stake his now vampiric mother to restore his memory of her as the nurturing mother who gave birth to him,[23] or Van Helsing must behead Dracula's three brides who seek to lure the 'good' Mina to their world (*Bram Stoker's Dracula*). In both cases, these violent deaths serve as precursors to the dramatically climatic destruction of the male vampire that closes the narrative. In other films, like *Near Dark, Fright Night* and *The Lost Boys*, the female vampire is reclaimed into normality by being cured of her vampirism – either through transfusion or by killing the head vampire – and reinstated into a heterosexual couple. In contrast, these indie vampire films are given far more open endings, in keeping with their independent nature. *Habit* ends with the disappearance of the 'vampire' Anna and the death of the film's protagonist Sam, suggesting that Anna has escaped as the film ends on a shot of 'her' boat leaving New York harbour, in reverse of the shot that opens the film. In *The Addiction* and *Nadja*, both Kathy and Nadja are seemingly reborn, although the implications of their rebirth are quite ambiguous. The religious overtones of *The Addiction*'s narrative infuse her rebirth with the theme of redemption, although this redemption does not seem to be at the expense of her narrative agency. In *Nadja*, Almereyda chooses to rework a form of rebirth that takes place in *Daughters of Darkness* in which the lead vampire, Elizabeth Bathory, dies violently but is then seemingly, and inexplicably, reborn in her protégé. In the film, Bathory burns in the sunlight after a car crash, but her lover Valerie, who should also have died in the car, appears three months later dressed in Bathory's clothes, speaking in her voice and seducing another young couple as Bathory did to her and her husband, suggesting that the vampire is trapped in a cycle of repetition. This cycle of repetition is also highlighted in the ambiguous conclusion to *The Hunger*, in which Sarah appears to have taken the place of the vampire Miriam Blaylock, who, due to accelerated ageing, has been transformed into living skeletal remains locked in a coffin calling for her lover. This cycle can be read in two ways. Either the female vampire cannot be destroyed or contained and therefore lives on, or she is trapped in an endless repetition, unable to evolve. The films are deliberately open to interpretation, with endings that are ambiguous and also darkly unsettling.

Nadja's rebirth, however, seems less random if equally ambiguous. Instead, it is a choice made by the vampire to break the vampiric cycle. Unlike Zaleska, who accepts her fate, Nadja chooses to transfuse her blood into the body of her brother's girlfriend, Cassandra, enabling her spirit to escape into Cassandra when Nadja's body is staked by Van Helsing and Edgar. Where in *Dracula*, Van Helsing and the other

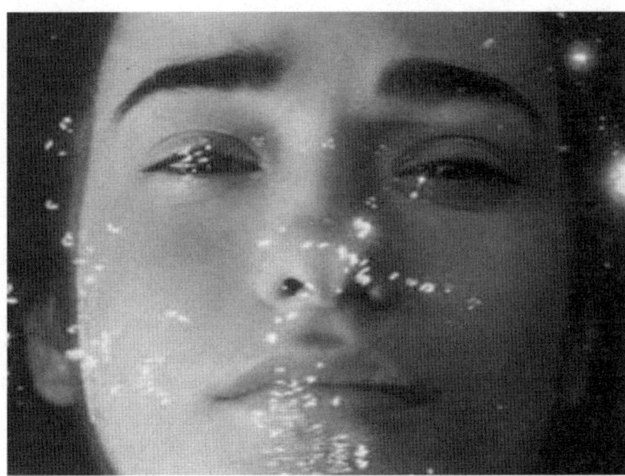

9. Nadja and Cassandra merge.

men presuppose that by staking the vampire Lucy they will save her spirit from damnation, in *Nadja* it is the vampire that manoeuvres the men into staking her in order to facilitate the transference of her spirit, allowing her to merge with Cassandra. As she explains to her servant Renfield, 'This is how I want it.' Here Almereyda also reworks the convention of the transfusion, made popular in Stoker's novel *Dracula* when Van Helsing unsuccessfully attempts to save Dracula's first victim Lucy by transfusing the blood of three men into her body. The convention was later adopted by Kathryn Bigelow for *Near Dark* when Caleb successfully 'saves' Mae through a blood transfusion. In this case, the transfusion is forced upon her and the implication of the ending of the film is unclear. When Caleb opens the barn doors to let the sunshine in, Mae cringes in terror, having run from the sun for four years. The final image of Caleb holding her as she stares into the daylight is unsettling. She may have Caleb, and is thus reinstated into a traditional feminine role as wife and mother to Caleb's sister, but she has lost the night and all of its wonder.

In the case of Nadja, her transference into Cassandra does mean that she is recouped into a heterosexual couple at the film's conclusion when she marries Edgar, but the implied incest of this union undermines any sense of this being a return to 'normality'. Furthermore, the film's conclusion is completely open-ended, inviting interpretation. The film ends as it begins, with Nadja's voice-over, spoken over a close-up Cassandra, in the daytime floating in a pool which slowly dissolves into the face of Nadja, both women living as one. Whether Nadja can ever take back the night and re-experience the 'whirl and rush' of the night-time city is unclear, as the pixelvision ceases to be used at this point in the film and the final images are all shot in the day. But what is clear is that, unlike so many of her vampiric predecessors, she is able to live, move on and evolve on her terms, and significantly her point of view still informs the structure of the film. Where her opening voice-over spoke of the sensorial excitement of the city at night, her concluding voice-over raises questions about identity – hers and Cassandra's:

> Sometimes at night, I hear a voice in my head. Who is it? Is it you? Nadja? Is it true that the beyond – that everything beyond is here in this life? I can't hear you. Who's there? Is it only me? Is it myself?

What this transference means for both women is unknown, but *Nadja*'s conclusion on a series of existential questions, rather than resolved absolutes, reasserts that in the indie vampire film, the female vampire's voice cannot be silenced.

Notes

1 Bram Stoker, *Dracula* (Oxford: Oxford University Press, 1897/1996), p. 20.

2 Stacey Abbott, *Celluloid Vampires: Life After Death in the Modern World* (Austin: University of Texas Press, 2007).

3 Christopher Frayling, *Vampyres: Lord Byron to Count Dracula* (London and Boston: Faber and Faber, 1991), p. 62.

4 Bram Dijkstra, *Idols of Perversity: Fantasies of Feminist Evil in Fin-de-Siecle Culture* (Oxford and New York: Oxford University Press, 1986), p. 351.

5 Stoker, *Dracula*, p. 3.

6 'Reunion', *Angel* (James Contner, 2000, 2.10).

7 'Redefinition', *Angel* (Michael Grossman, 2001, 2.11). As an example of serial television, *Angel* does grant Darla greater character development then most female vampires, particularly as she struggles with her conscience when she becomes pregnant with Angel's son. But even Darla's development is restricted, and while vampires Angel and Spike are shown to confront their evil pasts and atone for their sins by becoming champions fighting for good, Darla never fully seeks redemption except by killing herself in order to give birth to her son – 'The one good thing that she and Angel did together.'

8 For a more detailed discussion of the female vampire in relation to notions of the *flâneuse* and representations of New York, please see Abbott, 2007, pp. 141–62.
9 Michael Allen, *Contemporary US Cinema* (Harlow: Pearson Education Limited, 2003), p. 139.
10 Allen, *Contemporary US Cinema*, p. 139.
11 Allen, *Contemporary US Cinema*, p. 144.
12 Abbott, *Celluloid Vampires*, p. 144.
13 For further discussion of Almereyda's career, see Jeremiah Kipp, 'Michael Almereyda', *Senses of Cinema* 25 (2003), available at: http://www.sensesofcinema.com/2003/great-directors/almereyda/ (accessed 15 July 2010).
14 David Rudkin, *Vampyr* (London: BFI Publishing, 2005), p. 24.
15 Michael Almereyda, 'My Stunning Future: The Luxuries of Pixelvision', *Fleeting Joy: The Films of Michael Almereyda* (1993). Available at: http://fleetingjoy.fishbucket.com/writing.php?id=5 (accessed 1 July 2011).
16 Geoff King, *American Independent Cinema* (London and New York: I.B.Tauris, 2009), p. 137.
17 Anne Rice, *Interview with the Vampire* (London: Futura, 1976/1992), p. 24.
18 Anne Rice, *The Vampire Lestat* (London: Futura, 1985/1993), p. 110.
19 Abbott, *Celluloid Vampires*, pp. 146–47.
20 King, *American Independent Cinema*, p. 59.
21 King, *American Independent Cinema*, p. 174.
22 King, *American Independent Cinema*, p.174.
23 This is in many ways a repeat of the formula established in *Dracula* when Van Helsing, Arthur, Seward and Quincy destroy the 'thing' that has taken their beloved Lucy's form, described by Seward as 'a nightmare of Lucy' (Stoker, 1897/1996, p. 215). Once staked, however, Seward comments that, 'There in the coffin lay no longer the foul Thing that we had so dreaded and grown to hate that the work of her destruction was yielded as a privilege to the one best entitled to it, but Lucy as we had seen her in her life, with her face of unequalled sweetness and purity' (ibid., 216–17).

3

NORTHERN DARKNESS

The Curious Case of the Swedish Vampire

Peter Hutchings

Going Global?

On both occasions we begin with snow. It fills the screen, clearly visible against a night-time setting. In one instance it is Swedish snow; in the other it is initially Ukrainian snow although it quickly changes to Swedish snow, too, as the narrative proceeds. In the context of cinematic stories of the undead, this curtain of whiteness is provocative and a little unsettling. It bestows distinctiveness but at the same time it dislocates things; it is not really what you expect when it comes to vampires, at least not so far as their cinematic existence is concerned. Snow-laden vampire films are rare, until recently at least, with *Dance of the Vampires* (Roman Polanski, 1967) and the more recent *30 Days of Night* (David Slade, 2007) probably the only major examples. Yet snow is a constant presence in *Frostbite* (*Frostbiten*, Anders Banke, 2006) and *Let the Right One In* (*Låt den rätte komma in*, Tomas Alfredson, 2008), the two Swedish vampire films upon which this chapter focuses, and it acts as a reminder that there is something just a little bit out of the ordinary about them. Indeed, this snowiness seems not only to invite reflection on the unusual place of these films within vampire culture, but also drives the films themselves, pushing them in directions possibly not that common in vampire cinema. Underpinning this all is a preoccupation with qualities of coldness and whiteness as filmmakers and audiences alike are drawn inexorably towards one simple question. What the hell are vampires doing in Sweden?

Invoking the national in this way might well be seen as decidedly old-fashioned, especially in the face of a vampire culture that is often now viewed in terms of globalisation. Stacey Abbott concludes her book *Celluloid Vampires* by noting the association of the mobile modern vampire with a new era of globalisation, with vampire films appearing in a wide range of diverse locations; as she puts it, 'The modern vampire has gone global.'[1] Similarly, both Martine Beugnet and Dale Hudson have offered comparable theorisations of the vampire as a globalised presence in French and French-speaking cinema. For example, Beugnet has argued that the figure of the contemporary vampire 'comes to typify the emergence of a transnational era, conjuring up anxieties which represent but also exceed and, indeed, contradict its original role in the stigmatisation of a fantasised Eastern Europe'.[2] The sense of the globe-trotting modern vampire's uncanny return to its old European haunts is presented as something that throws traditional identities into disarray, with established national distinctions weakened or effaced in large part through the vampire's own increasingly borderless identity.

This way of thinking about the vampire is of obvious relevance to an understanding of any specific iteration of the vampire within a European context. It suggests an approach that is less focused on the psychosexual dimensions of the vampire, that for many critics in the past have comprised this monster's principal interest, and more attuned to the journeys undertaken by vampires through particular spaces and geographical locations. Yet at the same time, it becomes harder to pin down vampires to any specific place. It might be Sweden today but on another day it could be Korea (*Thirst/Bakjwi*, Park Chan-Wook, 2009) or Great Britain (*Lesbian Vampire Killers*, Phil Claydon, 2009) or the United States (*Twilight*, Catherine Hardwicke, 2008) or the Czech Republic (*Underworld*, Len Wiseman, 2003) or somewhere else entirely. From such a perspective, it follows that there is no specifically or exclusively Swedish explanation for the presence of vampires in Sweden. In fact, that presence might be seen as entailing a diminution of Swedish cultural identity precisely through the infiltration into it of entities with a strong international character that have similarly infiltrated other national cultures. The plague-like or viral proliferation of vampires evident in many vampire stories, especially in the contemporary period, thus becomes an image of globalisation encompassing the international flow of capital (that in many instances supports the production of vampire films), with the vampires themselves representing or symbolising globalising processes. In Beugnet's words, the modern vampire 'appears destined to thrive within this new global era ruled by transnational flows and the seemingly irresistible law of universal, deregulated greed'.[3]

But is this true? While it might be acknowledged that, hypothetically, vampires today can appear anywhere, in any country or any type of location, it is also undoubtedly the case that they have not actually appeared in every country or location. They have appeared instead in specific places, usually for reasons that arguably, at least to some degree, have something to do with the particularity of the places themselves. It is interesting in this regard that Beugnet's article views vampires as a kind of invasive force, albeit one that operates from within, that is mobilised against particular notions and models of Frenchness. In this sense, her vampires might be associated with a non-national and geographically elusive space – the global Transylvania, to use Beugnet's term – but their entanglement in French culture affords them a specificity that is presented as distinctly French and which does not obviously apply in general terms across other national or, for that matter, international or transnational contexts.

Vampire film production has always had an international character and it has also ranged freely across cultural hierarchies, with cinematic vampires featuring in upmarket 'art' projects and commercial mainstream films as well as in more outré independent offerings. In addition, horror film production itself has become more internationalised from the 1960s onwards, and in that period different national styles of cinematic vampirism – including American, British, Chinese, French, Italian, Japanese, Mexican and Spanish – have come into and then gone out of fashion. So one needs to ask what it is about contemporary vampire culture that renders it different, or more 'globalised', than what has gone before. Is the difference between the way things are now and the way they were then, absolute and epochal, or are we talking instead about relative degrees of difference, of shifts in emphasis in an ongoing story that cuts across various national contexts but within which notions of the national might retain some importance?

This chapter proceeds on the basis that the Swedishness of both *Frostbite* and *Let the Right One In* is a significant feature, albeit one that cannot be readily isolated from the international development of screen vampirism or indeed of the horror cinema within which much of this activity takes place. In doing this, it inevitably ends up exploring the relationship between what might be perceived as national and something that exists beyond that, with this involving not just textual detail in the films themselves but production and marketing contexts as well. However, notions of the global are arguably too abstract or generalising to be of much use in identifying what that something else might be or indeed the particular ways in which these films seek to connect themselves to what has gone before or what is happening concurrently in vampire cinema. The international qualities of vampire cinema in all its manifestations are more productively viewed not as expressions of or commentaries upon prevailing general economic or cultural conditions but rather as involving much more specific sets of connections and associations. Focusing on just two films, in both their distinctiveness and their connectedness to a wider body of work, reveals an internationalised vampire cinema not as an entity with its own overall cohesion and values but instead as a kind of loose historical network, with various pathways through it actualised in different ways by individual films. From such a perspective, it becomes easier to place these two Swedish horror films in relation to broader patterns of generic development that, rather than flattening out national distinctions, foreground and draw sustenance from such distinctions, with particular conventions and approaches reworked and re-energised and then sent back out into international markets.

Tracing the passage of *Frostbite* and *Let the Right One In* through vampire cinema and horror cinema more generally necessarily leads us back to the starting point of this particular journey, their Swedishness – which, in the context of the horror genre at least, turns out to be something of a problem.

Swedish Horror Cinema

Up until a few years ago, the concept of Swedish horror would have been seen as a contradiction in terms. It is certainly the case that throughout much of their histories the various Scandinavian cinemas have never featured sustained horror film production, at least not in the commercial and conventional sense of the term 'horror film' (a term that first appeared as a publicly recognised category in the United States during the early 1930s). It is surprising then to find a chapter in a recent book, *Horror International*, which takes as its subject the Scandinavian horror film and which, written as it was before the release of *Frostbite* and *Let the Right One In*, focuses precisely on that period where there does not appear to be any horror production taking place.[4]

What Rebecca and Samuel Umland, the authors of the chapter, do to establish a corpus of Scandinavian horror is in effect appropriate a series of films that were not generally thought of as horror films on their initial release but instead were offered as belonging to what might be termed an art tradition. To some, this might seem heretical, with what is generally perceived as a low-cultural format assimilating high-cultural forms at will, but it is a not uncommon feature of a contemporary horror criticism that is not especially respectful of traditional cultural hierarchies. So, in this instance, Danish director Carl Theodor Dreyer's *Vampyr* (1932) – although it is not actually a Danish production – and *Day of Wrath* (*Vredens Dag*, 1943) are featured, alongside fellow Danish director Benjamin Christensen's *Häxen: Witchcraft Through the Ages* (1922) and more recent work from Lars von Trier, notably his television series *The Kingdom* (*Riget*, 1994). The films of Swedish director Ingmar Bergman also feature heavily, among them *The Seventh Seal* (*Det sjunde inseglet*, 1957), *The Magician* (*Ansiktet*, 1958), *Through a Glass Darkly* (*Såsom i en spegel*, 1961), *Persona* (1966), and, most of all, *The Virgin Spring* (*Jungfrukällan*, 1960) – which was loosely remade as the American horror film *The Last House on the Left* (Wes Craven, 1972) – and *Hour of the Wolf* (*Vargtimmen*, 1968). In doing this, the Umlands identify what they see as the distinguishing features of Scandinavian horror, drawing upon particular, pre-existing notions of Northernness. Most of all they focus on the idea of North marking the location where modernity becomes tenuous, fragile, superficial, with powerful primal, elemental or atavistic forces at work.

Regardless of the credibility of the Umlands' critical calling into being of Scandinavian horror as a distinctive tradition or cultural continuity, it is clear that neither *Frostbite* nor *Let the Right One In* fit into this particular model. They are both self-consciously and manifestly horror films rather than the 'horror in disguise' projects focused on by the Umlands and they were unabashedly marketed in such terms (although *Let the Right One In* was presented in a more upmarket way than was *Frostbite*). In addition, neither goes anywhere near the set of pagan/modernity themes identified by the Umlands as core to the Scandinavian horror experience. On this basis it might indeed be argued that they represent a break in cultural continuity, something that would accord with the sense of modern vampires as agents of globalisation. However, such notions of cultural continuity are themselves arguably best viewed as ways of thinking that privilege certain types of cultural activity in order to support a particular reading or argument about a culture and its value. Bearing this in mind, perhaps one should not worry too much about whether new cultural developments – such as the introduction of vampires where none were before – breach any of those general and probably unreliable notions of continuity or tradition but instead focus on the specific ways in which particular films make sense of and connect with their locations.

Both *Frostbite* and *Let the Right One In* can more usefully be placed in relation to a broader revival in European horror production that has taken place since the late 1990s and which includes productions from Britain, France, Germany, Spain and other Scandinavian countries such as Norway and Finland. This has involved horror production in countries where no such production existed before, but even in those European countries which had produced horror films in the past the new horrors have usually had little or nothing in common with the horror that went before. It is also hard to find any clear thematic or formal links between what is a very diverse range of films (and indeed *Frostbite* and *Let the Right One In* are very different from each other), although many of them seem to share an ambition to be nationally distinctive while also displaying what might be termed a cult sensibility that has pronounced international qualities and which often manifests in the form of eclectic references within these films to horror films or generic traditions from other countries (for example, in the form of a reworking of American slasher traditions in the French production *Switchblade Romance/Haute Tension* (Alexandre Aja, 2003) or of Italian and American zombie conventions in the British horror *Shaun of the Dead* (Edgar Wright, 2004)).[5]

Put another way, this development of the new European horror, which includes the new Swedish horror, has not entailed a simple surrender to an overwhelming assault from outside a national-cultural identity (however that might be defined), but rather has involved the transportation of horror conventions and subject matter from diverse national contexts into other national cultural frameworks where they have been reworked and made sense of in relation to those cultures. There are obvious commercial imperatives driving this, with various European countries seeking to support their film industries through encouraging both local production and investment from elsewhere, with this often facilitated by national and regional film funds and companies. (One such company, Filmpool Nord, which is owned by several municipal authorities in northern Sweden, was involved in the production of both *Frostbite* and *Let the Right One In*.) However, at the same time, this kind of activity can also be seen as an expression of a sub-cultural or cult attachment to horror that does not just provide a basis for the creative commitment to horror evident in many contemporary European horror films – hence the loving references evident within them to original inspirational cult films – but which in recent years has also increasingly helped to organise specialist markets devoted to the circulation of cult horror material. Consequently, the films that emerge from this are often directed at very specific international markets for horror while also possessing a distinctive national address.

In their discussion of the Norwegian zombie film *Dead Snow* (Tommy Wirkola, 2009), Jo Sondre Moseng and Håvard Andrea Vibeto present a scenario in which a film can contain numerous national references but where these are mainly lost for international audiences: 'the cleverness of *Dead Snow* is that none of the national markers actually interfere or disturb narrative understanding. In other words, whatever the degree of nationally specific images, they are unnecessary, or redundant, in terms of grasping the action.'[6] While this might well work for *Dead Snow*, with its emphasis on low-cultural zombie action, the considerably more artful *Frostbite* and *Let the Right One In* present more complex interactions between that which might be deemed national and that which appears international. Their shared subject is the coming of vampires to Sweden from elsewhere, and their dramatisation of this does not just reveal a hinterland of cultish attachments and knowledge but also places the films themselves in relation to specific national spaces and locations. In both cases, the results are far from straightforward.

Snow Falling on Vampires

Solid Entertainment, one of the main Swedish production companies responsible for *Frostbite*, wears its pop-cultural credentials on its sleeve.

Its website unambiguously distances itself from the art film traditions that in the past have proved so important to establishing critically privileged national film cultures, especially in Europe, and instead pledges its allegiance to a kind of filmmaking that seems altogether more international and commercial: 'We've never been very keen on art-house films. We've never really been inspired by Bergman and that tradition of movie making, even though our staff writer would like to remake *Fanny and Alexander* and set it in space with Nazi aliens and kung fu-fighting nurses taking long showers.'[7] The tone is self-consciously arch, however, and *Frostbite* itself turns out to be not quite the hyperbolically exploitative and fully internationalised product that the Solid Entertainment credo might have suggested. Certainly it deploys some of the standard conceits of vampire cinema and literature – for example, the idea of vampires as a separate and superior race, the town that falls to vampires, vampirism as a quasi-scientific infectious organism. The film also draws eclectically upon other horror conventions in a manner likely to enhance the recognisability of the film to international horror audiences. For instance, the focus on teenagers as main protagonists and victims owes more than a little to the American slasher film – indeed Kim Newman has described the film as an '80s-style teen-skewed gorefest'[8] – while *Frostbite*'s climactic party sequence, during which the vampire plague takes full hold, arguably relies for at least some of its inspiration on the party sequence that concludes the American horror *Scream* (Wes Craven, 1996).

Even as it does this, however, *Frostbite* also pays attention to Swedish specificities of setting and history. It begins by directly addressing the question of how vampires get into Sweden. In so doing it manages both to maintain the traditional convention that vampires come from the East and to connect the narrative more specifically with one of the darker episodes in Swedish and European modern history. The film's opening sequence is set in Ukraine during 1942 and depicts a bloody encounter between soldiers from SS Panzer Division Wiking and a small group of vampires. The Wiking division was a real-life organisation comprised of volunteers from outside Germany and particularly from the Scandinavian countries that served the Nazi cause with some distinction, at least from the Nazi point of view, throughout World War Two. One of these Swedish Nazis, now himself transformed into a vampire, ends up bringing a girl vampire back to Swedish Lapland where he spends the decades leading up to the present day of the main narrative experimenting on her in order to produce a genetically 'pure' human/vampire hybrid. Although there is no explicit mention of it in *Frostbite* or in the film's marketing, the fact that Dr Josef Mengele served in the Wiking Division before undertaking his notorious medical 'experiments' in the Auschwitz concentration camp draws further attention to the connection made by the film between Swedish Nazism and eugenic beliefs.

In fact, *Frostbite* can be put alongside a small band of contemporary European horror-thrillers that also deal with the survival of eugenic and/or Nazi beliefs and which emphasise notions of racial purity – for example, *Anatomy* (*Anatomie*, Stefan Ruzowitzky, 2000), *Anatomy 2* (*Anatomie 2*, Stefan Ruzowitzky, 2003) and *Tattoo* (Robert Schwentke, 2002) from Germany, and *Crimson Rivers* (*Les Rivières Pourpres*, Mathieu Kassovitz, 2000) from France, as well as the aforementioned Nazi-zombie project *Dead Snow* from Norway. Viewed in this way, *Frostbite* becomes imbued with a sense of a particular national and European history rather than being a standard vampire film that just happens to be set in the snow; it can function, if only in a perverse sense, as a kind of heritage film in which nationally specific qualities help to bestow distinctiveness in an international marketplace.

Having noted this, *Frostbite* does not explain or explore this historical episode at any length. By the same token, it offers no sustained explicit engagement, perhaps surprisingly so, with the fact that the narrative takes place entirely during Scandinavian polar night. While this element is quite literally visible for all to see and might potentially have been developed as a distinctively Swedish characteristic, it is only mentioned twice in the film, once near the beginning and then again at the end when a vampire jokes that 'dawn is just a month away' as he looks at his watch. It is interesting in this regard to compare *Frostbite* with another vampire film that benefits from its own version of polar night, the Alaska-set *30 Days of Night*. The latter film presents polar night as an overwhelming event for the small town that is its main setting, an event that has to be explained and worked into the drama. Even before a pack of vampires arrive to exploit a month of uninterrupted darkness, the town itself is shown as isolated and embattled, with polar night representing the climactic environmental assault on the community. By contrast, in *Frostbite* the theme of isolation is much less prominent, with the polar night not inconveniencing the town unduly. It seems that what for the American film is a sufficiently unusual event – for its intended audiences at least – to be a main structuring concept (hence the film's title) is for the Swedish production more commonplace and less worthy of explicit comment or explanation.

Frostbite's unelaborated references to Swedish history and the Swedish environment might be viewed as, in Moseng and Vibeto's words, 'unnecessary, or redundant, in terms of grasping the action' if it were not for the fact that they are, in places at least, so obtrusive and noticeable. In other ways, too, *Frostbite* playfully and none too subtly mixes together local and internationally sourced elements in such a way that they are hard to disentangle. This often entails abrupt tonal shifts from moments of relative seriousness to sequences involving manic comedy as well as some self-reflexivity. So we are offered a flashback sequence – a redundant one, given that the information it contains could easily be provided in a more linear fashion – which concludes with the repetition of an encounter between two women that has already appeared earlier in the film. 'Wow, déjà vu,' comments one of the women second time round. Two talking dogs also show up (although it is not clear whether they arise from a character hallucinating as he transforms into a vampire or whether the ability to converse with dogs is a vampiric trait in this film), and in one striking sequence a vampire is 'staked' with a large garden gnome: 'What a totally uncool way to die,' she comments.

What *Frostbite* presents then is a series of attractions and events, with no clear privileging of one attraction over any of the others. There is an evident indifference here not only to the idea of cohesion but also to overall intelligibility. The film just does not seem to care whether its audiences know about the Wiking Division or Scandinavian polar night or indeed about vampires. Instead, these things and others pass by in rapid procession and in no particular order. This carries over into the film's treatment of vampires, which is variegated and fractured. The Nazi scientist vampire fits a certain generic template in his obsession with bloodlines and genetics and would not be out of place in, say, the bloodline-obsessed *Blade* or *Underworld* films. By contrast, the teenage vampires, who are completely disconnected from their older counterpart and only occasionally occupy the same space as him, offer a performative rendition of vampirism that is harder to place in relation to broader trends in vampire culture. Here it is vampirism as a game or as a role-playing activity completely bereft of the sensual or sexual elements

10. 'What a totally uncool way to die' – death by garden gnome in *Frostbite.*

more conventionally associated with young beautiful vampires. One of these Swedish teenage vampires – the same one who ends up getting staked with the gnome – goes so far as to offer advice to a potential victim on how to wield an impromptu crucifix effectively and, once this is done, acts out the appropriate response of snarling repulsion. It seems from this that, for these young vampires at least, vampirism is merely an extension of having a good time at a party, that is, wrecking the furniture and defying authority, with no thought of consequence. Add to this the idea of vampirism as something that involves social embarrassment – with one extended dinner party sequence depicting the attempts of a young man to conceal his transformation into a vampire from his prospective in-laws – and you end up with an energetic if ultimately incoherent mix of generic conventions and innovations. In this, vampirism itself seems drained of any core identity, but instead is characterised by its dispersal across different characters and dramatic situations and its fragmentation.

In contrast to *Frostbite*'s playful disrespect for tradition, *Let the Right One In*, the other Swedish vampire film, offers something more focused, univocal and upmarket in tone. Indeed it presents a canny mix of generic convention and art-house 'quality', to the extent that *Variety*'s review of the film indicated that it 'should click with cult and art-house auds'.[9] Underpinning this, however, is an eclecticism comparable with that exhibited by *Frostbite*, where references to a range of pre-existing vampiric and horror scenarios and conventions are reworked without ever fully losing that sense of allusion. In the case of *Let the Right One In*, it is a muted realism and an associated slow pacing that provide the context both for what might be seen as a generic revitalisation and for the film's claim to be a quality piece of work. In *Variety*'s blunt and industry-savvy words, 'Every decade or so, the long-reliable scare genre gets a reinvention. And some in the film biz are betting that Scandinavia will provide the newest twist as Scandi filmmakers add their own touches to the genre they grew up with ... The Scandi directors are bringing in elements of their arthouse heritage, with a brooding atmosphere, superstition, foreboding and romantic longing.'[10]

What this means for *Let the Right One In* are scenes that manage to be both generically familiar and toned down to the point where they become mundane. For example, the initial arrival of the vampire is often associated in horror with a hyperbolic display of bad weather and other sinister portents – from Bram Stoker's *Dracula* (1897) through Stephen King's *Salem's Lot* (1974) right up until the Guillermo Del Toro/Chuck Hogan vampire novel *The Strain* – but here she arrives via a taxi ride shot with no dramatic under- or overtones at all. Similarly, the scene in which an unfortunate victim is strung upside down and has his throat cut by the vampire's human companion clearly replays a comparable and generically iconic scene from Hammer's *Dracula – Prince of Darkness* (Terence Fisher, 1966). However, the Swedish version replaces Hammer's sinister manservant with a bumbling incompetent who is distracted by a curious poodle and bathetically ends up spilling the blood he was collecting from his victim. More obscure, to the point where even die-hard cultists probably missed it, is the association made by John Ajvide Lindqvist, the film's screenwriter and author of the novel upon which the film was based, between the Rubik's Cube that is central to the developing relationship between Eli, the film's young vampire, and Oskar, the film's 11-year-old main protagonist, and the Lament Configuration, the ornate puzzle box that opens up the way to hellish new dimensions in Clive Barker's horror film *Hellraiser* (1987) and its sequels.[11] A private reference perhaps (and indeed Tomas Alfredson, the film's director, seems startled by the revelation on the DVD commentary in which it features), but it does underline the pervasiveness of the intertwining of quotidian reality with

11. Eli's companion incompetently trying to procure blood for her: *Let the Right One In.*

established horror conventions in both the film and the novel upon which it was based.

Another aspect of this is *Let the Right One In*'s reticence when it comes to the representation of gore and violence. The novel upon which the film is based contains graphic details of vampire attacks and their aftermath and also does not flinch from depicting the paedophile predilections of Eli's adult companion (who in the novel is eventually transformed into a disgusting zombie-like creature). All this material is absent from the film. The vampire attacks tend to be filmed from a distance and often shrouded in darkness. This is most evident in the conclusion, which features three boys being torn apart by Eli by a swimming pool but which is filmed mainly from an underwater position, thus obscuring much of the flesh-tearing action (although a severed head and arm both make fleeting appearances). And Eli's companion, rather than a paedophile monster, becomes, if not innocent, at least more sympathetic in his bumbling and pathetic incompetence.

In this respect, it is striking that the film's most arresting and iconic bloody image is of the vampiric Eli herself bleeding profusely as a consequence of her entering Oskar's flat without his permission. This turns out to be an image not of violence but of submission and also a key moment in the development of the relationship between Oskar and Eli.

12. The ambiguous relationship between vampire Eli and human Oskar in *Let the Right One In.*

This elliptical quality also carries over into other parts of the film, with various elements left ambiguous. The most obvious example is Eli herself who in the novel is a castrated boy masquerading as a girl but who in the film is rendered more mysteriously. Although she tells Oskar at one point that 'I'm not a girl', and the film also offers a brief glimpse of what looks like a scar on her crotch, there is no moment where her masculinity is made absolutely explicit, and indeed critical discussions of the film routinely refer to her as a girl (as indeed does this chapter). Similarly, the relationship between Oskar and Eli can be viewed in different ways, with no definitive resolution ever emerging. On the one hand, and perhaps most obviously, it is a tender and fragile relationship between two isolated outsiders. More subtly, although not too subtly, it is an exploitative relationship in which Eli is, consciously or otherwise, grooming Oskar as her next companion. One by-product of rendering the older companion as a more sympathetic character is that it permits parallels to be drawn between him and Oskar as his possible replacement. So the film cuts from the companion stabbing someone to death to Oskar playing with his own knife, and when Oskar finally stands up to the school bully and hits him across the ear with a pole, it is the same pole earlier used by the companion to push a dead body under the water. (*Let Me In*, the American remake of *Let the Right One In*, removes these ambiguities, and makes the connection between the companion and his replacement yet more obvious by having the boy discover a photograph of the vampire with the companion at the same age as the boy himself.)

Let the Right One In comes out of this as an innovative film that makes sense in relation to a 1980s Swedish setting conceived both realistically as a slightly down at heel location and expressively in terms of social *anomie*, with characters – and not just Oskar and Eli – isolated in an alienating urban landscape (and an understated sense of social and familial dysfunctionality is also a property of *Frostbite*; it is as if vampires require a degree of societal weakness in order to function). Yet it also connects with various threads in vampire and horror fiction, both through its allusions to specific texts and more generally as a vampire story featuring (apparently at least) a vampire that is both a child and female; in the latter regard, as noted by J. M. Tyree, links are made to literary and cinematic texts as diverse as Sheridan Le Fanu's *Carmilla* (1872), Anne Rice's novel *Interview with the Vampire* (1976) and its 1994 screen adaptation, and the films *Vampyr* and *The Hunger* (Tony Scott, 1983).[12]

As was the case with the thematically and formally very different *Frostbite*, it is hard to separate out the nationally distinctive from the generic and the internationally marketable in *Let the Right One In*. These elements interact with each other in productive and sometimes surprising ways. The film is unthinkable without the generic associations that it calls into being, but this generic stuff is not simply reproduced or reiterated. There is selectivity at work and deformation and idiosyncrasy. Indeed, it is the idiosyncrasy, perhaps more than anything else, more even than the snow, that links together *Let the Right One In* and *Frostbite*. Both *Frostbite*'s manic excess and *Let the Right One In*'s art-house restraint can be seen in this respect as responses to the oddness of the idea that vampires might be in Sweden. The result in both cases is a simultaneous assimilation of those vampires into particular locales and milieu and a generic placing of them via a series of allusions to non-Swedish vampire stories.

Tensions between these two apparently countervailing tendencies tend to be mediated through the idea of the vampires' journey. Their travels through Sweden, or parts thereof, help to articulate a broader generic mobility as horror conventions associated with the figure of the vampire also pass from one country to another and are transformed and developed in the process. It is perhaps appropriate then that both *Frostbite* and *Let the Right One In* conclude with scenes in which vampires leave to go somewhere else. In *Frostbite*, it is the little girl vampire – the source vampire in the story – and the heroine's vampirised mother, along with the non-vampiric teenage heroine, who drive away into the snow; in *Let the Right One In*, Eli leaves by train with her new protector-companion Oskar. In both, it is unclear where precisely these vampires are now going, but that does not really matter. What matters is that they have moved through the spaces and places of Sweden, have been animated by and interacted with these, and finally have been transformed, refreshed and renewed by the experiences thereby generated. This comes over in each film as a kind of liberation, with *Frostbite*'s girl vampire freed from her imprisonment in the hospital, and Eli freed from her awkward and tired relationship with her adult companion. And as they go, each vampire takes something of Sweden with them, not just in the memories of their time there but in the people who now travel with them.

The historical model of vampire culture suggested by this is one predicated on the specificity of localised encounters and their accretion over time rather than on any broad or underpinning thematic or ideological cohesion or meaning. In this regard, the oddness of the Swedish vampire, while important to the films themselves, simply adds to a more general oddness as vampires continue to career across the world in erratic and unpredictable ways, challenging all the time fixed definitions of what they are or might be.

Notes

1 Stacey Abbott, *Celluloid Vampires: Life After Death in the Modern World* (Austin: University of Texas Press, 2007), p. 215.

2 Martine Beugnet, 'Figures of Vampirism: French Cinema in the Era of Global Transylvania', *Modern and Contemporary France* 15:1 (2007): 77. Also see Dale Hudson, 'Transpolitical Spaces in Transnational French Cinemas: Vampires and the illusion of National Borders and Universal Citizenship', *French Cultural Studies* 22:2 (2011): 111–26.

3 Beugnet: 'Figures of Vampirism': 78.

4 Rebecca A. Umland and Samuel J. Umland, 'Burn Witch Burn: A First Look at the Scandinavian Horror Film', in S. J. Schneider and T. Williams (eds), *Horror International* (Detroit: Wayne State University Press, 2005).

5 For a discussion of the new European horror, see Peter Hutchings, 'Resident Evil: The limits of European horror', in Patricia Allmer and Emily Brick (eds), *European Nightmares* (London: Wallflower Press, 2012).
6 Jo Sondre Moseng and Håvard Andrea Vibeto, 'Hunting High and Low: Notes on Nazi Zombies, Francophiles and National Cinema(s)', *Film International* 9:2 (2011): 37.
7 http://www.solidentertainment.se/faq.html (accessed 17 October 2011).
8 Kim Newman, *Nightmare Movies: Horror on Screen Since the 1960s* (London: Bloomsbury, 2011), p. 356.
9 *Variety*, 18–24 February 2008: 33.
10 G. Rehlin, 'Horror gets Swedish massage', *Variety*, 30 March–5 April 2009: 8.
11 Referenced in the commentary track on the DVD.
12 J. M. Tyree, 'Warm-Blooded: *True Blood* and *Let The Right One In*', *Film Quarterly* 63:2 (2009): 31–37.

4

LET THEM ALL IN

The Evolution of the 'Sympathetic' Vampire

Milly Williamson

It is now a truism to suggest that the vampire is no longer a monster dramatising the fear of the Other, but has been rendered sympathetic, knowable, a figure of empathy. So what does the vampire *mean* in this landscape when so much of the audience identifies with many of the positions of otherness that the vampire is said to represent? What can we make of the many sympathy-inducing performances of the vampire on screen? The late twentieth-century vampire predominantly enacted our own pain of outsiderdom and a desire for redemption and crucially for significance;[1] its appeal lay in its ability to echo our predicament of meaninglessness and disconnection. But the vampire ceaselessly transforms, rendering meanings anew even while it pulls remnants of its past signification into the present. What do the sympathetic vampires of the twenty-first century tell us about our age, our desires and our fears?

The Career of the Sympathetic Vampire

The sympathetic vampire actually has a very long history – it is not an invention of twentieth-century culture. Indeed, the vampire that most British Victorian readers would have been familiar with was not the menacing Dracula of the late Victorian era, but the tortured vampire Varney in 'Varney the Vampyre' – a figure who was 'driven by a disease of the mind and body', a condition that he tried to rid himself of.[2] *Varney* was a bestseller which ran to 108 instalments between the years 1845 and 1847 when it was finally published as a novel. Varney's was not a threat of domination, but instead the lure of intimacy. The sympathetic vampire of this tradition has been immensely popular in the twentieth and twenty-first centuries, perhaps because it is simultaneously enduring and mutable. This vampire continues to depict the essence of the outsider, the tortured soul, a figure at odds with its ontological being in a way that resonates with many different experiences of the self over the last century and a half. But romance was added to this sympathetic articulation of outsiderdom at the moment when the outsider became a glamorous figure in popular culture, a figure of the counterculture. Margaret Carter suggests that while the nineteenth-century vampire might have inspired sympathy *despite* its curse, in the late twentieth century it 'appears as an attractive figure precisely *because* he or she is a vampire'.[3] Vampires in the second half of the twentieth century are rebels who become heroes and heroines of their time because of the way they speak to the changed attitudes towards authority and sexuality. The cultural politics of these vampires were seen as progressive, liberating and against the confining moral and sexual codes of the previous decades. This vampire's sympathetically depicted 'otherness' lured us, not simply with the promise of intimacy, but with its rebellious pose and its refusal (or inability) to live by the rules of the day. Nina Auerbach explains what these 'shadowy monsters' meant to her growing up in 1950s America: 'Vampires were supposed to menace women, but to me at least, they promised protection against a destiny of girdles, spike heels, and approval.'[4]

The career of the vampire in the twentieth century *might* suggest that, in its transformation from blood-sucking menace to sympathetically depicted rebel, it is a figure bound on a progressive journey, subtly critiquing established ideas about sexuality, belonging and identity. Indeed, as Richard Dyer has noted, there is something fundamentally 'queer' in the image of the vampire. Because it is a borderline figure, and one that resounds so much with sexuality, the vampire can articulate the joy (and the pain) of forbidden desire. Perhaps this is why, as Dyer comments, the vampire has come to stand for homosexuality.[5] But like Dyer, Andrea Weiss and Bonnie Zimmerman note that the figure of the homosexual vampire is highly ambivalent, for it is presented as both attractive and loathsome.[6] The gay male vampire has stood for corrupt desire and liberated desire, while the lesbian vampire in the twentieth century has often been used to perform for male pornographic fantasy. But it can also provide images of same sex desire which offer something far more enthralling. A significant example of the alluring portrayal of same sex desire is to be found in the film *The Hunger* (Tony Scott, 1983), which comes a decade after the deluge of lesbian vampire films of the 1970s, many of which, like *The Hunger*, draw on the nineteenth-century sympathetic vampire tale *Carmilla* (Sheridan Le Fanu, 1872).

Produced in the early 1980s, *The Hunger* completely did away with the conventional signifiers of the traditional vampire film associated with Hammer and Universal. There are no dreary Gothic castles, no bats or cobwebs, and the beautiful and elegant vampires in here do not even possess fangs. The mise-en-scene of this film has more in common with fashion photography and music videos than it does with the traditional vampire movie. The film has glamour; it is chic and achingly hip. This is one of a number of elements that the film borrows from the Belgian film *Daughters of Darkness* (Harry Kumel, 1971) which also replaced fangs and castles with (retro) fashion and glamour.

The tale centres on Miriam Blaylock, played by the stunningly beautiful and graceful Catherine Deneuve, an ageless vampire who falsely promises immortality to her male and female lovers. When her current lover (played by the legendary gender transcender, David Bowie) begins to deteriorate, he seeks out a specialist doctor, Sarah (Susan Sarandon), whom Miriam chooses as her next lover and companion. Miriam seduces Sarah in a highly erotic lesbian encounter which begins Sarah's vampiric transformation. The scene is set to Léo Delibes' beautiful piano adaptation of the *Flower Duet*, and is shot in the light of a dreamy afternoon haze. The mutual attraction is palpable, especially when Sarah asks with a smile, 'Are you making a pass at me, Mrs Blaylock?', to which Miriam replies seductively, 'Miriam, please.' Female vampires, although fewer in number than male vampires, do have their own notoriety, and although this is often of the misogynist kind, in this scene the vampire offers a sensuality that is both unconventional and deeply attractive. There is no visual menace in this scene, only seduction and erotic pleasure, and the peril is rather hinted at in a few off-key musical chords. The film cuts to Sarah sitting at a meal with her husband in a scene which alludes to fractured gender relations. Tom is trying, unsuccessfully, to persuade Sarah to eat the steak he has ordered for her. But Sarah refuses – she has clearly been unutterably altered by her encounter with Miriam, and the argument that ensues between man and woman is resonant of the battle for female autonomy. This too harks back to *Daughters of Darkness*, when newlywed Valerie discovers that her husband is a brute and is instead drawn to the tender embraces of the vampire Countess Bathory.

But it is important to note that the lesbian vampire, like all vampires, is highly ambivalent. So while tales inspired by Carmilla tend to present a sensitive portrayal of the female vampire, misogynistic depictions of the lesbian vampire also stretch back to the nineteenth century where this image was also used as a motif of women who take too much pleasure in sex and exhaust with their embraces. Coleridge portrays the female vampire as an evil seductress in his unfinished poem *Christabel* of 1816,[7] while Baudelaire uses vampiric imagery to portray the lesbian as decadent and morally corrupt in *Les Fleurs du Mal*.[8] But the lesbian vampire is a figure imbued with ambiguity, even in her perceived origins, and this ambiguity infuses the portrayal of lesbian vampirism in *The Hunger*, for implied in the film is the more sympathetic lesbian vampire, Carmilla.

Barbara Creed suggests that the lesbian vampire, while a symbol of the abject and monstrous, is also highly attractive because she threatens the symbolic relations between men and women 'essential to the continuation of the patriarchal order'.[9] The lesbian vampire evades the trap of conventional female domesticity; she has autonomy, and her relations with women run counter to the ties of marriage; she may appear unnatural, but she simultaneously emerges as a symbol of female power. But the female and lesbian vampire is perhaps inevitably situated on the dangerous border between oppressive and liberating meanings. The association of the lesbian vampire with death, which is very strong in this film, is the homophobic side of the connection between vampires and homosexuality. Because sex between two woman (or two men) is not directly linked to reproduction, homosexuality in our culture is problematically associated with sterility. This is figured in the film as decay. Miriam's partners lie rotting in the attic, decomposing but undead, a symbol of the bareness that lies behind the surface values of beauty and elegance. But on the other hand, here is an erotic image of sex for pleasure – a challenge to the most repressive ideas about human sexuality, that sex should *only* be for reproduction inside marriage. The vampire here, like the lesbian, continues to pursue an alternative lifestyle, and despite persecution she continues to survive.

The Shifting Cultural Politics of the Sympathetic Vampire

However, one might argue that there has been a recent shift in the sexual politics of the sympathetic vampire. While the pathos-filled vampire of the 1960s and 1970s and into the 1980s ended the sexually-conservative reign of the early twentieth-century Dracula cycle, offering polymorphous perversity and an alluring ambiguity, today's sympathetic vampire seems determined to return desire to heterosexual normativity. Contemporary sympathetic vampires are as mutable as their ancestors, but a dominant trend in today's fiction is the heterosexual 'paranormal romance'. This recent trend surfaces as a significant theme in the enormously influential television series *Buffy the Vampire Slayer* (Joss Whedon, 1997–2003; henceforth *BtVS*). Forbidden love grows initially in a pairing that is decidedly not 'queer' – Buffy, whose purpose is to 'slay' vampires, and Angel, the vampire she comes to love and who is an embodiment of the male romantic lead. The complex narrative of *BtVS* has been identified in the academic industry that has grown around it, and its themes are too numerous to outline here (including the destabilisation of normative heterosexuality). However, the series puts romance at the centre of the vampire's meaning, and its success has encouraged a cycle of highly popular vampire romances – notably the television series *True Blood* (2008–) and the film *Twilight* (2008). But paranormal romance in *BtVS* operates through two parallel sites which also influence these later narratives – the family and youth.

In fact, the vampire was heading for the young prior to *BtVS*, particularly in two films of 1987: *Near Dark* (Katherine Bigelow) and *The Lost Boys* (Joel Shumacher). These films begin a cycle of sympathetic vampire fiction in which youth and the broken family emerge as significant themes. Both of these broken-home narratives, like *BtVS*, connect youth culture to unease about the family. In both films the young male protagonist is lured by the cool vampire gang/family while the protagonists' family is incomplete; Caleb's family is missing a mother in *Near Dark*, and in *The Lost Boys*, David's family is missing a father. But both films show the protagonist rejecting the lure of the vampire gang/family and returning to the family, the return signalling a completion of previously broken families and patriarchal norms. *BtVS* differs from these films because romance is centred on a young female protagonist and is connected to questions of female empowerment.

Also, unease about the family is never resolved in *BtVS*; families remain incomplete and unstable, and romance operates outside of marriage and the ties of the family. Nevertheless, the success of *BtVS* spawned a new and highly lucrative industry of paranormal romance. The enormously popular *Twilight Saga* seems to be a case in point.

Twilight is also a broken-home romance which seems to be built on restraint and a regressive postponement of desire. It appears to have removed the polymorphous sexuality of earlier sympathetic vampires (including *BtVS*) and entrenched an insipid and rather soppy heterosexuality as the centre of desire. At one level, this saga returns us to a 1950s narrative of sexuality that seems to be built on a repression of desire – or at least postponement until after marriage. While earlier vampires, such as those of *The Hunger*, disturbed the patriarchal family, these vampires seem to reinstate it.

If vampires are personifications of their age, then surely the vampires in the *Twilight Saga* (*Twilight*, 2008; *Twilight Saga: New Moon*, 2010; *Twilight Saga: Eclipse*, 2010; *Twilight Saga: Breaking Dawn I*, 2011–12) are a reminder of the ongoing conservative backlash which is trying to roll back the advances of the liberation movements of the 1960s. The main protagonist, Bella Swan, arrives in the relentlessly dismal and damp Forks, Washington, to live with her father because her mother is going on the road with her new husband. Ms Swan, we soon discover, feels very much the ugly duckling. Clumsy and accident prone, this is a coming of age saga in which the central female protagonist seems determined to misrecognise herself as insignificant and invisible, despite the attention of the boys at her new school. However, if Buffy originally misrecognised herself as an ordinary teenage girl when she actually had superhuman powers, Bella's sense of self comes not through learning about her own strength, but by falling in love with a boy at her school who turns out to be a vampire. Bella's main preoccupation at the beginning of the first film is to go unnoticed because she seems to embrace her insignificance. When the editor of the school magazine tells her she is 'front page news', Bella pleads, 'Please don't.' So while the twentieth-century vampire expressed insignificance both ontologically and in emotional suffering, in this new tale, meaninglessness is not projected onto the vampire, but is enacted through the main character, Bella, whose growing desire to become a vampire stems less from a longing for supernatural power, and more because of her romantic

13. Bella learns that Edward is a vampire.

attachment to the sympathetic vampire, Edward Cullen. Insignificance, then, turns to meaning through the experience of romantic love. Edward is formally a reluctant and therefore sympathetic vampire, but he lures not as a symbol of excess, rebellion or the forbidden, but quite the opposite. He demands restraint and self-control of himself and of Bella and insists that all expressions of desire, vampiric or otherwise, are postponed until after marriage.

Edward's domineering and controlling attitude towards Bella is depicted as a sign of love and, for Bella, a mark of significance, rather than a potential loss of autonomy. Their relationship is redolent of abuse, hidden beneath the commitment to marriage and the family; he often unintentionally hurts her physically, followed by expressions of regret and remorse.

Unlike the human protagonist, Edward belongs to a stable and supportive vampire family. The vampire family in previous narratives is depicted either as a dangerous lure or a monstrous force, but in the *Twilight Saga* the vampire family is venerated and is depicted as desirable and absent in relation to Bella's own broken family; the lure of the Cullens is family stability and unity. After Bella and Edward's marriage in the penultimate film (2011–12), father figure Carlisle Cullen repeats the family mantra on a number of occasions – Bella is one of the family now and 'we look after our family'. Rather than critique the patriarchal family, this narrative seems to censure family breakdown with ineffectual parenting, liberal values and permissiveness. Bella's mother has abandoned Bella to pursue a new relationship, and her father is depicted as aloof, awkward and lacking in parental authority – neither are able to offer guidance to Bella or manage her problems; she must manage them herself. This is in stark contrast to the vampire Cullen family that has a paternal father figure in the character of Carlisle Cullen whose parental efficacy contrasts with the human parents. Unlike the film's human family, Carlisle heads a complete family – Carlisle's wife Esme is the mother, and Edward and his adopted brothers and sisters complete the family as siblings. Carlisle 'sired' all of the family members, including Esme, turning each into a vampire to prevent an untimely death. Carlisle is a figure of authority, but this is not the totalitarian authority of a monster. Instead, he represents parental responsibility; he cares for his family and guides them; he demonstrates the self-restraint that he teaches and has earned the respect of his family. Carlisle represents the paternal authority missing in the film's other family constructions. By recuperating paternal authority, the film rehabilitates the traditional patriarchal family and depicts it as the most desirable social unit on offer. In *Near Dark* (1987) and *The Lost Boys* (1987), the patriarchal family is restored only when the male protagonists finally reject the allure of the rebellious vampire cult, but in *Twilight*, the vampires seem to represent the patriarchal family and a return to conservative family morals and gender politics.

However, it is worth remembering Nina Auerbach's observation that vampires are 'dramatically generational'.[10] For instance, while I have argued here that *The Hunger* offers a depiction of alluring lesbian desire, Nina Auerbach sees in the same film a deeply conservative tale. As a teenager watching the film for the first time, I was struck by vampires whom I regarded as alternative, hip and arresting. In contrast, Auerbach argues that far from being timeless, Miriam is actually stuck in the consumerism of the 1980s, making us envy her accoutrements rather than her immortality and offers of intimacy. Auerbach declares that 'Vampires in *The Hunger* are not their powers, but their assets.'[11] The homoerotic possibilities of the intimacy between Miriam and Sarah are repudiated in favour of a fetishistic consumption. These different readings do suggest that the lure of the vampire is indeed generational and this precisely because of its mutability. No doubt, just as there are meanings in *The Hunger* that jostle with Auerbach's consumerist narrative, beyond the conservative narrative that presents itself in the *Twilight Saga*, there are other readings and meanings for a younger generation that are rooted in the concerns and dilemmas that young readers and viewers face today.

Also, it is untenable to suggest that the young today are more duped by mass culture than the generation reaching adulthood in the late 1980s, or that they imbibe conservative narratives that the so-called more sophisticated reader rejects. I resist such a view not least because these films (and the books they are based on) predominantly appeal to adolescent girls and young women, a group who have long been derided for their cultural tastes and who have symbolically been aligned with denigrated mass culture. It is important, when offering critiques of the objects of mass culture, particularly those with a shady history such as horror, not to simply reinscribe the taste dispositions of dominant social groups. That is not to say that one should not offer critiques of conservatism and consumerism; quite the opposite. Rather, one must take care to consider in whose interests such critiques are made.

The Denigration of the Female Gothic

The example of horror and its ancestor the Gothic are a case in point. It is well documented that in the eighteenth and nineteenth centuries, the Gothic was defined as a women's genre and was, as a literary genre, downgraded in the cultural hierarchy of the day because of the association with femininity, the irrational and the supernatural (which today is echoed in the critical reception of the *Twilight Saga*). However, the Gothic has a hidden but firm connection to the canonical Romantic movement, and its themes of the passions (found at the centre of the *Twilight Saga*) have long influenced Gothic fiction. The vampire became an instant Gothic success with the publication of Polidori's *The Vampyre* in 1819 in Henry Colburn's *The New Monthly Magazine*, not least because of the tale's association with the Romantic poet, Byron. Polidori, employed as Byron's personal physician, is reputed to have based his vampire on Byron, whose renown was based as much on his outrageous lifestyle and sexual antics as it was on his writing; his magnetism lending force to a pre-Dracula vampiric imagery which was as attractive as it was dangerous. But Gothic became critically dissociated with the concurrent Romantic movement, despite, as the critic Gamer points out, Gothic's 'widespread but uneasy presence in romantic writing' which contrasts sharply with its 'almost unanimous critical vilification'.[12]

In the early nineteenth century the public taste for all manner of Gothic tales was at its height. But the critical reception of Gothic was disparaging. Gothic from its inception was regarded as of low cultural status, despite – or perhaps partly due to – its immense popularity; for it emerges concurrently with an expansion in the literate population. According to Maggie Kilgour, the extension of literacy and the proliferation of the press produced 'a wariness of the potentially pernicious influence of literature on what was considered to be a broad but naïve market'.[13] The early nineteenth century witnessed an outpouring of 'bluebooks', which were short, cheap derivatives of the Gothic novel that could be purchased for sixpence, taking their name from the flimsy blue paper that covered them. These publications have become more commonly known as 'shilling shockers', and later 'penny dreadfuls', and they were considered to cater to 'the perverted taste for excitement among degenerate readers'.[14] According to Kilgour, early critics thought shilling shockers encouraged an 'amoral imagination that was a socially subversive force'. In particular, there were concerns that the imaginative world created by the Gothic offered a 'tempting alternative to the mundaneness of everyday life'.[15] Bluebooks were said to have corrupting effects, in particular, among their lower-class and youthful readership.

Singled out as particularly vulnerable to the pernicious influence of bluebooks were young women, predominantly of the lower classes. Indeed, such was the close association between Gothic's devalued status, notions of 'pulp popularity' and femininity, that one Gothic scholar, Anne Williams, has hesitated about defining Gothic as feminine because of the way that critics have used this label to scorn texts.[16] Fred Botting suggests that Gothic actually depended on women readers and writers who were excluded from 'the male dominated "high arts" of poetry and politics'.[17] For Botting, there was a 'feminisation of reading practices and markets'[18] which in a patriarchal age helped to ensure Gothic's low status in the eyes of the critical establishment. Gothic's cheap spin-off bluebooks were replaced in the 1820s by monthly magazines which continued the tradition of terror, and they provided the bridge between the Gothic novel and the mass circulation of horror tales in the twentieth and twenty-first centuries, including a pejorative association with femininity and related concerns about the effects of such fiction, which persist into our own time. However, as Kilgour points out, while early conservative moralists found 'Gothic's offer of an imaginative retreat from reality' a potentially dangerous amoral threat, 'to many modern critics this, contradictorily, has proved it to be a reactionary, socially conservative form'.[19]

Mass culture and mindless consumerism have replaced the notion of the feminine irrational in the twentieth and twenty-first centuries; or rather these have been added to the denigration of the female in a cultural hierarchy which continues to be gendered, but in different ways. Today, 'real' horror is seen to be a man's game; it is no longer associated with the feminine irrational; instead it is 'extreme' and associated with a savvy and knowing (male) cult reader, who, as Mark Jancovich has pointed out, shares many aesthetic dispositions as the art house and cultural elite.[20] While the cult horror fan is seen as transgressive and male, rereading old narratives with the eyes of a connoisseur and appraising new films with the connoisseur's erudition, the young female fans of *Twilight* are castigated for their consumption of conservative narratives and obsession with the books, films, stars and the tacky merchandise. In the US, MTV, *Time* magazine and the *New York Times* have all described *Twilight* fans with adjectives like 'shrieking' and 'squealing'. *People Magazine* tells us, 'You'd have to be an already ardent *Twilight* fan – girls and moms, you know who you are – to get moony over this teen twaddle.'[21]

The media has heaped this kind of derision of female fans throughout the twentieth century and now into the twenty-first. Invoking the language of the cynical and in-the-know cultural commentator, the *Guardian*'s Stuart Heritage blames *Twilight* for transforming vampires from things that 'used to scare the hell out of people' to 'little more than sensitive glittery emo types who enjoy poetry'. That this is inaccurate (we have already noted that this 'new' vampire goes back to the early nineteenth century) is less significant than the mockery of the female fans of this 'new' vampire; fans of *True Blood* are described as women who dress their cats up as butlers, while the fans of *Twilight* are scornfully described as 'grown women referring to themselves as Team Jacob'. Heritage spells out two choices – either ignore the 'madness' or embrace it, which means 'kissing posters of Robert Pattison before you go to bed'.[22] The whiff of sexist condescension is very strong in this article, and his pejorative association of the feminine with excessive patterns of consumption has a history as long as that of the sympathetic vampire, as we have seen.

Instead of deploying cultural distinction to elevate one's taste above those they mock, what if critics offered a serious examination of the meanings and pleasures of the saga and considered what it offers to its young female audience? We have already noted above, the very strong submerged connections between the Romantic movement and the Gothic and I would like to suggest that key themes from Romanticism are a structuring force in the *Twilight Saga*. At the centre of the saga is the emotion of passion which is so strong that it transcends all barriers (including those between the human and the non-human) and gives meaning. Fred Inglis has recently reminded us that passion is as historical as anything else and I want to suggest that the meaning and importance of passion in Bella's self-definition, and for the pleasure of the readers/viewers, stems from a reassertion of a modern conception of emotion that emerged out of the Romantic movement to jostle with contending meanings given to the passions.

The role of the passions in driving human action shifted in the eighteenth century from one that can be summed up in Hume's *Dissertation on the Passions* to 'passion' as redefined in the Romantic movement. For Hume, while the passions drive reason, reason has a significant role in selecting a reasonable course of action for our feelings. Morality drives passion toward appropriate and reasonable conduct. There is a sense here that social man acts in and for the gaze of others. However, by the end of the century this sense of passion was challenged by the more revolutionary but also more individualised notion of passion emerging out of the Romantic movement. Social man acting in the gaze of others gives way to Romantic man acting 'true to the self'. The meaning of passion shifts from reciprocal moral conduct to centre on the self and on spontaneity. Jean-Jacques Rousseau, for instance, scorns Hume's dependence on the gaze of others to advance a philosophy in which being true to ones feelings is the surest guide to proper conduct. The English Romantic poets raise the stakes on this new principle of feeling, 'learned by opening oneself to the chance of personal spontaneity, and catching it on the wing, above all in the passionate love affair'.[23] Romantic women

14. Bella's love for Edward transcends all boundaries (including life) and gives meaning.

of course were constrained by the impositions of gender and could *only* be spontaneous in the arena of passion (Romantic man had the thrill of passion and of money), but for both it is the passionate love affair 'which triumphed as the key lesson in, and example of, the advent of Romantic feeling'.[24] The iconoclastic centre of Romanticism connects passion to the flouting of social convention through the life and work of the poets Byron (perhaps the first modern vampire) and Shelley. This is the moment in which 'true love' as we understand it today was born – for these poets, true love, passion, transcends social convention and enables us to act on the basis of passion, for the feeling and its intensity is its own rational justification for action. Passion becomes close to the meaning of life for the Romantics for it is what gives meaning; it is the place of signification and the grounds for action.

In the late eighteenth century and today, this new philosophy did not completely supersede the old; instead, it contended for legitimacy with the established rules governing social correctness. But what we see in the *Twilight Saga* is homage to the philosophy of passionate love born of the late eighteenth-century Romantic movement. For Bella, significance and meaning come through passionate love, and this love justifies any action, with a grandiosity borrowed from Romanticism – including her own death. Edward Cullen is less a vampiric projection of the self here and more a foil.

The intensity of her feelings for Edward Cullen is underlined in the erotic triangle between Bella, Edward and Jacob, who, as a 'sensible' boyfriend for whom she cares deeply, is rejected for an all-encompassing dangerous love which makes its own rules. The experience of this emotion becomes the basis of Bella's action and the purpose of her life. Indeed, Bella's voice-over opens the first film in the saga with the lines, 'I'd never given much thought to how I would die, but dying in the place of someone I love seems to be a good way to go.' By the film's end, because of her love for Edward, Bella is determined to end her human life and become a vampire. Edward asks her, 'Is that what you dream of, becoming a monster?', to which she replies, 'I dream about being with you forever.' In this tale, passion is legitimised by being enacted and it is the place of personal meaning. The old debate is presented here in order that passion can triumph. In contrast to the reckless spontaneity that marks Bella's passion for Edward Cullen, the older mores of conduct such as duty and the importance of social bonds are represented through Jacob and his Native American/werewolf community. An uneasy truce exists between the vampire family – the projection of romantic passion – and the werewolf tribe – who are a supernatural projection of duty. Choice and spontaneity which shapes the passionate love between Bella and Edward is in contrast to the predetermined process of 'imprinting' which shapes the parings in the werewolf Native society. And while the conversation between passion and duty continues throughout this saga,[25] passion is ultimately endorsed *because* it gives meaning; it transforms insignificance into significance. Perhaps this can account for the enormous popularity of these books and films among young women and adolescent girls. The coupling of passion and meaning are a significant and pleasurable contrast to the fetters affecting the ability to act meaningfully for young women and girls and the difficulty in finding the occasions for significant action in a cultural moment which promises the democratic possibility of achievement for all, but doesn't deliver it. The sociologist Chris Rojek argues that in our 'acquisitive' society, most people suffer from 'achievement famine'. For Rojek, the democratic ideal of being recognised as 'extraordinary, special or unique collides with the bureaucratic tendency to standardize and routinize existence'.[26] Fame and wealth, the marks of success in the social order, are closed to most. In this context, deep romantic love is a form of significance that all can seemingly aspire to – one that girls can own for the self. Just as the action hero provides the male with a fantasy of power – where brute strength is the basis for action and meaning – here the fantasy of power is based on the transcendent power of love. It is a reason for being and meaning. And of course there is a link between meaning and power. For in the end the vampire is a projection of the self and it is though the course of passionate love that Bella not only flouts conventional wisdom but becomes herself a powerful vampire. The validation of Romantic passion also raises individualism as the centre of modern ethics, an individualism with which the vampire is imbued – in contrast to the more collective meanings of the zombie undead. Romantic passion in the sympathetic vampire tale offers the pleasures of individual significance, then, by validating the importance of the individual as being in possession of her feelings. Bella's final voice-over in the first film tells us that in love, she will win: 'I won't give in – I know what I want.'

In this alternative reading of the *Twilight Saga*, I have suggested that there is a problem with invoking a cultural hierarchy to legitimate socially dominant tastes over others, and I have suggested readings of the films which remind us of the link between venerated Romanticism and the vilified Gothic. However, it is another step to simply applaud any offering from what is an increasingly consumerist, merchandise-bound, branded and profit-driven cultural field, simply because it is consumed by non-dominant social groups. Because if the vampire is a metaphor for anything in our time, perhaps it can be seen to be a metaphor for money – it is spilling as much green as it is red. It is estimated that in the last three years, vampire films, books, TV shows, DVD and merchandising sales, games and other publications have generated revenue of $7 billion. The *Twilight Saga* is one of the top earners. The first three films made $1.76 billion – *New Moon* alone grossed $309 million at the box office, $160,000 million in video/DVD sales. Franco Moretti, back in the early 1980s, suggested that Dracula was a metaphor for monopoly capitalism, traversing national boundaries with the ease of capital. Perhaps today's vampires are more a case of capitalist oligopoly – the profits being shared by the top media conglomerates that have come to dominate global media with the frenzy of mergers and acquisitions following deregulation in the US and Europe. This is a case of culture for profit, rather than the expression of our human desire for stories and myths. The large corporations who profit so well from the new vampire industry want complete control of their portion of the brand. For instance, Summit Entertainment, which owns the licensing rights for *Twilight*, have sued Zazzle for infringement of trademark and copyright. Zazzle (a print-on-demand service for T-shirts and other objects) were inundated by teenage *Twilight* fans with orders for their own designed *Twilight* goods.[27] Summit Entertainment attempted to put a stop to do-it-yourself merchandise in an effort to have complete control of its 'product' and the revenue generated from it. Perhaps not surprising given that the magazine *License! Global* estimates that the saga has so far made $500 million in merchandising sales.[28]

Let The Right One In: Whose Right One?

However, those critics who ridicule the fans of *Twilight* and other more mainstream vampire stories, as being dupes of consumer capitalism and naïve prey to marketing strategies, ignore how cult or quality horror films address their own audiences. Contrast the critical reception of *Twilight* with that of a contemporaneous vampire film *Let the Right One In* (Tomas Alfredeson, 2008). This low-budget Swedish film was critically acclaimed and celebrated at the time of its release in Sweden in 2008 and later elsewhere. In October 2010, the critics' website Metacritics awarded it best foreign film since 2000,[29] and respected critic and vampire author Kim Newman gave it 5 out of 5 stars in *Empire* magazine, rating it as a classic. Newman writes that 'In a season where *Twilight* – which also hinges on a school-set friendship between a vampire and a human – has become, by a wide margin, the most profitable vampire movie ever made, *Let The Right One In* trumps the Hollywood vision by landing an instant, secure place on the list of the ten best vampire movies.'[30] Indeed, the film already has a monograph devoted to it in the 'Devil's Advocate' series.[31] The film's bleak depiction of outsiderdom, chilling cinematography and art-house connotations won it fans among the critical establishment. It has been noted that *Let The Right One In*'s marketing appeal lay in its crossover status. Peter Hutchings points out in this book that although horror has not featured as part of Swedish film culture, *Let the Right One In* was marketed specifically as a horror film, but in an up-market, art-house way. The film combines multiple addresses. Its 'muted realism' and 'slow pacing' combines art-house restraint with the transportation of horror conventions from diverse national contexts into the Swedish context. The film thus addresses a Swedish national cinematic context, a European art-house sensibility and a European cult or sub-cultural attachment to horror. The aesthetic crossover between these traditions has been noted above via Jancovich's critique of cult. For Hutchings, this combination not only demonstrates a 'creative commitment to horror', but also part of a European marketing strategy for the circulation of cult horror material to specialist cult markets. It is important to note that the film is marketed as carefully as the Hollywood blockbuster – but to very different audiences whose cultural (or cult) capital distinguish them from mainstream horror sensibilities. Hence the film's 'ambition to be nationally distinctive while also displaying what might be termed a cult sensibility'. Hutchings suggests that European horror films like *Let the Right One In* are 'often directed at very specific international markets for horror while also possessing a distinctive national address'.

But as Newman hints in his *Empire* review, there are thematic links between the Hollywood blockbuster and the art-house cult film. As different as *Let the Right One In* and *Twilight* seem, they have more in common than perhaps appears at first. Both are films where broken families haunt the emotional landscape, unspoken but ever present. Indeed, despite some critics' complaints that the vampire has become domesticated,[32] the sympathetic vampire has always been concerned with the domestic. The central character, Oskar, is a 12-year-old boy who lives with his mother on a bleak council estate on the outskirts of Stockholm, whose contact with his father is depicted as intermittent and odd. He is badly bullied at school and is a withdrawn and sensitive boy. He befriends Eli, who appears to be a girl his age but who is actually a vampire. There are hints in the film that Eli is a boy (the novel makes explicit that he is actually a castrated boy) and so the homoerotic possibilities of the vampire partially resurfaces. What unfolds is the growth of a rather disturbing friendship, and the film leaves a terrible sense of unease – the sort of unease that Freudian psychoanalysis associates with guilt.

Ernest Jones, writing in the 1930s about the psychology of the nightmare, suggests that belief in, and fear of, the vampire stem from guilt arising from the emotions of love and hate in the drama of infantile sexual urges towards one parent and murderous jealousy of the other.

For Jones, the vampire is a projection of our guilt, and guilt turns to fear. Jones argues that love does not give rise to fear when it is accepted by the ego. It gives rise to fear when it is guilty and repressed. Dread, he says, always signifies suppressed sexual wishes. Certainly on the surface of the narrative, this film presents us with a rather unhealthy relationship between Eli and her father figure, Hakkan, who tries to procure blood for Eli. There is a strong insinuation of incest in this relationship and the guilty love to which Jones refers. But perhaps it is written too obviously on the surface of the narrative as a motif for other concerns. Eli's relationship with Hakkan is undoubtedly disturbing; parental care is depicted as a form of perverse devotion. In one of the film's most unsettling scenes, Hakkan is in hospital after having deliberately burnt his own face with acid so that Eli will not be implicated in the murder he has been caught committing on her behalf. His devotion, although creepy, seems absolute. Eli creeps into his hospital room through a window where he offers his neck so the she can feed and then he falls to his death from the window. The film here differs from the novel, where Hakkan is overtly depicted as a paedophile and Eli draining him does not actually kill him but turns him into a monstrous undead paedophile. Nonetheless, Hakkan is one of the film's key symbols of parental care and it is shown to be deeply troubling.

Indeed, all of the parental relationships in the film are disturbing and depicted as unwholesome and as harsh an environment for children as the film's landscape itself, for the adult world is populated by drunks, incompetents and hucksters. Whether perversity (as in the relationship between Hakkan and Eli) or alcoholic brutish neglect (as in the case of Oskar and his father), paternal affection and protection is deficient. Mothers in this film are spectral, and maternal care is marked by its absence. The family in this film is not simply in crisis; its very existence is tenuous and fragile.

The Lost Boys and *Near Dark* resolve their family crises through the restoration of the patriarchal family, and *Twilight* solves its own family crisis by presenting the vampire family as complete and ideal. However, *Let the Right One In* does not resolve its crisis – instead it displaces it. The guilt induced by the film seems less to do with our child selves being projected onto Eli – the devouring love/hate for the parent – and perhaps more to do with parental/adult guilt. Jones comments that projection is always a 'circuitous method' of

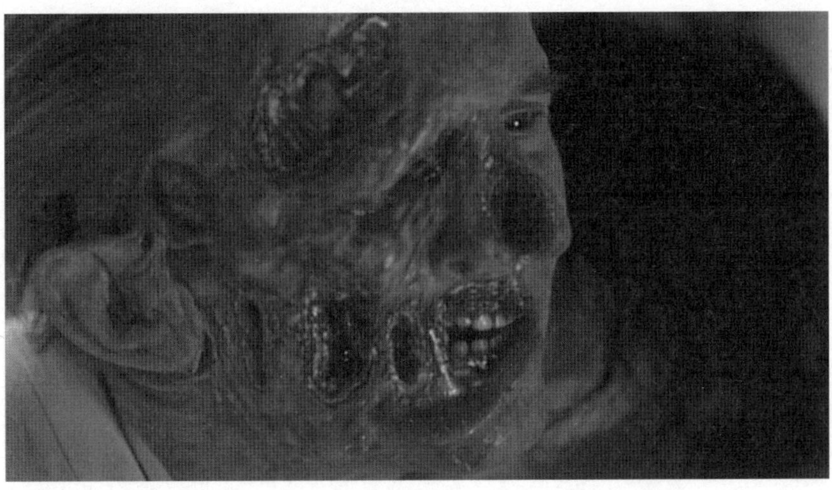

15. Disfigured Hakkan letting Eli into his hospital room to drain him of blood and kill him.

expression.[33] The image that is projected is warped by the very need to do so. If projection is not straightforward, then it is possible to suggest that Eli the child does not represent our child selves – indeed, as s/he tells us, she is not a child at all, but a vampire. Perhaps Eli is not a projection of child guilt towards the parent, but of parental guilt towards the child, or rather towards broken childhood. Oskar, perhaps more heart-wrenchingly than the young protagonists of the other films, is a broken-home child, left to his fate unprotected by parental love or care. He is weak and vulnerable and deprived. If Eli is a projection of the guilt, then it is because she is a mirror image of Oskar, the film's symbol of childhood isolation and suffering. However, the repressed guilt is mitigated in two ways in this film, in the first instance by appearing to be its opposite. Eli is a projection of adult guilt that has taken the form of a child who is not a child. Eli is a nightmare version of Oskar, one who simultaneously evokes sympathy *and* creepiness; one whose plight cannot, unlike Oskar, be left at 'our' door as adult and parent society; one for whom guilt can thus be displaced by subtle dread and revulsion. When Eli tells Oskar to 'be more like me', we almost want him to, because Oskar *is* needy childhood, innocent and neglected by adult society, but unable to cope on his own. In becoming like Eli, love/hate turned to guilt for innocent childhood broken can also be transformed into revulsion and dread.

Guilt is mitigated in another way, in the visual quality of the film, and in its invitation to the audience to appreciate the film's aesthetic quality and to deploy our (adult) ability to discriminate. It emerges from and speaks to a particular cinematic sensibility, as discussed above. The haunting beauty of the film contributes, I am suggesting, to the displacement of guilt. *Let the Right One In* invites interpretation and appreciation, it encourages us to be aware of its 'Swedishness', its artiness and its 'cultishness', and in doing so, we are one step removed from what is so disturbing about the film.

So where have we ended up and are we any closer to what the vampire means? It seems that the vampire, despite its ability to mutate and to traverse national boundaries, cannot entirely step outside of the national or the logic of the economic; it can be shackled to capital and its image can be made to work for consumer culture and media. But my own affection for the vampire makes me resist this as a total conclusion of what the vampire means. For surely the vampire also persists as an image in popular culture because of its ability to represent what is disavowed, to speak to anxieties and desires that are difficult to name. The Gothic form has persisted beyond the life of the Gothic novel into contemporary horror fiction both on the screen and on the page because, like its ancestor, it is concerned with the troubles and contradictions of contemporary society that lurk beneath the surface of reality or rather, hover in the half light dusk of the undead. The outsiderdom and ambiguity of the vampire speaks not to one set of disavowed experiences, but many. In *Twilight*, it perhaps speaks to the loneliness of the young, who, in dreaming of belonging and significance in a culture which demands individualism, idolise romantic love. In the case of *Let the Right One In*, it perhaps speaks to the adult who is both horrified and moved by the unrelenting depiction of precisely that loneliness in child vampiric form. Both films, like many vampire films, draw on the vampire to articulate hidden pain, and they speak to different audiences in different ways. In light of what the vampire can tell us about ourselves, our socio-historical moment and our cultural denials, I say, don't just let the right one in – let them all in.

Notes

1 Milly Williamson, *The Lure of the Vampire: Gender Fiction and Fandom from Bram Stoker to Buffy* (London: Wallflower Press, 2005).
2 Alain Silver and James Ursini, *The Vampire Film* (South Brunswick: A S Barnes, 1997), p. 89.
3 Margaret L. Carter, 'The Vampire as Alien in Contemporary Fiction', in J. Gordon and V. Hollinger (eds), *Blood Read: The Vampire as Metaphor in Contemporary Culture* (Philadelphia: University of Pennsylvania Press, 1997), p. 27.
4 Nina Auerbach, *Our Vampires, Ourselves* (Chicago and London: Chicago University Press, 1995), p. 4.
5 Richard Dyer, 'Children of the Night: vampirism as homosexuality, homosexuality as vampirism', in S. Radstone (ed.), *Sweet Dreams: Sexuality, Gender and Popular Fiction* (London: Lawrence and Wishart, 1988).
6 Andrea Weiss, *Vampires and Violets: Lesbians in the Cinema* (London: Jonathan Cape, 1995) and Bonnie Zimmerman, 'Daughters of darkness: the lesbian on film', in B. Grant (ed.), *Planks of Reason: Essays on the Horror Film* (Metuchen: The Scarecrow Press, 1984).
7 Samuel Taylor Coleridge, *Christabel* (1816).
8 Charles Baudelaire, *Fleurs du Mal* (1857).
9 Barbara Creed, *The Monstrous Feminine: Film, Feminism, Psychoanalysis* (London: Routledge, 1993), p. 61.
10 Auerbach, *Our Vampires*, p. 5.
11 Auerbach, *Our Vampires*, p. 58.
12 Michael Gamer, *Romanticism and the Gothic: Genre, Reception, and Canon Formation* (Cambridge: Cambridge University Press, 2000), p. 23.
13 Maggie Kilgour, *The Rise of the Gothic Novel* (London: Routledge, 1995), p. 6.
14 Peter Haining, *The Shilling Shockers: Stories of Terror from the Gothic Bluebooks* (London: Gollanz, 1978), p. 12.
15 Kilgour, *Gothic Novel*, p. 7.
16 Anne Williams, 'The Fiction of Feminine Desires: not the mirror but the lamp', *Women's Writing* 1:2 (1995): 229–39.
17 Fred Botting, *Gothic* (London: Routledge, 1996), p. 6.
18 Botting, *Gothic*, p. 4.
19 Kilgour, *Gothic Novel*, p. 8.
20 Mark Jancovich, *Defining Cult Movies: The Cultural Politics of Oppositional Taste* (Manchester: Manchester University Press, 2003).
21 Leah Rozen, 'Only Fervent Fans Will Believe New Moon Shines Brightly', *People Magazine*, 20 November 2009; http://www.people.com/people/package/article/0,,20316279_20321383,00.html?xid=rss-topheadlines (accessed 21 October 2011).
22 Stuart Heritage, 'Being Human, I'd say True blood is in its Twilight years', 4 February 2012; http://www.guardian.co.uk/film/2012/feb/04/being-human-true-blood-twilight (accessed February 2012).
23 Fred Inglis, *A Short History of Celebrity* (Princeton, NJ: Princeton University Press), p. 26.
24 Inglis, *A Short History*, p. 27.
25 Fans adopting Team Edward or Team Jacob can be interpreted as participation in cultural debates about meaning – one representing duty and honour and the other spontaneity and passion.

26 Chris Rojek, *Celebrity* (London: Reaktion, 2001), p. 149.

27 Chloe Albanesius, 'Zazzle.com Sued for Infringement Over "Twilight" Merchandise', *PCMag.com*, 30 October 2009; http://appscout.pcmag.com/news-events/271265-zazzle-com-sued-for-infringement-over-twilight-merchandise#fbid=FzJN7aLGWjx (accessed 9 December 2010).

28 *License!Global* July 2010; http://www.licensemag.com/licensemag/article/articleDetail.jsp?id=681472 (accessed 8 December 2010).

29 http://www.metacritic.com/feature/best-foreign-horror-films-since-2000 (accessed 17 January 2011).

30 Kim Newman, 'Review', *Empire*, 2010; http://www.empireonline.com/reviews/review.asp?FID=135765 (accessed 17 January 2011).

31 Anne Billson, *Let the Right One In* (Leighton Buzzard: Auteur, 2011).

32 Jules Zanger, 'Metaphor into Metonymy: the vampire next door', in J. Gordon and V. Hollinger (eds), *Blood Read: The Vampire as Metaphor in Contemporary Culture* (Philadelphia: University of Pennsylvania Press, 1997).

33 Ernst Jones, *On the Nightmare* (London and New York: Read Books, 2007 (1931)), p. 102.

Part 2

REWRITING THE LIVING DEAD – THE ZOMBIE IN POPULAR CULTURE

5

DEAD METAPHORS/UNDEAD ALLEGORIES

Jeffrey Sconce

Monsters are meaningful: this maxim enjoys almost universal agreement now, equally at home in pages of a weekly movie guide as in the most obtuse schools of psychoanalytic theory. Whenever a monster appears on page or screen, it skulks about as the distorted ambassador from some absent psychic empire, be it the unconscious proper, a repressed historical imaginary, or an ever-nebulous 'cultural anxiety'. The Cold War thus gave the free world alien intruders and irradiated insects, material symbols of the invisible threats posed by communism and radiation. Slashers are Oedipal creatures, of course, rehearsing traumatic memories of psychosexual development and the original implantation of castration anxiety.[1] Vampires, too, are all about sex, a revelation that no doubt would have surprised John Polidori, Sheridan Le Fanu or Bram Stoker in their respective eras, but now circulates as common knowledge even among most teenage girls. Born of repression and displacement, the vampire, thanks to writers like Anne Rice and Stephanie Meyer, has now largely fulfilled the Byronic destiny of his Byronic origins – mad, bad and dangerous to date.

And then there is the zombie: undead and usually unlovable, a creature without depth, desire or mystery of any kind. Troubled vampires may crowd the shelves of the teen fiction aisle, but it is the zombie that trudges on as perhaps the last remaining monster capable of generating any actual *revulsion* in its audience. The basic template of the George Romero zombie series has, over the past 30 years, spawned a truly global empire, and like all mature bodies of work, circulates now in proliferating copies, clones, remakes, reinterpretations and parodies. As with all genres, subsequent filmmakers have offered key inflections – new origin myths, more disgusting modes of transmission, ever-faster zombie land speeds. Yet it remains, at its heart, a genre of the glacially besieged, a constrictive horror of the social body's inexorable implosion.

For nearly a century, we have looked to Freud's Gothic theatre of the mind to explain what scares us and why, and in particular his influential essay of 1919, 'The Uncanny'.[2] Over time, Freud's dissection of Hoffman, the sandman, castration and all things *unheimlich* has increasingly become a cousin of the folktales it once sought to explain. As Richard Davenport-Hines argues in his book on Gothicism, Freud may well have been the last of the great Gothic novelists, transforming the genre's obsession with the hidden family secret, unmentionable horror and secret architecture into an entire science of the mind.[3] Then again, Freud may have found in the Gothic what he found in the Greeks: evidence of certain psychic structures that will not be denied – in the unconscious, in the dreamwork, in the pages of the Victorian fantastic. Either way, there remains something decidedly *ungothic*, *unFreudian*, *un-uncanny* about the zombie – he, she or it staggering about as an irreducible bio-core wholly resistant to traditional terms of analysis. Perhaps this explains, in part, why Gilles Deleuze and Felix Guattari, in their own ambitious attempt to slay Freud and Oedipus, nominated the zombie as the only salient mythology remaining within the capitalist era. 'The only modern myth is the myth of zombies,' they note in *Anti-Oedipus,* 'mortified schizos, good for work, brought back to reason.'[4] Like the schizophrenic, extolled elsewhere in *Anti-Oedipus* as a subject heroically resistant to Freud's mamadrama, the zombie is also a 'body without organs', although one suspects the zombie experiences this less as the liberated ecstasy of deterritorialised desire than as the plodding negation of non-being. The zombie is quite literally a body without organs, or at least without the apparent need for any organs, save the brain of course. In any case, zombies appear to have no secrets, no interiority, no conflicts, and are thus immune to neurosis. They know what they want and they know how to get it, to quote another rotten body, a society where instinct and drive are perfectly integrated around a simple economy of brains. Zombies take the stage when the theatre of the mind, so central to psychoanalysis and the modern subject, at last goes dark. When there is nothing left to repress, one might say, the dead will walk the earth, not as phantasmic projections of some occult psychic force, but as an obscene parody of positivist sociology – blank bodies on an empty march toward absolute massification. Once the world's standing reserve of bio-power, now they will stand no more!

Many would no doubt argue that the zombie film does have another level, a deeper, latent meaning to be excavated from beneath its anarchistic spray of blood and viscera. *Night of the Living Dead* premiered in the autumn of 1968, a year of dramatic unrest and upheaval in the Western democracies: the student and unionist uprisings in Paris, Enoch Powell's 'River of Blood' speech in England, the assassinations of Martin Luther King, Jr and Robert Kennedy in the United States, leading in turn to the tumultuous riots of the Democratic National Convention in Chicago that autumn. As *Night of the Living Dead* played on the screens that October, the war in Vietnam continued seemingly without end and Richard Nixon battled Hubert Humphrey for the US presidency. This historical context is well known, and it is tempting to read Romero's zombie horde as symptomatic of this social unrest. And it is, of course, *manifestly so*. Romero's penchant for political parable has become ever more pronounced as the series develops. But again, this is not an unconscious process – a distortion or displacement. As carefully crafted allegories, zombie movies are often meant to be read as political statements, and like most science-fiction, they are more about the present moment than future predictions. And, much as the structural positions of cowboy and Indian reversed during the course of the western, we now increasingly root for the zombies. Wealth, power, imperialism, military force – all are useless in perpetuating tyranny and injustice over the rotting dispossessed. They will win, for their cause is just. It is now or soon will be their world and we are only living in it; that is, until the moment when we cross over and join them. Such allegory is perhaps most successful in the second instalment of the Romero series, *Dawn of the Dead* (1978), in which the United States stands as a barricaded shopping mall, protected by brute force, foolishly hoping to hold off an advancing army of second- and third-world marauders who want brains, of course, but also a taste of the good life. This allegory of the West in escalating crisis and decline has become ever more salient over the past 30 years – the unrest of the late 1960s setting the stage for the eventual rise of Reagan and Thatcher, the third way compromises of Clinton and Blair, the inexorable transfer of economic and cultural power to the Pacific rim, the inadvertent revelation that the world's last remaining superpower, like the Soviets before it, was more a house of

16. Undead allegory: the shopping mall in *Dawn of the Dead.*

cards, in this case one built on manic consumerism. It turns out that the US was a giant shopping mall after all, and a poorly run one at that.

Psychoanalytic metaphor and political allegory remain durable and compelling models, to be sure, and they continue to inform the majority of zombie theory – a surprisingly fertile corpus of work in recent years. The zombies lurking in *Anti-Oedipus* enact a myth of labour pushed beyond even alienation, reduced to such pure automatism that there is no longer a consciousness to alienate or mystify. In their recent 'Zombie Manifesto', meanwhile, Sarah Lauro and Karen Embry present the zombie as embodying tensions between global capitalism and the dawn of post-humanism, offering the zombie as a more probable future compromise than the cybernetic feminism offered in Donna Haraway's celebrated 'Cyborg Manifesto'.[5] Slavoj Zizek, finally, makes the characteristically perverse argument that the zombie's apparent absence of subjectivity presents a challenge to its still human observers. If a zombie is a creature devoid of consciousness and yet nevertheless appears to have coherent control over its goals and behaviour, who, asks Zizek, is deceived in this performance of subjectivity – the humans or the zombie?[6] This question, of course, must lead – as do most Zizekian riffs on Lacanian theory – to the theory-fiction of one's own consciousness. We are all zombies, in other words, only some of us are more adept than others at shielding our egos from its fictional foundations.

These are all interesting readings of the zombie, and to the extent that one wants to make sweeping claims about the nature of Western consciousness based on a movie monster, I see no reason *not* to believe them. Still, I would argue that the zombie remains a much more *manifest* creature than this, a monster that does not necessarily demand recourse to the interpretative gymnastics of encrypted metaphor, latent allegory, or political symptomology. The modern zombie is a creature of the *post-uncanny* – an era when models of horror born of modernity and repression become improbable, if not completely impossible. Like the rest of the cinema, horror long ago passed over from the mystery of eerie indeterminacy to embrace the more obscene fascinations of suspense and spectacle intertwined. Horror in the Victorian and modern eras revelled in the ambiguities haunting an allegedly rational mind in an allegedly rational world. Zombie horror, on the other hand, is *all there,* wholly of the surface, a saga of unambiguous confrontation rather than tentative interpretation. There is no element of 'fantastic hesitation' in the zombie, only a single, obvious and inviolable ground rule of the genre: *don't let yourself get bitten by a zombie.*[7]

If zombie horror no longer resides in the unconscious, where then do we look for it? Zombie films are about blood, guts and the abject body, certainly, but this promiscuous slathering of viscera remains meaningless without the genre's other structural demand – the spectacle of social disintegration. The zombie genre is really the story of two bodies in decay – the individual corpses of the undead and the social body as a whole. Taking up the horror of banal multiplication foretold in Hitchcock's *The Birds* (1963), the zombie film presents a social horror of arithmetic and aggregation.[8] Typically, a lone zombie poses little threat, especially the lumbering dimwits of the Romero mythos. They are easy to evade, easy to trick, relatively easy to kill. Encountered one at a time, cut off from their horde, they can even be rather poignant in their baffled isolation. They only become truly dangerous once they achieve an irresistible mass, a type of lumpen lump wherein the brute strength of numbers negates individual stupidity. Moreover, zombies play a zero-sum game: once you go zombie, you can't come back – so the more living souls who cross over into the zombie nation, the more likely the ultimate zombie victory, their numbers growing in direct proportion to ours shrinking. When the tipping point arrives at last, the only options are to escape to a new zombieless land mass or to blow one's brains out, preferably before the zombies catch your scent.

This elemental conflict between the besieged subject and the zombie as a structural menace finds its most characteristic expression in the genre's almost obsessive fixation on the tactics of evasion. In what stands as a metonymy for the genre as a whole, almost all zombie films feature multiple scenes where agile human subjects – still illuminated by the light of consciousness – must negotiate and evade various configurations of zombie obstacle. For example, once the zombies have invaded the previously secure shopping sanctuary in *Dawn of the Dead,* much of the film's subsequent suspense involves the humans' constant cogitation over changing vectors, possible escape routes and unexpected dead-ends. The adrenalised *28 Weeks Later* foregrounds this ghoulish geometry as its opening set piece. Seeing that zombies have trapped his wife and son in an upstairs bedroom, a man assesses the space and the possible angles of attack, making the quick calculation that he cannot intervene without sacrificing his own life. Fleeing the house in a primal fear response, he quickly attracts the attention of several dozen free-range zombies milling about outside the home. There follows a full-on sprint across an open field as the man attempts to escape the flanking manoeuvre of the converging zombie columns. Those familiar with football, on either side of the Atlantic, will recognise these manoeuvres for what they are: splitting the defenders, a dummy run, a bootleg, an open field offence. And, as in football and otherwise ordinary life, success in zombie evasion depends on seeing how the play is developing down the field – much like anticipating a path through Harrods' shoppers to the Knightsbridge stop, finessing testy co-workers to institute a policy reform, tip-toeing through a minefield of family dysfunctions to make it to the end of holiday. Once conventional society begins to disintegrate, this is what remains – politics at its most primal: me versus not-me, my autonomy versus their incessant demands, my flesh versus their teeth, my subjecthood versus their objecthood.

In *Fatal Strategies,* Jean Baudrillard observed that the proliferation of objects in the modern world has at last 'defeated' the subject's attempt to remain the (illusory) master of history and destiny. Given the accelerating logic of excrescence, a culture wherein information and commodities multiply according to their own occult agendas and in excess of any human ability to contain or control them, the subject finds itself overwhelmed by the object at every turn, becoming increasingly adrift and impotent in its illusions of agency. Baudrillard posited two possible 'strategic' responses to this state of affairs. In 'banal strategies', the subject continues to imagine that it has power over the world of objects, forging ahead with the familiar yet increasingly untenable Enlightenment proposition that 'objects' serve us in fulfilling our needs and desires. More useful (or at least honest), Baudrillard argues, are 'fatal strategies', engagements that recognise that the 'object' has won, that we now serve at the pleasure of a world of commodities that need us more than we need them. 'Doubtless the only difference between a banal theory and a fatal theory is that in one strategy the subject still believes himself to be more cunning than the object, where in the other the object is considered more cunning, cynical, talented than the subject, for which it lies in wait.'[9] The zombie film, one might argue, is a particularly poetic treatment of this dilemma, narratives that are explicitly concerned with tracing the line between the subject and a hyperactive multiplication of encroaching objects, a band of humans fighting to preserve their precious illusion of autonomous self versus zombies who have passed over into the 'evil genius' of the object. Not only are zombies generally 'unthinking' and 'unfeeling' (negating the signature properties of the Cartesian ego), they are also little more than oddly motile matter, able to 'survive' as long as the motive brainstem remains in some way connected to some form of tissue, no matter how rotten and dysfunctional. They thus defy even the biological-materialist fantasy that the body (and thus the self) is a complex machine of interrelated systems in functional balance; instead, the zombie's residual, frequently twisted human form mocks both the human mind and body. No longer caught up in the endless circle of this 'duality', the zombie is simply a thing, a thing *out there* that reduces both mind and body to little more than pure mass. In this respect, the zombie film is a more playful expression of a delusion frequently encountered among the psychotic – the belief that everyone else is a robot, or that loved ones have been replaced by automatons, aliens or other imposters. Sent to the madhouse in 1891, psychiatry's most famous psychotic, Daniel Paul Schreber, recalls being beset by 'fleetingly improvised men', souls that he believed only briefly took material form in order to trick or harass him. 'When my wife visited me in person ... I believed for a long time that was only "fleetingly improvised" for the occasion,' he recalls in his memoir, 'and that she

17. Underestimating the zombie horde: an unwise biker checks his blood pressure in *Dawn of the Dead*.

would therefore dissolve, perhaps even on the stairs or directly after leaving the Asylum.'[10] Zombies do not dissolve when out of sight (as far as we know!), but they certainly stage a very similar mode of alienated suspicion. Zombies mirror the horror of imagining our own subjectivity gone dark, or maybe even worse, in the Lacanian/Zizekian mode, that we are ourselves only a temporarily animated and woefully deluded bag of bones and meat.

This all sounds very dire, as if watching a zombie film might trigger an existential crisis or a fatal brush with the real. But often as not, zombie films are also very funny. Mixed with the dreadful revulsion, there is also an often cruelly comic pleasure in seeing our on-screen human surrogates exert their clever mastery over a hapless field of drooling zombie idiots, using the hard-fought victory of coherent subjectivity to trick, taunt and otherwise torment the slow-witted body-object that is the zombie. 'Deluded' or not, our best hope against the zombie horde is our seeming ability to outsmart them. Using a flare to trick a small child or the mentally challenged would just be mean – but as the zombie has seemingly renounced all claims to subjectivity, it opens itself up for all manner of righteous and/or hilarious abuse. But this humour goes both ways. There is also the lesson of the boastful human subject who, having become a little too cocky in his presumed mastery over the stupidity of the undead hordes, finds himself unexpectedly trapped and

18. The living and the undead co-exist in zombie comedy *Shaun of the Dead.*

violently defeated after having fatally miscalculated the volume and persistence of the zombie mass. Typically, this is a minor, disposable character inserted briefly to enact this cautionary fable, like the biker in *Dawn of the Dead* who, in the midst of an epic zombie battle, calculates that he still has time to stop and take an automated blood pressure test (turns out, he doesn't). Like all other stolid but diabolical objects, zombies are relentless, and much like the petty annoyances and daily grind of human life in a world increasingly beyond our control, they will eventually wear you down, forcing you to make that one error of judgement that finally results in absolute annihilation. The zombie-comedy *Shaun of the Dead* (2004) plays this divide brilliantly, the politics of the living and undead existing more or less side-by-side and indistinguishable in their banality, at least initially. Indeed, much of the humour centres on the solipsistic efforts of the living to maintain the quotidian routines that come with subjectivity (like dating), even as the world gradually collapses around them. The Danny Boyle *28*-franchise, on the other hand, reimagines this founding political divide through a logic of catastrophic acceleration, quite literally in the truly horrifying development of a sprinting zombie, but also in the films' radical erasure of the genre's conventional process of zombie incubation. A superficial zombie bite used to mean a period of gradual transformation, and with it, a little time to consider one's fate, to say goodbye to friends and family before committing suicide or begging for euthanasia. This melodramatic convention speaks to just how horrific the prospect of objecthood is for the subject. Is becoming a zombie really a fate worse than death? Might not some of the afflicted wish, during the time of their incubation, to get far away from friends and family (so as not to eat them) and at least give zombiedom a try? The *28* films remove this option, of course, by making the contagion instantaneous – the once familiar companion converted immediately into a putrid sack of rage and adrenaline, the loyal opposition to life itself.

Of course, one might argue that this Manichean political dynamic of subject/object emerges in any apocalyptic scenario. As society and then the world comes to an end, the politics of basic survival become raw and direct, our duty to nation, community and family put to ever more drastic tests until we, like the zombies, are guided only by the logic of our limbic system. Again, it is tempting to read the zombie as some veiled allegory for this threat. But what, exactly, is *displaced* in the zombie scenario? Most of us probably realise, somewhere in the back of our rational and yet highly defended ego formations, that the human race will certainly come to an end one day, and that the most likely culprit will be either an unlucky asteroid strike or a raging global virus. Zombies do not disguise or displace this rather brutal realisation; in fact, they revel in it. The genre reminds us that we are all doomed – individually and as a species – and that the world will most likely end in some cataclysm of mass anarchy and decay. *Mad Max*, the *Terminator* and other post-apocalyptic narratives involving only the politics of the living inevitably hold out some hope that humanity will reorganise and return, perhaps wiser and with a greater capacity for empathy and peace. Zombie films typically dispense with such sentiment, instead heralding absolute and irretrievable annihilation. No government, no God, no triumph of the human spirit is going to save us.

How different this is from the monsters of yore. Ghosts, for example, remain perhaps the distilled essence of the Freudian uncanny – a creature of pure spirit, pure psychic (and thus subjective) energy. It is no coincidence that the physics of spiritualism, occultism and psychoanalysis should overlap at the dawn of modernity – all were in search of a haunted force that exerted invisible influence. As an avatar of some distant emotional trauma – a curse, a betrayal, a life left unresolved – the ghost could not help but become the featured player in the uncanny wing of psychoanalytic theatre. Beyond rational time and space, the ghost can never be truly escaped or be contained because, like the unconscious itself, it obeys the irrational logic of another world. Only when *haunter* and *hauntee* come to some mutual agreement, a talking Ouija cure perhaps, does the *revenant* agree to no longer *revenir.* And, as *Ghost* (1990) demonstrated, the disembodied spirit is such a pure essence of selfhood that it can remain an acceptable, even passionate romantic partner. Zombies, on the other hand, present a complete inversion of this scenario. If the ghost is a spirit without body, the zombie is body without spirit, unburdened by either the conscious or unconscious mind. The zombie simply is and does. It has no interest in the mysteries of mind and memory, only in the brain as protein. And to 'love' a zombie is not an expression of timeless romance – it is only one step up from necrophilia (as in the case of serial killer Jeffrey Dahmer, who used sedatives, a power drill and muriatic acid in an attempt to transform at least one of his victims into a submissive zombie companion).

Though both are putatively 'dead', the zombie lumbers toward a different truth than the ghost, one found not in the recesses of the individual psyche, but in the externalised social field. What is this truth? Perhaps it is the apocalyptic insight posited in 1978 by Baudrillard in his polemical break with sociology, *In the Shadow of the Silent Majorities.* In this wickedly prescient volume, Baudrillard likens the 'masses' to a black hole that absorb any and all attempts to define, inform, educate, survey, reform or govern them. For Baudrillard, the mass does not exist in any real sense – it is more a concept that gives illusory form to what is otherwise an abyss of meaning, an ultimately formless void that will consume any and all attempts to subject it to rational debate and analysis. The 'mass' is a political term sociology employs so as to believe politics is itself still possible, when in fact the modern experience has long ago passed over into spectacle, fascination and irrational obscenity. Of the masses, Baudrillard writes, 'They are neither good conductors of the political, nor good conductors of the social, nor good conductors of meaning in general. Everything flows through them, everything magnetizes them, but diffuses throughout them without leaving a trace ... They are inertia, the strength of inertia, the strength of the neutral.'[11] Of course, this could easily serve as the zombie manifesto as written by zombies themselves; that is, of course, if zombies still suffered from the delusion of believing in organised political action – which they do not.

Ghosts must 'make peace' with the world before they proceed into the light, on to heaven, or wherever else we might imagine they go after exiting the body, arriving at last at a transcendental tranquillity evocative of the quintessence posited by Freud as the motive force in the 'death drive'.[12] But if 'the aim of all life is death', as Freud cheerfully reminded us, then zombies would counter that 'the aim of all society is anarchy'. They do not seek peace, but rather appear to revel in mayhem. No one wants to be bitten by a zombie, of course, nor does anyone really want to become a zombie. But there remains a certain thrill in seeing zombies lay waste to the cities and civilisation of the living, a chaotic exhilaration of collapse that speaks to what we might call a *social* death drive. In this respect, the zombie genre thrives on the same energy informing so much of J. G. Ballard's fiction. But while Ballard's great novels of social collapse such as *The Drought* (1965) and *High Rise* (1975) evoke a melancholy unravelling of the present, zombie films speak to the new and ecstatic order to come. Zombies appear to have the courage we often lack, willing to imagine (or at least simply enact) a new world where the various discontents of civilisation are finally and definitively cast aside. Zombies do not have jobs, mortgages, bank accounts, property, household chores, utility bills, laws, marriages, children or any other discernible obligations. Want to wander off into a field and snarl at crows for the rest of the day? Your zombie peers will wish you well, or more to the point, they will not even notice you are gone. Drained of all duty and desire, they appear to have achieved a Zen-like state in their aimless wandering, a mode of existence only occasionally disrupted by the sudden proximity of brains. In some iterations of the zombie mythos, moreover, even this basic 'need' remains unexplained and maybe even unnecessary (some zombies, for example, appear quite capable of functioning for days, months and years without need of food, water, sleep or sex – suggesting their compulsion to eat brains is a sport born of bored malice or residual contempt for the living). The zombie is truly 'centred' and living 'in the moment', a state of being that the living often spend huge amounts of money on each year attempting to achieve. Meanwhile, those who survive the zombie apocalypse are no less impacted by this radical reordering of the social imaginary. The living may claim to fight for the traditional values of a world temporarily disrupted, one that they vow to restore (usually for the sake of the children), but in the meantime, daily existence becomes intensely focused on the most elemental aspects of survival. The post-zombie subject no longer has the time and energy to indulge the luxuries of anomie, repression, modesty, neurosis and alienation, and that in itself is also a form of 'liberation'.

This 'social death drive' is central to Seth Grahame-Smith's surprisingly successful literary 'mash-up' of Jane Austen, *Pride and Prejudice and Zombies* (2009). The book reimagines Austen's world of elaborately formalised courtship rituals as having been overrun by an outbreak of zombies. Not only must Elizabeth Bennett and her sisters find worthy husbands, but they must also do so in a world where the undead might attack at any moment. The book's opening lines have become almost as famous as Austen's original: 'It is a truth universally acknowledged that a zombie in possession of brains must be in want of more brains. Never was this truth more plain than during the recent attacks at Netherfield Park, in which a household of eighteen was slaughtered and consumed by a horde of the living dead.'[13] In theory, one could 'mash-up' any classic of English literature with the zombie action film to achieve a similar sense of comic incongruity. But I would argue that Grahame-Smith's use of *Pride and Prejudice* was a particularly inspired choice. Zombies in Dickens? Funny, perhaps, and yet in the highly stratified and sprawling world that is Dickens' England (or even just London), zombies are not so improbable an addition. Austen's comedy-of-manners, on the other hand, amplifies the claustrophobic social constraints that are so central to the indulgence of a social death drive, making the middle-class Regency parlour a much more satisfying site for zombie violation. With the French and American Revolutions still within a generation's memory, Regency England witnessed not only the era of E. P. Thompson's 'making of the English working class', but also the radical institutional changes that would shape modern forms of industrialism, government, law, science, gender and sexuality. Indeed, Regency England has become – perhaps even more so than the Victorian era – a stuffy signifier of the most 'civilised' of civilised civilisations, marked by an emerging middle class emulating the very 'proper' codes of conduct that Austen (and others) would so often play for humour (Thackeray's Becky Sharp, it should be noted, would excel as a zombie fighter). What better place, then, to locate a fantasy of the social in collapse than the very crucible in which this social order was forged (at least for the Anglophonic world)? Clearly, all the wit, cunning, scheming and social dissimulation that still make Austen popular among a certain readership also provide the fuel for fantasies of that 'refined' world's utter destruction.

In addition to Austen/Grahame-Smith's drawing room dead, the publishing industry has for almost a decade now hawked such titles as *The Zombie Survival Guide* (2003) and *The Zombie Handbook* (2009), books that indulge most directly the fantasy of witnessing a seemingly inevitable zombie apocalypse. Crucially, all of these books amplify the inherent comedy of this scenario, transforming the genre's bloody horrors into an ongoing joke at the expense of the social, reasserting (like the death drive proper) a certain ecstatic inevitability at the thought of social implosion. The zombie's ludic call to a social death drive can be witnessed most explicitly (if also somewhat ironically) in the increasing presence of the socialised/socialising zombie in everyday life. While dressing up as a zombie was once a masquerade typically confined to Halloween, various zombiphilic organisations now regularly organise zombie pub crawls at various times of the year – events wherein revellers shuffle in zombie gear from bar to bar, culminating in a contest for best costume and make-up. Like many other rituals of costumed drinking, zombie crawls present a carnivalesque reversal of power – but one that goes beyond the mere inversion of king and serf to reverse the entire category of the sentient human into its negated Other: the zombie object. When zombies 'play' in public, they provide a mirthful nod to the eventual collapse of the very public they invade. The city of Chicago, for example, now hosts an annual 'Zombies on Ice' event at the downtown skating rink, offering this iconic social ritual back to bemused passers-by as either a vision of the future or a sign that the apocalypse has indeed begun.

Particularly inspired in this respect have been the 'Run for Your Lives' charity events for the American Red Cross. Hosted in various US cities during 2011 and 2012, this 5k event pitted runners against a course infested with zombie attackers. 'Run For Your Lives is a first-of-its-kind event, one part 5k, one part obstacle course, one part escaping the clutches of zombies – and all part awesome,' boasts the event's website.[14] It would appear that the American Red Cross, an organisation long dedicated to rescuing human subjects in distress, has itself now adopted the logic of a fatal strategy, pitting healthy human runners against a zombie apocalypse as nothing less than a drill for the subject-destroying crises the organisation may well be called upon to service in the future. As with Grahame-Smith's choice of *Pride and Prejudice,* the marriage of zombie and jogger presents a particularly inspired collision of the social and the anti-social. Baudrillard noted some 20 years ago that the 'jogger' is already a subject that flirts with the annihilation of ecstatic non-being:

> Decidedly, joggers are the true Latter Day Saints and the protagonists of an easy-does-it Apocalypse. Nothing evokes the end of the world more than a man running straight ahead on a beach, swathed in the sounds of his walkman, cocooned in the solitary sacrifice of his energy, indifferent even to catastrophes since he expects destruction to come only as the fruit of his own efforts, from exhausting the energy of a body that has in his own eyes become useless. Primitives, when in despair, would commit suicide by swimming out to sea until they could swim no longer. The jogger commits suicide by running up and down the beach. His eyes are wild, saliva drips from his mouth. Do not stop him. He will either hit you or simply carry on dancing around in front of you like a man possessed.[15]

Pitting fit, healthy and well-accessorised runners – deluded as to their own immortality – against a field of slovenly zombies is the height of black comedy. Emblematic of the West's cult of the body and self-realised individualisation, the runner here finds himself attempting to outmanoeuvre the rotting bodies of a rotting society. And once runner and zombie meet on the open field, who can resist rooting for the zombies? If nothing else, it is simply more entertaining to play zombie and be in the company of other zombies. As opposed to the solitary exclusivity of the long-distance runner (one is tempted to say 'the loneliness' as well), zombies are a much more inviting, convivial and egalitarian community.

By portending the end of the subject and the end of the social, the zombie somewhat ironically makes available a profoundly social form of play. Consider performing the part of a zombie in comparison with performing the role of a vampire. By virtue of their mythology and codification, vampires assume a narcissistic air of aristocratic self-pity and weary solipsism, invoking an intrinsic hierarchy of preening: who is the best? the most convincing? the most tragic? the most sexy? and so on (thus the appeal of the vampire within the tortured adolescence of the 'Goth' teenager). But playing a zombie allows one to simply go blank, to 'turn off' the self so as to better assimilate alongside one's similarly brain-dead peers. A good zombie event requires the entire ensemble to act en masse, each individual player evacuated of any pretence to intelligence, rank or attraction. To be a vampire, one must presume to be extraordinary and expect to be seen. To be a zombie, one has the freedom to be nothing at all, to be 'inertia, the strength of inertia, the strength of the neutral'.

A final meme of zombie humour is perhaps the most literal in articulating this social death drive, and serves as a fitting coda for considering the zombie's oddly alluring presence in twenty-first-century popular culture. Over the past few years, several ingenious pranksters have hacked into the electronic traffic signs that stand alongside major urban thoroughfares in order to warn: ZOMBIES AHEAD – EXPECT DELAYS. An unexpected delight for the bored commuter, this gag's brilliance is obviously a function of its site-specific installation. Targeting commuters trapped in their cars and cars trapped in traffic, making their way day after day into the urban core to perform eight hours of often mindless labour, only to repeat the same traffic jam on the way home – the ZOMBIES AHEAD – EXPECT DELAYS sign is the gallows humour of the slow-motion damned. The sign reminds them (and us) of the fate that slowly engulfs us all – a zombified repetition of social obligations that does a little more each day to destroy the self and the planet. With every 10k trip in and out of the city, staged five times a week, the soul becomes a little duller and the planet a little more toxic. The sign is funny because, on the one hand, the commuter recognises himself in the figure of the zombie, ceaselessly and often blindly forging ahead for the tasty 'brain' that is a paycheque. But there is also a form of longing in this warning. What if there really were zombies ahead? Not only would life be on the verge of becoming much more interesting, but there would also be the promise that one's quotidian routines would not simply be 'delayed', but instead radically and irretrievably destroyed. Facing an 8.00 am meeting at the office about new strategies for monitoring paper clip allotments, who wouldn't hold some hope, however small, that zombies might actually be around the next corner of the expressway, waiting as an immovable object to put our social subjectivity into a perspective both drastic and delirious?

Notes

1 The definitive psychoanalytic account of the slasher genre remains Carol Clover, *Men, Women, and Chainsaws: Gender in the Modern Horror Film* (Princeton, NJ: Princeton University Press, 1993).
2 Sigmund Freud, *The Uncanny* (London: The Hogarth Press, 1957 (1919)), pp. 219–56.
3 Richard Davenport-Hines, *Gothic: Four Hundred Years of Excess, Horror, Evil, and Ruin* (New York: Northpoint Press, 2000).
4 Gilles Deleuze and Felix Guattari, *The Anti-Oedipus* (Minneapolis: University of Minnesota Press, 1983), p. 335.
5 Sarah Juliet Lauro and Karen Embry, 'A Zombie Manifesto: The Nonhuman Condition in the Era of Advanced Capitalism', *boundary 2: An International Journal of Literature and Culture* 35:1 (Spring 2008): 85–108.
6 Slavoj Zizek, *Organs without Bodies: Deleuze and Consequences* (New York: Routledge, 2003), pp. 135–36.
7 In his study of the 'fantastic' in literature, Tzvetan Todorov famously argues that the essence of the genre consists of placing competing systems of explanation in dialogue with one another, maintaining uncertainty ('hesitation') in the reader for as long as possible. See Tzvetan Todorov, *The Fantastic: A Structural Approach to a Literary Genre* (Ithaca, NY: Cornell University Press, 1977).
8 Romero's *Night of the Living Dead* remains the most direct translation of Hitchcock's structure of domestic besiegement, installing it as a central feature of the genre from the very beginning.
9 Jean Baudrillard, *Fatal Strategies* (New York: Semiotext(e), 1990), p. 219.
10 Daniel Paul Schreber, *Memoirs of My Nervous Illness* (New York: New York Review of Books, 2000), p. 119 (originally published in 1903).
11 Jean Baudrillard, *In the Shadow of the Silent Majorities* (New York: Semiotext(e), 1983), p. 36.
12 Sigmund Freud, *Beyond the Pleasure Principle* (London: The Hogarth Press, 1957 (1920)), pp. 1–64.
13 Jane Austen and Seth Grahame-Smith, *Pride and Prejudice and Zombies* (Philadelphia: Quirk Productions, 2009), p. 7.
14 http://runforyourlives.com/ (accessed 1 April 2011).
15 Jean Baudrillard, *America* (New York: Verso, 1998).

6

NIGHTMARE CITIES

Italian Zombie Cinema and Environmental Discourses

Russ Hunter

Recent debates over GM crops, animal and human cloning, the future status of nuclear energy and the potential for toxic spillage in the aftermath of the 2011 earthquake in Japan, have all pointed to the ways in which the alliance of scientific and technological developments have been increasingly scrutinised. Such interventions have sparked intense discussion over the extent to which the unpredictability of scientific creation means that caution is required in knowing exactly what the long-term implications of any experiment, creation or action might be on nature and man's relationship to it. Cinema has consistently engaged with environmental concerns, often expressing an ambivalent relationship to technology and science as a site of progress. Whilst films as diverse as *Frankenstein* (1931), *Dawn of the Dead* (1978) and *Fern Gully: The Last Rainforest* (1992) have displayed concerns over the scientific and technological impact of man on his environment, little academic attention has been paid to a cycle of films originating mainly in Italy in the late 1970s that linked the undead to fears of environmental catastrophe. Often dismissed as examples of pure exploitation cinema, little thought has been given to the ways in which several films of this cycle actively engaged in entering environmental debates (however crass or ineffective these interventions may have been). Although more recent examples of popular horror films and their sequels, such as *28 Days Later* (2002), *Resident Evil* (2002) and the remake of *The Hills Have Eyes* (2006), contain narratives that emphasise man's complicity in the disasters they portray, they form part of a much longer tradition of the horror film as a conduit for exploring the environmental impact of human beings.

Recent work by Austin Fisher on the Italian western has stressed the ways in which various cycles of popular Italian cinema are open to more dynamic textual readings, rejecting the conventional perception of 'a politically-engaged native cinema set against an anodyne, imitative genre cinema'.[1] In contrast to a wider film studies tradition that has generally seen socio-political metaphors as being unable to emanate from Italian horror cinema, this chapter argues that in fact such cinema can, and often does, have a very real message and one that their dismissal as examples of ephemeral trash has often ignored. Crucial here is a stress that, despite often low budgets and poor production values, 'exploitation' (or trash) movies, as exemplified by the Italian zombie cycle of the late 1970s and early 1980s, *can* engage very specifically with broader social concerns. That is to say, they *did* partake in contributing to a form of national discourse that was current in Italy with regards to environmentalism in the late 1970s. The subtlety or profoundness of precisely *what* was being said is less important than the fact that the films were entering the debates at all, contrary to both what might be expected from exploitation/genre cinema and the way in which their dynamics have previously been explored.

Jeffrey's Sconce's seminal article on paracinema cinema explored the often celebratory way in which fans engage with certain kinds of cinema and was an important step in a recognition of the cultural uses and exchanges that 'trash cinema' can often have.[2] However, whilst this rightly salvaged many films from being utterly dismissed in that it showed that they were taken up and explored in a variety of previously unconsidered ways, this has also tended to ghettoise conceptions of genre cinema in ways that can negate more mainstream textual readings. Steve Chibnall has offered a word of caution in this regard, noting that 'we should be wary of dismissing cheap genre productions as "paracinema", dumb sensationalism which can only be camply appreciated as "bad film"'.[3] Central to the kind of genre cinema that has often been associated with such paracinematic readings, low-budget Italian horror films of both the 1970s and 1980s have been dismissed as examples of, at best, derivative recycling or at worst have even been linked to deeper moral concerns about the impact of excessive onscreen violence and viscera.

This chapter examines two specific examples of Italian 'undead' films (featuring a variety of zombies and 'the infected') that seem to approach environmental concerns from a different angle, offering a less metaphoric and more literal ecological position. Both *Nightmare City* (Umberto Lenzi, 1980) and *The Living Dead at Manchester Morgue* (Jorge Grau, 1974) were products of a cycle of 1970s and 1980s Italian exploitation cinema that was – in a British context at least – most notably caught up in moral panics (most notably the 'video nasties' in the UK) and debates around trash cinema.[4] Yet despite their position within a critically lambasted cycle of Italian horror, these films, released between 1974 and 1980, put ecology at the heart of their narrative development and in ways that suggest an extended engagement with some of the concerns of the deeper ecological movement that began to gain momentum in the latter half of the 1970s. As Donato Totaro has noted, subsequent to both *The Living Dead at the Manchester Morgue* and *Zombie Flesh Eaters* (Lucio Fulci, 1979), Italian zombie films tended to offer one of two explanations for the cause of any outbreak of the living dead. The existence of zombies was thus either explained as some sort of supra-natural phenomenon or, importantly for my argument here, as being the fault of 'science' as evidenced by its role in creating or provoking biological, chemical and geological disasters.[5] In itself this was not a new explanation for zombie outbreaks in horror cinema, given that in the *Night of the Living Dead* (1968) George Romero tentatively suggested via the conceit of an 'emergency broadcast' that the dead had arisen as (possibly) the result of radioactive contamination from an exploded space probe. Undoubtedly, *The Living Dead at the Manchester Morgue* draws a great deal of influence from Romero's work. But in line with both Romero's film and later Italian horror films (as well as Romero's own later work), it places the blame for the existence of zombies on the scientific-technological developments of mankind.

Central to the ways in which these films frame the root causes of 'the zombie', and science's role in creating the circumstances for their existence, is an adherence to what environmental thinkers term the 'precautionary principle'. The nihilistic tone of the films explored here is tempered to some extent by their evocation of this precautionary principle and stand against what has been identified more broadly by Green theorist Andrew Dobson as 'drawing board' environmentalism.[6] The precautionary principle has been central to the logic of deeper forms of ecological thought whereby:

> Risk-aversion [is] the path of prudence. When new technologies, or new social practices, have consequences that are large and unpredictable. Especially when they are unquantifiable but potentially catastrophic risks associated with intervention.[7]

Italian zombie cinema of this period tended to stress the ways in which failing to adhere to an environmental 'precautionary principle' was (and is) likely to have unpredictable and dire environmental consequences.

The inherent cautionary-green politics of these films place them firmly against drawing-board design environmentalism, suggesting an underlying suspicion of unguarded scientific development and environmental interventionism. The reason for this difference lies in the films' unwillingness to engage in progressive possibilities for the relationship between scientific/technological development and ecological concerns, which I argue is derived from the impact of several environmental disasters in Italy in the period under consideration (most notably Seveso in 1976) and the reinvigoration of environmental discourses that followed these events in the country. As such, whilst they most certainly are examples of low-budget, exploitation films, they also offer the possibility of accessing other forms of filmic engagement with environmental concerns.

It is important to briefly consider the context within which the films under discussion here were conceived and produced. The 1970s was a turbulent and significant decade in the development of environmental thought. The era was important for broad debates about man's impact upon the environment and popular debates and action around what broadly began to be termed 'green' thought. Importantly, this move towards more radical ways of thinking about man's relationship with his natural environment was inspired by several important events that would later play out in direct and indirect ways in a number of the era's horror films. A string of ecological disasters (or near disasters), such as those at Seveso and Three Mile Island, combined with a growing awareness of the potential limits to economic growth based upon unlimited usage of the earth's natural resources, meant that environmental concerns began to spill over into popular consciousness. The 1973 oil crisis, in particular, demonstrated the potential dangers of an economic model that relied upon the continued exploitation of non-renewable natural resources. In fact, the crisis itself, characterised as it was by fuel shortages, price rises and panics, was instrumental in leading to a popular understanding that there might be limits to natural resources such as gas and oil. Environmental campaigners in particular were keen to point out that domestic and commercial consumption of fossil fuels would need to be either curbed or regulated if they were not to be exhausted completely. The most notable consequence of a growing understanding of such considerations was the result of the Club of Rome's[8] report into the possible limits on the earth's natural resources and how this might impact upon the ways in which man should relate to his environment. Called 'The Limits to Growth thesis', the report is the cornerstone of much radical (and deep) ecological thought. In stressing that there were very real limits on the earth's natural resources and that they could one day run out, it argued that rates of economic growth in industrial societies are often exponential, meaning that there is a danger that there could be sudden and unconsidered issues arising.

Andrew Dobson has argued that 'Greens' 'have all along been confronted with rebuffs to their belief in limits to growth' and broadly speaking the more radical movement has concretised around three main principles. As he notes:

> They are, first, that technological solutions (broadly understood; i.e. solutions formulated substantially within the bounds of present economic, social and political practices) will not bring about a sustainable society; second, that the rapid rates of growth aimed for (and often achieved by) industrialized and industrializing societies have an exponential character, which means that dangers stored up over a relatively long period of time can very suddenly have a catastrophic effect; and third, that the issues associated with the interaction of problems caused by growth – i.e. solving one problem does not solve the rest, and may even exacerbate them.[9]

The defining events for Italian debates around environmentalism in this respect were triggered by the Seveso chemical plant explosion of 1976.[10] The plant in question was located in Seveso (a town close to the northern Italian city of Milan and in the heartland of the country's industrial north) and specialised in manufacturing herbicides and pesticides. Due to a problem with the site's reactor, which produced the chemical trichlorofenol (more commonly known as dioxin), a thick cloud of the poisonous and carcinogenic tetrachlorodibenzoparadioxin (TCDD) was released into the atmosphere. The significance of this event cannot be underestimated as although fatalities were not reported immediately, 'kilogramme quantities of the substance lethal to man even in microgramme doses were widely dispersed which resulted in an immediate contamination of some ten square miles of land and vegetation'.[11] In fact, ultimately in excess of 600 people were evacuated from their homes and over 2,000 suffered the effects of dioxin poisoning and required medical attention.[12] More importantly still, the long-term effects of the spill meant that the dire health effects and environmental impact of the incident were unpredictable and long lasting. The incident was major news in Italy and at a Europe-wide level and resulted in 1982 in legislation aimed at preventing such serious industrial chemical leaks and ensuing environmental disaster, the 'Seveso Directive' (and its later replacement the 'Seveso II Directive'). But whilst Seveso and its lingering aftermath were important legislatively, they also had an important cultural impact, raising issues of environmental concern that were expressed in a number of ways. So, whilst newspapers of the time debated the details of the event, popular Italian film also engaged with the event.

Italian zombie films seem, at first glance, an unlikely repository for engagement with such a serious national issue. Typified, or perhaps made risible, by scenes such as those in *Zombie Flesh Eaters* in which a water-based zombie wrestles with a shark, it is easy to view them in light of their excess and visceral extremes. Their status as exploitation films and as part of generic cycles would naturally seem to suggest a form of repetition that was not conducive to references to issues of social, environmental and political concern. Yet, the films under discussion here evinced a clear concern for and with environmental issues in a way that reflected the importance of Seveso within the national consciousness. In fact, it is precisely their excessive, over-wrought style that allows for a very direct form of address in relation to environmental issues that, whilst not subtle, is at least clear.

If it is possible to identify a 'typical' Italian horror film that was part of the exploitation cycle of zombie movies that developed in the wake of the domestic Italian success of George Romero's *Dawn of the Dead* (1978) and the subsequent bankability of Lucio Fulci's *Zombie*

Flesh Eaters, then *Nightmare City* comes close. Filmed on location in Madrid and – along with numerous examples of Italian genre cinema in the 1970s and 1980s – in Rome's famous De Paolis studios, its multinational cast meant that it was produced in dubbed version in all markets. An Italian–Mexican–Spanish co-production released with a variety of names in different territories, it featured a largely Italian crew, a leading man from Mexico (Hugo Stiglitz, chosen as he was seen to have box-office cache of sorts in his native Mexico), an American 'star' whose film career had long passed its peak (Mel Ferrer) and a series of Italian and Spanish leading cast members (including former Luis Buñuel favourite Francisco Rabal). Its director, Umberto Lenzi, had up until that point variously directed spy thrillers, *gialli*, soft-core erotica, *polizieschi* and laid claim to directing the prototypical cannibal film, *Deep River Savages* (1972).

Yet the film, like several others of those under discussion here, also fails to conform to dominant expectations of Italian genre cinema. Its apartness lies in two key factors. First, its antagonists are not technically speaking zombies (or even undead) but rather are 'the infected', humans that have been turned into bloodthirsty savages due to a radioactive spill at the state nuclear power plant (run by scientist Dr Otto Haggenbach). Second – and somewhat innovatively at the time – the infected run and chase their victims rather than shambolically stumble towards their prey in typical zombie style. Such considerations demonstrate the ways in which the film both conformed to the typical conventions – so far as they existed – of Italian genre cinema at the time and stood slightly apart from it. In fact, although the nature of *Nightmare City* as a product of what we might broadly term the 'zombie cycle' of Italian genre cinema of the period meant that it was inherently exploitative in borrowing and copying from what had gone before, it also contains allusions to specific and significant aspects of Italian socio-environmental history.

Arguably, the film is the most obvious example in Italian cinema *as a whole* that is most intimately linked to the Seveso disaster, a local event whose impact was such that it is not an exaggeration to say that it became – and represents – a national trauma. Not only has director Lenzi gone on record as saying that the magnitude of the situation and its consequences inspired *Nightmare City*, but the film itself focuses upon the after effects of a spill at the local state-run power plant and its underlying narrative-drive is one that explores the potential (albeit extreme) consequences of such a disaster. Central to Lenzi's film is a stress upon the ways in which human attempts to defeat potential fossil fuel shortages by using scientifically engineered alternatives are unpredictable and therefore potentially catastrophic.

The film follows television news reporter Dean Miller (Hugo Stiglitz) after he is assigned to meet the scientist in charge of the state power plant, Professor Hagenbach, at the airport and quiz him about the precise nature of the spill. However, the Hercules military transport that is bringing him arrives off course and Miller begins to sense that something is very wrong (unpredictability is thus enshrined into the narrative from the very beginning of the film). When it lands, the professor leaves the plane but it is immediately clear that all is not well. Hagenbach has been infected and altered by the effects of the disaster and he is quickly joined by a horde of infected power plant workers who rapidly move to attack anyone in sight. What follows is carnage as the infected invade the city and begin infecting the local population, whilst the military headed by General Murcheson (Mel Ferrer) procrastinate over how to deal with the catastrophe. Miller's attempts to warn the population of the unfolding disaster are stymied by his editor, who after receiving a call from General Murcheson refuses to let him broadcast news of the event. Several plans are incompetently put into practice by the military, all of which are shown to come just 'too late', and the infected eventually completely overrun the city. Miller takes off to the countryside with his wife Anna (Laura Trotter), a doctor at the recently overrun local hospital, in order to escape the rapidly growing contagion. However, it offers only brief respite from the terror that has engulfed the city, as the previously serene country is rapidly overtaken by the infected. Eventually it seems that both Miller and Anna are doomed as, cornered in a fairground, the infected close in. A rogue military commander, Major Warren Holmes (Francisco Rabal), who has been sceptical about the military's response from the very beginning, attempts to rescue them both but Anna is killed in the process. Before Miller himself can be killed he wakes up with a start, realising that the whole episode has just been a nightmare. But as his day quickly begins to play-out in exactly the same way as his dream and we again return to Professor Hagenbach disembarking from his Hercules transport, we freeze-frame on Miller's face as a caption reading 'The Nightmare Becomes Reality ...' is emblazoned across the screen.

What the film does is tie a specific environmental disaster into a narrative that constantly stresses the broader and deeper ecological implications of what is presented as man's exploitative relationship with nature. The film's Italian title, *Incubo sulla città contaminata*, is significant in understanding the way in which it seeks to position itself environmentally. Translating into English more or less directly as 'Nightmare of the Contaminated City', it alludes much more directly to the environmental concerns at the heart of its narrative structure. Opening with an establishing shot of a grey industrial unit spewing out smoke that we later understand to be the state power plant run by Hagenbach, from the outset the film stresses the 'unnaturalness' of the facility in its natural surroundings, a device that is used at the start of *The Living Dead at the Manchester Morgue* and a number of other Italian zombie films of the period.

Crucially, it offers a note of caution in ignoring warnings of impending disaster. Several characters have visions and forewarnings that something is wrong but they are ignored, their concerns seen as frivolous products of overactive imaginations. Prior to the disaster fully unfolding, Major Holmes's wife creates a horribly disfigured sculpture of a humanoid face that mirrors the look we later associate with the infected, and at the hospital where Anna works, an injured boy dreams of his own limbs being severed (he is chastised and told that it is just a product of his imagination). Importantly, when Miller attempt to engage his boss at the start of his assignment in a discussion of the rights and wrongs of the work going on at the state power plant, he is dismissively told to 'forget the philosophy, just do what you're told'.

The dream sequence that ends the film stresses that the events of the preceding narrative are not only possible but appear to urge the breaking of a cycle, projecting what might happen and suggesting that it is all *really* happening and will do so endlessly in a loop. As Totaro has noted, the freeze-frame was 'a common formal method for ending the Italian zombie film, which helps to underscore the often ambiguous or open-ended conclusion'.[13] *Nightmare City*, however, uses the dual device of using the freeze-frame in combination with a dream sequence in order to lay stress upon the *possibility* of ecological catastrophe if humankind continues along the path the film presents it as being on. Miller's character therefore seems to be a cipher for the ways in which questioning the assumptions about man's exploitative relationship with nature are seen to be both necessary and potentially likely to be met with resistance.

Representatives of the state are largely absent from the film, being present only in so far as the army attempt to stop the encroaching infected. Yet all their attempts to do so fail and they seem just as concerned with suppressing the truth of what is occurring as resolving the ensuing crisis. Ultimately when General Murcheson tries to formulate one last attempt at defeating the contagion, he is told by his scientific officer that 'every treatment known to science' has been tried but that there is no solution. The film's tinge of despair and nihilism is enshrined in Murcheson's final upward call of 'God help us all!' As culpable as government and 'science' are in environmental terms, the apathy and complacency of society as a whole is just as significant in creating the conditions that allow them to develop. In particular, the young, whom it suggests are more interested in leisure pursuits than listening to ecological warnings, are positioned as lacking the appropriate interest in their natural environment and surroundings that would allow for a rigorous interrogation of scientific and technological developments. This indifference is represented by General Murcheson's daughter as she fails on several occasions to heed warnings about the outbreak of the infected on her radio, seemingly more interested in either sunbathing or taking a trip to the country with her boyfriend. This merely reflects a broader focus upon the way in which human nature is constructed as being the ultimate problem in preventing environmental disasters and is addressed by Miller as he wearily notes that, 'It's not the fault of science and technology, but man.' In fact, when Dean sadly observes to Anna that 'all this had to happen to realise the truth', the film reveals the double-bind central to many green narratives: whilst the catastrophe is seen as necessary to make humanity realise the dangers of its approach to nature, it also means that humanity will end.

The precise blame for the outbreak is situated in two particular places. One is very specifically the avaricious representation of those working in science (as a general entity) and more broadly as a pessimistic comment on the nature of humanity and its capacity to anticipate and learn from its own mistakes. The military are seen as inept in their response to the crisis, merely serving to deny that any problem exists that cannot be dealt with by pure military force. And, whilst the general populace are shown to be helpless to do anything that would stop the contagion once it has spread, they are also shown to be indifferent to its root causes.

Very few of the infected are killed, and those who are not infected merely run around in blind panic. So, whilst the individual is presented as being powerless post facto to stop what has been started, they are also shown to be complacent in the faith they place in government in relation to managing their natural environment. In fact, this is a narrative tendency that is reflected in several of the Italian zombie films of the late 1970s and early 1980s.[14]

Ultimately, *Nightmare City* suggests that human nature is to blame for both the existence of and failure to deal with the results of the contagion. Thus not only are the young and those in potential positions of power to stop or contain the spread of the contagion seen as complacently ignoring warning signs of impending environmental catastrophe, but mankind also (and by direct implication, science) is to blame. The slightly nihilistic tone of the film is borne out by Anna who mournfully intones that the whole disaster is 'part of the vital cycle of the human race – create and obliterate until we destroy ourselves' and that the infected are nothing more than 'monsters created by other monsters who have only one thing on their mind, the discovery of greater power'. Besides, in addition to strong textual allusions to Seveso in suggesting the damaging impact of industrial accidents involving man-made chemical compounds, the make-up effects are crucial in drawing a link between the film and the disaster. In fact, a widely circulated photo of four-year-old Stefania Senno, taken by noted photo journalist Mauro Galligani shortly after the chemical explosion at Seveso in the village of Meda, is illustrative of this link. Franco di Girolamo and Giuseppe Ferranti's make-up design gives the 'infected' deeply ridged, uneven and burned looking faces that ape the effects of chloracne poisoning suffered by the victims of Seveso and almost perfectly mirrors the way in which it affected Senno's face (and several thousand like her). This is perhaps the most explicit allusion to Seveso within the film and points to the ways in which it engages with the specificities of the disaster as well as acting as a more general allegorical tale on the dangers of experimenting with nature.

Whilst in *Nightmare City* the government and the military are seen as being slow to react and to grasp the scale of the problem that quickly unfolds, in Jorge Grau's earlier *The Living Dead at the Manchester Morgue* this relationship was taken one step further. Although the military are absent from the film – replaced instead by a cynical and

19. Make-up designs in *Nightmare City* – reminiscent of victims in the Seveso disaster.

incredulous local police force run by a character known simply as The Inspector (Ray Kennedy) – the government is seen as being more actively complicit in the disaster that befalls the countryside. The film follows antique shop owner George (Ray Lovelock) as he leaves a smog-filled inner city and heads to what he hopes will be an idyllic weekend away in the countryside. After he encounters Edna (Cristina Galbó), a city-dweller off to visit her recovering drug-addict sister on the farm she shares with her husband, the pair get lost and seek directions from a local farmer who has just installed a new machine on his land that is part of a government sponsored initiative to improve agricultural productivity. Use of the machine, however, has unexpected consequences and the vibrations it emits cause the dead to come back to life. After reports from the local hospital of babies being born with 'aggressive' and 'homicidal' tendencies, events quickly take a turn for the worse. The ensuing zombie outbreak slowly engulfs the countryside and George and Edna attempt to persuade the local sceptical and belligerent police force chief to take action. In the end, George is mistaken for a zombie and shot dead as he attempts to rescue Edna. In a final ironic twist, he later returns as a zombie and kills the previously sceptical inspector. The film ends with a lingering and ominous close-up of the machine.

The spread of the contagion is presented in a very different way to *Nightmare City*. Here the infection *originates* in the countryside but the city is presented from the beginning of the film as a place to escape from for very different reasons. Like Lenzi's film, it stresses the distancing and depressing nature of the industrial landscape of 'the city' from the off. Opening on a grey traffic-clogged cityscape, where people are so preoccupied with their daily routine that they fail to notice a nude woman cavorting through the streets, the sequence is accompanied by the kind of low-intensity sounds that act as pre-echoes of the sounds we will later hear of the agricultural machine. The grimly industrial nature of the city is stressed as we see a montage of buses, steam, dirt, people wearing 'anti-smog masks', smoke rising, litter on the streets, dead birds, and blank-faced people at a bus stop. All of which is intercut with flashes of verdant and still countryside, foreshadowing the way in which the problems of the city will later infect the countryside.

Both films present the countryside as ultimately being no safer than the city – it is not presented as a simple idyll to escape to – but rather the *effects* of indifference, governmental short-cuts and an ambivalence to the activities of science, means that it too becomes a place of danger, inverting the image of what Norman in *A River Runs Through it* (1992) termed 'the world with dew still on it'. Tellingly, in *The Living Dead at the Manchester Morgue*, George removes the scarf that has been protecting his face from the pollution of the city as soon as he enters the countryside. The hoped-for contrast between city and countryside is summed up by him after his bike breaks down and he hitches a ride with Edna, to whom he explains why he so desperately wants to get out of the city and to Lake Windermere: 'Beautiful countryside, low-industry and a nice little house that is all mine. Where from Saturday to Sunday I listen to grass grow – very restful.'

There is a further and important inversion of the usual cinematic and popular convention of the countryside as being a place to escape to. Although George cannot wait to escape the smog of the city, he cannot escape the impact of his fellow man on the peace and quiet of the countryside he so craves. Indeed, it is as soon as he makes contact with other men that he encounters problems and has to face the consequences of man's active intervention in the countryside – it is simply impossible for him to find a 'restful' place that has not been influenced by the activities of humankind. The impact of the Ministry of Agriculture's new machine on the countryside ensures that this is impossible. Turning on the radio in Edna's car, he catches the tail-end of a news broadcast and hears the announcer refer to 'so-called ecological problems, many of which have been exaggerated'. Half-jokingly he sardonically says to Edna, 'Of course ... when we all die, only the scientists will survive.'

The main obstacle in the way of addressing the zombie outbreak is seen to be a combination of the local populace's blind faith in the government science project that has put the machine in their vicinity and the way that those who speak out are seen as unreasonable, crazed or merely no-good 'hippies'. *The Living Dead at the Manchester Morgue* almost perfectly exemplifies the precepts of the precautionary principle approach to environmental debates in showing how the effects of 'the machine' – despite laboratory testing – cannot be anticipated once it comes into contact with the natural earth. Throughout the film, George, who is dismissed as a 'hippy' by the inspector and treated with disdain by the government scientist in charge of the agricultural project, is sceptical of the potential for harm of testing the machine in the countryside, unsure of its possible impact. Tellingly, when one of the Ministry of Agriculture men in the field, proudly demonstrating his equipment to George and a local doctor, cheerfully notes that 'not even DDT was this effective when it first came out', George replies snappily that 'DDT causes cancer.' In response to this, the government scientist asks George why he doesn't just go and find himself 'a nice Pacific atoll somewhere', to which he responds, 'Sure, all I'd have to worry about then would be atomic fallout.' In making reference to previous examples – both specific and general – of scientific interventions in the countryside that had disastrous and unanticipated side-effects, *The Living Dead at the Manchester Morgue* stresses the need to take a precautionary, conservative approach to man's relationship with the natural world. Notably, any urge towards caution is, however, met with a consistent rebuff. The Ministry of Agriculture workers insist that the machine has undergone rigorous testing and that they are confident that it will only harm insects and microbes. Yet, in line with precautionary environmental thinking, George is incredulous, insisting that the scientist in charge of the project 'do more tests'.

In fact, George's doubts and urge for caution are dismissed by the scientist who is apparently responsible for the machine, who tells him, 'It's never wise to exaggerate ... We can't get the government to act on more serious and concrete facts these days. Imagine what success we'd get to do anything on a mere hypothesis?' The government scientists working on the machine refuse to accept George's dire warnings of the impact of their work when he confronts them with what he has seen and as such he resolves to destroy their machinery (*à la* Edward Abbey's

20. Environmental undead: the resurrected tramp Guthrie in *The Living Dead at the Manchester Morgue*.

The Monkey Wrench Gang), direct and destructive action being seen as the only way to stop the potential for further harm to the ecosystem. A very direct connection is made between the work of the machine and the problems that have been afflicting the 'Manchester' countryside. Not only is the death and subsequent 'resurrection' of local tramp Guthrie seen to coincide with the installation of the Ministry of Agriculture machine, but in quick succession we are shown the machine being fixed after George's attack on it, then a dead man being taken to the mortuary, who then returns to life. All of which is underscored by the droning sound of the machine whirring away.

The film, then, very explicitly addresses the dangers of failing to be cautious in relation to environmental intervention. From the start, George is cynical about the need for scientific intervention in relation to the countryside, forcefully stating that he'd 'send it straight back – keep the insects and the parasites nature's given you' and that the machine is 'just another machine to pollute the earth'. Although the film does not suggest that there is a governmental–scientific conspiracy in order to introduce the machine at all costs, it does show the ways that both act in accord but ultimately in ignorance of the final outcome of their faith in their new machine. In fact, stress is laid upon the fact that the Ministry of Agriculture are there to help farmers and that their new machine works by ultra-scan radiation with 'not a chemical in sight'. Ultimately, *The Living Dead at the Manchester Morgue* is as pessimistic

21. Environmental horror: George attacks the agricultural machine in *The Living Dead at the Manchester Morgue.*

as *Nightmare City* in its presentation of the possibilities for change. At the end of the film, a policeman, on passing the machine in a field, admiringly says 'They say that machine's performing miracles – we'll have a marvellous crop this year. I'm mad about apples,' his flippancy and complacency in the face of what has happened perfectly reflecting the grim message the film purveys.

Several other Italian zombie films of this period also explore the potential dangers of man attempting to deal with the problems of diminishing natural resources through unguarded scientific solutions. They, too, present an image of human scientific intervention in nature that suggests a position in line with the precautionary principle of green thought. In Bruno Mattei's *Zombie Creeping Flesh* (1980) – a film that also opens with a montage sequence of a concrete-grey industrial complex – a leak at a chemical research centre leads to an outbreak of the undead. In a similar vein to *The Living Dead at the Manchester Morgue*, it is the unintended (and unpredictable) consequence of a well-intentioned scientific project aimed at improving food production (in this case for the 'Third World') that initiates the disaster that follows.[15]

Both of the films that have been under consideration here are, in many ways, archetypical 'trash' films: a combination of low budgets, variable production values – an arm is chopped off at one point in *Nightmare City* but it is evident that it's a man with an arm inside his jacket – poor dubbing, incoherent plotting and flat, lifeless performances by some of those involved. Yet whilst it is tempting to therefore either dismiss them entirely as pieces of exploitation ephemera or to embrace them paracinematically, either approach would ignore other aspects of these films. In particular, it would detract from the ways in which they attempt to contribute to public debates over the nature of humanity's relationship with nature, impelled in part by the socio-historical context of their production. *Nightmare City* and *The Living Dead at the Manchester Morgue* are an agglomeration of ecological standpoints and neither is entirely consistent in their standpoints. The dominant strand of ecologism is that of a shallow ecology, where the concern is for man's well-being rather than any systemic concern for non-human nature. Although both evince strands of social ecology, where man's relations with each other and capitalism is considered problematic, the real problem is seen to be the 'unknowable' nature of any of man's interventions with non-human nature. Thus science and its application to technology is not seen as troublesome in itself, but man's usage of them to underpin a capitalist system based on greed has made them instruments of his own destruction. The implication is that a fundamental value change is needed and this is what makes the films truly ecological.

This hostility to the unfettered reliance on scientific solutions to human problems is also evident in a number of other popular Italian films of the period, most notably *Zombie Creeping Flesh*, *Zombie Flesh Eaters* and *Zombie Holocaust*. Here, too, scientists are seen as dangerous when unchecked (showing the effects of a kind of 'feral' scientist) and also – importantly – even when supposedly constrained by their involvement with the state. The latter is particularly notable in the unquestioning faith placed in them by the national government in both *Living Dead at the Manchester Morgue* and *Nightmare City*.

Italian zombie films therefore do not offer the 'secure' form of horror that Andrew Tudor speaks of, where disorder is always defeated and there is a return of sorts to an equilibrium of peace, order and tranquillity.[16] Instead, the emphasis is on a far more nihilistic vision, a cautionary representation of the power of man to change and (mis)manage the ecosystem. There are echoes here of the underlying assumption of the precautionary principle that you can do, but you cannot undo. The films therefore invite us to reconsider the dangers of state-sanctioned environmental 'experimentation' and suggest that the consequences of any such act are entirely unpredictable.

In this sense, the films align with Andrew Tudor's conception of what he terms 'paranoid horror', whereby 'human activities are routinely unsuccessful, order far more precarious and boundaries between known and unknown rarely as clear as they first might seem'.[17] The feeling of collective disorder that is evoked in these films therefore runs in parallel with the ways in which the precautionary principle of environmentalism suggests the natural environment might react if treated in the wrong way. Here, expertise – and specifically scientific expertise – is seen as less effective in both the short and long term as practical, common sense. Indeed, scientific and technological expertise are often presented as the *least* effective of all and are often portrayed as being responsible for the events that occur in each film. In contrast to this, workaday reporters like Dean Miller and antique shop owners George – the common man with an enquiring mind and a suspicion of authority and 'expertise' – are seen to be the most valuable members of society from an ecological standpoint.

The sense of nihilism that runs through both films can be viewed in light of Italy having seen a major environmental disaster at Seveso, as well as the broader impact of the oil crises of the 1970s and the growing concern over the limits to growth, nuclear winters and toxic waste. Given their prominence in debates around the growing environment in the 1970s, it is easy to see why filmmakers – even those operating in the low-budget end of a particularly low-rent end of Italian horror cinema – thought that the nightmare might indeed become reality.

Notes

1 Austin Fisher, *Radical Frontiers in the Spaghetti Western: Politics, Violence and Popular Italian Cinema* (London: I.B.Tauris, 2011), p. 3.

2 Jeffrey Sconce, '"Trashing" the Academy: Taste, Excess, and an Emerging Politics of Cinematic Style', *Screen* 36:4 (Winter 1995): 371–93.

3 Steve Chibnall, 'Double exposures: Observations on the Flesh and blood show', in Deborah Cartmell, I. Q. Hunter, Heidi Kaye and Imelda Whelelan (eds), *Trash Cinema Aesthetics: Popular Culture and its Audience* (London: Pluto, 1997), p. 98.

4 *The Living Dead at the Manchester Morgue* is often seen as an example of 1970s Spanish horror cinema. However, there are good reasons for including it within the broad sweep of 1970s and 1980s Italian zombie cinema. While director Jorge Grau is

Spanish, the film's two credited writers, Sandro Continenza and Marcello Coscia, are both Italian. Similarly, the presence of co-producer Edmondo Amati, who produced *Lizard in a Woman's Skin* (Lucio Fulci, 1971), *The Crimes of the Black Cat* (Sergio Pastore, 1972), *Cannibal Apocalypse* (Antonio Margheriti, 1980) and a number of other Italian exploitation films of the period, as well as Carlo Leva, iconic Italian make-up artist Giannetto De Rossi and genre star Ray Lovelock suggest a film as Italian as it is Spanish. The co-production status of *The Living Dead at the Manchester Morgue*, made as it was by both the Spanish Star Films S.A. and Italian Flaminia Produzioni Cinematografiche, means that, in line with other Italian horror films of the time, it fits the prevailing production logic of 1970s exploitation cinema, which means that any assignation to either Spain or Italy is problematic.

5 Donato Totaro, 'The Italian zombie film: from derivation to reinvention', in Steven Schneider (ed.), *Fear Without Frontiers: Horror Cinema Across the Globe* (Godalming: FAB, 2003), p. 164.

6 Andrew Dobson, *Green Political Thought*, 2nd edn (London: Routledge, 1995), p. 78.

7 Dobson, *Green Political Thought*, p. 32.

8 The name applied to the mixture of scientists, researchers and environmentalists who had taken a serious interest in the impact man might have on his natural environment and the extent to which a consideration of the limits of the earth's natural resources needed to play into economic thinking and patterns of consumption.

9 Dobson, *Green Political Thought*, p. 73

10 The explosion has often been talked about in ways that compare its significance to Italy with that of both Bhopal and Chernobyl.

11 European Commission, Chemical Accidents (Seveso II) – Prevention, Preparedness and Response; http://ec.europa.eu/environment/seveso/index.htm (accessed 12 October 2011).

12 European Commission, Chemical Accidents (Seveso II); http://ec.europa.eu/environment/seveso/index.htm (accessed 12 October 2011).

13 Totaro, 'The Italian zombie film', p. 164.

14 There is an important distinction between it and other films of the cycle in that the infected do not kill for the sake of it, but seek human blood in a vain attempt to purify their own destroyed cells. Zombie- and infection-based horror narratives tend to stress the exponential way in which the contagion spreads, much in the same way that advocates of the precautionary principle identify the potentially exponential fallout of any environmental disaster.

15 Other films of the period, most notably *Zombie Holocaust* (Girolami, 1980) and *Zombie Flesh Eaters*, offer a slightly different position, whereby the remote and hidden-from-view nature of the scientists' work allows them to develop their ideas unchecked and keeps their growing megalomania dangerously hidden from public view.

16 Andrew Tudor, *Monsters and Mad Scientists: A Cultural History of the Horror Movie* (Oxford: Blackwell, 1989), p. 214.

17 Tudor, *Monsters and Mad Scientists*, p. 216.

7

DIARIES OF A PLAGUE YEAR

Perspectives of Destruction in Contemporary Zombie Film

Emma Dyson

'Our responsibility is finished.'
Camera Operator, *Dawn of the Dead* (Romero, 1978)

The past 20 years has seen a steady flow of productions of zombie film globally, in both 'independent' and studio-based productions of horror film. This infective genre spans different countries and concerns, notably at a time of rising global communication and subsequent shifts in global film markets. While economic imperatives may explain the rise of fan-created material, notably through the affordability of camcorder and now digital video equipment, it does not satisfactorily explain how the concept of global infections and the culpability of news media is such a strong thematic consideration of contemporary zombie film. The notion of fictional 'reportage' is not new to literature – notably in Daniel Defoe's *A Journal of the Plague Year* (1722) – but in zombie film it may well be a seminal shift in the social critique and reimagining of horror considered a hallmark of the diverse film texts that comprise zombie film.

As a genre predicated on establishing and destroying social spaces of freedom and containment, some contemporary zombie texts address concerns relating to the visual representations of protests, uprisings and disasters in news media reportage and the possibly conflicting viewpoints of 'official' news and those arising from first-person perspectives of events. In order to understand how the perspective of destruction changes in zombie films, we must discuss both the production factors that have resulted in the use of mediated perspectives to construct a narrative, and the impact this has had on the visual and thematic concerns of zombie film after the 1990s. As with most histories of zombie film, we can place George Romero as an influential figure in the utilisation of news media in zombie film. The survivors in *Night of the Living Dead* (1968) cluster round the radio and television for information, relying on a newsman and roving camera crews to fill in their own experience of the situation. This allowed Romero to indicate the scope of the disaster, while maintaining the claustrophobic setting of the isolated farmhouse. This was repeated in *Dawn of the Dead* (1978), where the frantic atmosphere of the television studio degenerates into the listless emergency news broadcasts that the appalled survivors watch in the mall. This use of media footage indicates the essential uselessness of media information in the crisis, and underlines that the careers of both Fran and Steven were as useless as many of the consumer goods they idly play with in the mall. The critical acclaim accorded to Romero within the zombie film genre does not need to be reiterated, but he has also had a much more lasting influence within the consolidation of the zombie film as a recognisable, popular and economically viable sub-genre within horror film.

Following the period in the late 1970s and early 1980s where the rising popularity of home video initially challenged then supported the exhibition of studio films, the introduction of accessible video technology led to an increase in independent and fan filmmakers' portrayals of the zombie during the late 1980s and early 1990s.[1] These representations were based on previous portrayals and narrative styles of the zombie sub-genre, with varying levels of commercial success; as Meghan Sutherland notes, the zombie genre's 'affiliation with a no-frills B-film production-style, and its record of solid returns in the Hollywood mainstream surely contribute to the high concentration of remakes'.[2] In the various reclamations of *Night of the Living Dead* as a seminal text during the early to mid-1990s, and the ongoing use of the zombie figure by 'established' horror directors, such as Brian Yuzna, John Carpenter and of course George Romero, we can confidently place the period from the mid-1980s onwards as marking a boom in the production of zombie film.

In the larger context of American horror films overall, the production of horror film arguably becomes less easily isolated as either independent or 'mainstream' during the 1990s onwards. This is linked directly to another shift in technological developments in two key areas: digital filmmaking and the rise of global communications, notably in the form of the internet. Rick Worland makes these connections between horror film production and film content in his chapter dealing with the American horror film post-1995. In particular, the success of *The Blair Witch Project* (Daniel Myrick, Eduardo Sánchez, 1999) acts as a key case study of the changed production and reception constructs of horror film at this point, as Worland argues:

> *Blair Witch* added an original notion of style to the genre – horror effects based on a technological and ontological appeal to truth and reality. The ready availability of consumer-grade video cameras in middle-class homes since the 1980s has greatly affected how a younger generation thinks about film and television. In addition ... the 1980s home-video revolution encouraged the theatrical and/or video release of the 'director's cut' or other 'special editions' of some movies.[3]

The marketing of the film – on the internet – created the illusion of the film as 'reality', a documentary film made by young people. That the film went on to return over $245 million indicates the strength of the stylistic approach to both marketing and filming that the creators engaged in. This innovation was set against the availability of film texts that the contemporary audience of teenagers would not have accessed on their initial release, alongside the introduction of Digital Video Discs (DVDs) in 1997 and the shift away from video cameras to digital cameras as an accessible filming technology in the mid-1990s. This introduction of new technology offered immediate economic benefits to the filmmaker. The cheapness of the recording format, and the computer packages to edit the recorded material offered, as video had, presented an approachable method of filmmaking outside of traditional production budgets and constraints. Unlike video, however, this format could be downloaded to the internet, edited to include more detailed special effects and, in the shape of DVDs, could hold much more information. The quick production methods offered by this technology mean that the fan production of zombie film has now shifted in terms of audience – the internet is now *the* key exhibition space for fan filmmakers. But the availability of zombie texts in terms of cinematic releases has not diminished as a result. Instead, the rise of global communications, and the need for Hollywood to maintain some form of market dominance, has led to a startling change in how the American zombie film responds to these global shifts, taking account of other national film productions and international co-productions between 2000 and 2008.

These cinematic texts both draw upon and extend previous thematic uses of the figure of the zombie. In particular, the strength of epidemic narratives continued, remaining as the primary narrative impetus for many zombie texts. This is partially due to the increase of zombie films released after the mid-1980s onwards that focused on replicating previous successful films, and also the visual references to what we might term the *spectacle of destruction*, a useful definition of the content of contemporary horror texts. The success of high-budget films such as *The Exorcist* (William Friedkin, 1973) and *Jaws* (Steven Spielberg, 1975) focused on special effects as a factor for maintaining audience interest, while other producers of films attempted to re-create elements of the blockbusters for smaller budgeted productions – hence the spate of monster films after *Jaws*.[4] The majority of smaller budgeted productions could not hope to replicate these expensive spectacles of destruction, so chose to focus on smaller, but still explicit, depictions of the individual body. In zombie films from 1976 onwards until the 1990s, the majority of portrayals and narrative uses of the zombie body reside within this overall concept of individual destruction. Rick Worland charts the parallel prominence of the contemporary splatter film's interest in 'its construction of detailed, often breathtaking gross effects of bodily destruction, decomposition or mutation',[5] claiming that the increase in popularity of these film texts indicates a return to the concepts of *grand guignol* and the 'cinema of attractions' in vivid spectacles. This visual use also coincided with what William Graebner describes as a cultural perspective on 'a disastrous era that defined life as survivorship',[6] expressed in American disaster films of the 1970s. The conclusion we can draw from this is that the personal impact of destruction became a key visual and thematic concern for zombie films specifically and horror texts generally.

As several commentators have noted, the growing fascination with 'body horror' during the 1970s and 1980s indicates a shift in audience tastes that recognised and expected to see the fragmentation of the social body as well as the personal one.[7] In particular, narratives surrounding disease became prominent, notably within the works of David

Cronenberg who positions his texts as part of the approach to horror that Romero had used in *Night of the Living Dead*: making his horrors contemporary and focused on the familial and social body.[8] As Jesse Stommel notes, for Cronenberg, the abject nature of the human body is a recurring theme, perhaps most clearly displayed in his first feature film *Shivers* (1975).[9] This physical focus on the body perfectly mirrors the concerns within zombie film following Romero's *Dawn of the Dead*, but also, chillingly, refracts mediated images and concerns of the time. We should take into account that in the 1980s reports of the supposedly 'homosexual' disease AIDS became prominent in mainstream media. The media reportage of the time, argues Harry M. Benshoff, indicates that the definitions and limits used by horror narratives to determine the monstrous were quickly reiterated in media discourses:

> Perhaps expectedly, an ideological approach to fictional monsters frequently bleeds into an accounting of real-life horrors such as AIDS: recent critical essays on the mass media have demonstrated how the representational codes and narrative tropes of the monster movie (plague, contagion, victimization, panic) have been grafted onto much television and newspaper coverage of AIDS.[10]

This use of recognisable fictional tropes within news reportage offers a potential explanation of recurring epidemic horror narratives during the 1980s and 1990s, as the scale of AIDS became understood. Both Rick Worland and David J. Skal tentatively argue that this may be understood as the impetus for the revival of vampire films in this period.[11] If this is a partial explanation of the surge in vampire films, it is advisable to extend this argument to the zombie film also, as post-*Dawn of the Dead* the infective zombie is the key thematic figure within zombie films. David J. Skal continues his discussion of how the AIDS 'viral epidemic' was refracted in film, by arguing that the twin spectres of AIDS and anorexia nervosa stand as key visual symbols of body trauma within horror film of the 1990s onwards.[12] This can be linked to representations of the diseased and failing human body that reached greater discussion in mainstream media during the late 1980s and throughout the 1990s. Roberta McGrath's comments on medical photography in the media indicate the impact of these dialogues:

> They impinge on and break the fragile base upon which our lives are built – the disavowal of mortality, of disfigurement; a breakdown of barriers between the internal/external. We are shown the body cut open, flesh minus skin.[13]

This description of factual documentations immediately brings to mind the portrayal of the body within zombie films of the period discussed in this chapter, where the diseased individual body should be feared, as a holder of the potential for transformation and degradation from external infections: themes that are a strong precursor to contemporary zombie films. The spectacle of destruction, rendered as realistically as possible through effects and digital photography, became a site of pleasure for the audiences in their suspension of disbelief and a contemporary *memento mori* of images easily accessed through global media, whether in fictional or factual popular culture. In these examples of the 1980s and 1990s, news media reportage echoed horror tropes in order to offer a recognisable discussion of the monstrous; however, later horror films reversed this trend to use global media as a thematic and visual threat within their fictional worlds. The fear of mediated epidemics arguably provided another vital narrative shift in the modern zombie film, beyond the distrust of the vacuous media portrayed in Romero's *Dead* films.

In particular, I would select certain texts from Britain as exemplifying an aesthetic shift when using the cheaper production equipment of digital video, in an age of global news media. The British zombie film remained a marginalised part of a decimated horror film industry. Andrew Parkinson's *I Zombie: A Chronicle of Pain* (1998) is arguably of import, as it focuses on the personal documentation of the physical and emotional degradation of a man infected by a zombie. The same discussion of isolation underpins his later *Dead Creatures* (2001), though, as Jonathan Rigby notes, both films' gore and low-budgeted philosophical narratives have ensured that they are subject to 'ghetto-isation' within film markets.[14] The same could be argued of Conor McMahon's *Dead Meat* (2004), a lively discussion of BSE or 'mad cow' disease that creates zombies in the Irish countryside. What is clear in these films is an adherence to national concerns.[15] Foremost amongst these 'Brit pics', as Rigby notes, is the output of Danny Boyle.[16] Boyle's *28 Days Later* (2002) is both innovative and derivative, in that its

22. Apocalyptic zombie narrative comes to London: *28 Days Later.*

visual style and use of the bleached, overexposed colours of digital camerawork separate it from previous British (and American) zombie film. The derivation comes from the narrative touches that link the film to others; while Boyle dismissed the assertion that this was a zombie film, the writer Alex Garland makes his links to previous zombie and apocalyptic narratives in the screenplay clear:

> Our male protagonist, waking up in hospital ... will be familiar to anyone who has read *Day of the Triffids*. The scene in which our heroes loot a supermarket ... the empty mall of *Dawn of the Dead*. Mailer, the chained 'infected', is in some ways a refugee from *Day of the Dead*. And Selena's race is a kind of reference to George Romero's Night-Dawn-Day trilogy, which was notable for the black leading characters. Other influences I should mention would certainly include David Cronenberg, Stephen King, Capcom's *Resident Evil* video game series.[17]

While the visual references are clear, what is of much more import in this text is the specifically national concerns that emerge from focusing on the devastation of London and the quarantine imposed upon the

British Isles. Given the relevance of the contemporaneous BSE crisis, with media images of pits of burning corpses, the concept of viral outbreaks in a national context, placed against global concerns, seems particularly relevant and is noted by several critics.[18] Within the film text itself, global news media are culpable in the actual devastation: the infection is rage, first glimpsed in the laboratory where the apes are infected through drugs and televisual violence – multi-screens in front of one experiment subject show a stream of fights, riots and burning, taken from news media. The global medium is the message here, and infection is a result.

The idea of media as an infective medium is not new to zombie films – we can cite the *Demons* films of Lamberto Bava, or *The Video Dead* (Robert Scott, 1987) as relevant examples. However, I would argue that *28 Days Later*, by its foregrounding of this concern as the centre of the virus, instigates a new direction in zombie film narratives. The zombie genre is completely self-referential by this stage in its history, cannibalising previous narratives and spreading these images through new texts, in different production contexts. As such, this *infective* genre spans different countries and concerns, notably at a time of rising global communication and subsequent shifts in global film markets. *28 Days Later* exemplifies this perfectly. Benjamin Svetkey notes that the opening weekend returns in America garnered $9.7 million from 1,260 cinemas, eventually returning $42 million.[19] As several articles in *Variety* noted, 'There's a growing belief in some quarters that hitching a ride on Hollywood's global superhighway offers the best hope for local filmmakers to escape their national ghettos.'[20]

This occurred at the same time as a general change in zombie narratives in larger budgeted productions. George Romero hinted at the global scale of devastation in *Day of the Dead* (1985), but succeeding films, limited by budgets, could not hope to envisage this. Instead, it is arguable that the American zombie film, pre-2004, is distinctly insular in its conception of a zombie apocalypse, preferring to envisage destruction within recognisable American cityscapes. This is not a criticism, as horror film from differing national cinema responds to differing economic, historical and social contexts. In the case of American zombie film of 2000 onwards, given the influence of foreign film texts (especially *28 Days Later*), it is notable that global concerns do start to emerge in zombie films distributed by major studios. The initial presentation of these ideas emerged in the first large budget remake of George Romero's *Dawn of the Dead* (Zack Snyder, 2004). Snyder's interpretation of Romero's premise avoids overt social criticism, relying on an action narrative that echoes the *Resident Evil* series.[21] Therefore we can place this film as a text that references Romero's work, and indeed Snyder's *Dawn* uses some of the undeveloped concerns of Romero's film to great effect – notably when indicating the global scale of the zombie epidemic and the impact of global media. After the opening sequences, which briefly use a distanced aerial perspective to track the devastation in one town, the credits are superimposed on a montage of news footage of riots and conflicts, taken from reported events. This is interspersed with fictional 'news' reports and images of multiplying viral cells, a sadly underdeveloped rhetoric of infectious images and narratives. The links to Romero's chaotic news station in *Dawn*, and Boyle's lab tapes are clear to see, alongside the use of fast moving, snarling zombies, another innovation of *28 Days Later*.

The distanced perspective of destruction, that Snyder makes such effective use of in Ana's flight, is one that Romero himself replicates in his later film *Land of the Dead* (2005). While concerned with larger social critiques as in his previous films, the final onslaught of the zombies against the tower block Fiddler's Green encapsulates Romero's criticisms, as the insular wealthy are trapped by their own lifestyles. The city becomes a death trap, vividly conveyed in Romero's use of aerial shots of the encroaching mass of zombies, a telling visual link to factual news reports filmed from helicopters of riots and street protests against globalisation, the twenty-first-century fear of loss of identity. The distanced camera perspectives used in zombie films of 2002 onwards display not only the advancement of digital effects to replicate 'reality', but an acknowledgment of the changing depictions of violence and resistance present in global media. The scale of devastation, these images imply, is larger than before. These apocalyptic texts indicate that for the American box office, the zombie was a viable source of narratives intended for a mainstream audience. That so many rely on images of fighting, global unrest and the destruction of buildings may also replicate the climate of uncertainty that America was feeling at the time, as Tom Shone argues in a 2005 article:

> In an article entitled Gory Gory Hallelujah, the New York Times relates the public's love of horror movies to 'the national frame of mind. Hollywood, always quick to reflect or stimulate mass appetite' is simply 'satiating the bloodlust of non-combatant Americans'. This article appeared ... as stormclouds gathered over Europe. But with America now entering the fourth year of its war on terror, and the public monitoring its fear levels ... on CNN, the national mood appears to have hit Hollywood in the only way it could: by becoming big business again.[22]

If we also consider the widespread media coverage of the SARS epidemic of 2002–04, and ongoing concerns over the growing AIDS epidemic, especially in Africa, zombie narratives dealing with destructive infection and conflict, linked with an acute distrust of media reportage, become more apparent. Joe Dante's television film for the *Masters of Horror* series, *Homecoming* (Showtime, 2005) is a particularly notable example. Reworking the premise of *The Monkey's Paw*, the returned are dead soldiers. The imagery of flag-draped coffins, so widely publicised during the Iraq War, are here used in a chilling sequence, as the soldiers rise to claim their democratic right to vote against the administration that sent them to their deaths. The political anger embodied in the undead figures is set against a cynical view of mass media manipulation, as Brian Lowry notes:

> Meanwhile, a Karl Rove-like presidential adviser and Ann Coulter-like pundit (the names have been changed, but just barely), manipulate a talk circuit where gaseous windbags presume to speak for the fallen. When exec producer John Hyde told the Associated Press the goal was to allow the filmmakers to operate 'with no restrictions, no second-guessing,' he wasn't kidding – though in this case, that freedom allows for a bare-knuckled political statement, not buckets of Zombie blood.[23]

What is notable here is the thematic concern – the 'truth' behind news stories – and a visual reminder to the audience of the images used by the same media to summarise the situation.

The film is playing on two levels, using and critiquing the media's ubiquitous presence in contemporary society, and allying itself with those who refuse to believe in spin. The individuals' moral choice is applauded here, and this is at the same time that the production values and visual representation in zombie film were echoing the same concern with the individual. A shift in the presentation of zombie narratives was occurring, reflecting back to the impact of digital filmmaking since the 1990s. These texts took the concept of the aesthetic values of 'reality' embodied by the modern documentary style of the first-person perspective, and linked it to the preponderance of digitally-produced zombie films of 2002 onwards. *28 Days Later* utilised digital cameras to invoke a grainy immediacy in sequences, the handheld cameras adding to the visual impact of attacks by the infected. The same is true for *Dead Meat*'s roving camera. Characters within Snyder's *Dawn of the Dead* record their eventual fate on digital video cameras (notably the plight of the marginal character Andy, as an 'extra' on the DVD release). The self-reflexive filmmaker, charting the impact of destruction on characters in a restricted milieu, becomes a significant trope, in itself a refraction of the independent filmmakers who accessed and created zombie films in the wake of affordable video recording technology in the 1980s. This production ethos and visual style is perhaps best exemplified by the production of the zombie film *Pathogen* (Emily Hagins, 2006) by a 13-year-old girl whose effort attracted the attention of other independent horror filmmakers.[24]

This symbolic use of handheld video cameras – whether digital or video – intimates a return to the personally specific impact of infection, against a global backdrop. The implication that this medium for recording is accessible to all, regardless of experience, is at once the production instigator of many low-budget zombie films and also a thematic signifier in extolling the 'democracy' of information, set against those narratives that are selected by larger media as worthy of attention. This accounts for the rise in first-person perspectives within zombie film and the subsequent small-scale narratives of destruction and isolation that these films present. Grace Lee's *American Zombie* (2007), alongside Bruce LaBruce's *Otto; or, Up With Dead People* (Germany, 2008), use the format of the 'mockumentary' to comment on those isolated within society – that Otto is a gay zombie adds a clear discussion of homophobia to an otherwise comedic text. Michael Bartlett and Kevin Gates's *Zombie Diaries* (Britain, 2006) positions a shattering first-person perspective on a supposed Avian Flu epidemic that gradually decimates the characters, while the Spanish film [*Rec*] (Jaime Balaguero, Paco Plaza, 2007) charts a television crew's reportage on a quarantined building while trapped inside with demonic zombies. The two latter films eschew soundtracks and non-diegetic sound, focusing instead on the aesthetics of the first-person perspective of horror, a factor that leads to a disorienting experience as the audience are positioned, both as witnesses and survivors, alongside the protagonists. The narratives both use the element of reportage to situate the aesthetic – *Zombie Diaries* begins with a TV news group leaving London to report on Avian Flu in the countryside – indicating that the unedited presentation of information is what determines 'reality' and 'reliability' in these narratives.

This final thematic shift in the narratives and presentation within zombie film reaches its apogee in the final key zombie film of this period discussed in this chapter. Fittingly, it is the progeny of the modern zombie film instigated by the same director: George Romero's *Diary of the Dead* (2008). *Diary of the Dead* is filmed on two cameras, one video, one digital, and the narrative follows a group of student filmmakers as a zombie epidemic unfolds. Here, Romero has returned to the timescale of apocalypse begun in *Night of the Living Dead*, as the plague begins. His reasons for returning to this stage of his zombie mythos are debatable – Robin Wood theorises that the previous film, *Land of the Dead*, offered no chance of development into another sequel, while Mark Kermode argues that the low financial returns of *Land* forced Romero into a low-budget production context.[25] Another interpretation is that Romero feels directorial freedom in low-budget filmmaking. As he commented on *Diary*, 'The financial risk was so low that I could afford to gamble ... and it was like going home.'[26] This return to the roots of his career – the filmmakers are from the University of Pittsburgh, arguing over the conventions of the horror film they are making – is at once ironic and telling. Part of the pre-release advertisement for the film was a direct challenge by Romero to independent filmmakers to compete for the chance for their short horror film to be included on the DVD release of the film.[27] His acknowledgment of his fan base and the growing numbers of independent filmmakers is clear. This explains the aesthetic of the film, as an ironic comment on low-budget filmmaking, but also allows Romero to air the particular social concerns that overshadow this film.

23. A 'diary of cruelty'? Jason Creed films the undead in *Diary of the Dead.*

Primarily, Romero castigates the reliance on mediated information, whether from mainstream media suppliers or the students themselves. For Romero, the media is always culpable, as seen in *Night* and *Dawn of the Dead*. From the first news report shown in *Diary*, which is later edited to minimise its impact on the public, to the lecturer's assertion that the filmmaker, Jason Creed, is merely making a 'diary of cruelty', Romero's attacks on mass media are clear. He makes this explicit in an interview issued as part of the supplementary extras on the DVD release of *Diary* when he discusses the failings of the internet and personal footage of disasters to maintain integrity when reporting events.[28] This seems a particularly conservative viewpoint, given that the freedom Romero enjoys is because of his position as an established director who has control over his texts. However, there is another interpretation. Romero's films constantly argue for individual responsibility, and the character of Jason Creed encapsulates this dilemma: is he hunting for internet approbation, or is he trying to inform others of the 'truth'? The overall message of Romero's film is that there is no absolute truth. As is made clear from the beginning, this text had been edited and enhanced (with a soundtrack) by Jason's girlfriend 'to scare you'.

The inclusion of 'news' footage and personal appeals online adds to the pathos of the situation, and also invokes the global context of infection that the contemporary zombie film relies upon. This is reinforced by the inclusion of 'news' sound bites voiced by iconic horror figures. Romero is not just including an in-joke here (though the humour in the film is ironic when discussing horror), but is invoking specific national and personal concerns as reported by the fictional media.[29] The 'news' footage used at the beginning of the film clearly places the dead as immigrants, and the re-editing of the same footage gives the characters in the film their impetus to provide their own 'truth'. However, it is in the real news footage included in the film that Romero's ongoing concern with mediated representations becomes clear. The film refers to the proliferation of personal cameras that record the violence of everyday life, but more poignantly the social destruction caused by Hurricane Katrina in August 2005 that resulted in the destruction of large swathes of New Orleans and the deaths of over 1,800 people, with 705 missing.[30] The brief moments of footage Romero uses include the evacuation and unrest following the flooding, where those people who had not been evacuated attempted to survive by looting. Romero makes his criticism of the situation explicit through the fictional media that distorts situations and the implied racial bias of news reports in *Diary*, and his use of the Katrina images showing desperate flight from the area, which emphasises the race and economic status of those left behind.

Diary of the Dead, in the final analysis, may be referring to global communication, but firmly within an American context of destruction. In this respect, *Diary* brings us full circle to the original fears espoused in the earliest American zombie films, of the silent dispossessed, ignored and enslaved. That representations of the zombie re-emerged during the late 1960s and the 1970s in American film is not a simple manifestation of the cyclical nature of genres, but rather a response to the images of brutality – in America and abroad – that fuelled the social changes and unrest of the decades. As Henry Giroux argues:

> From the beginning of the Civil Rights Movement to the war in Vietnam, images of human suffering and violence provided the grounds for a charged political indignation and collective sense of moral outrage inflamed by the horrors of poverty, militarism, war and racism[31]

But this social rebellion against injustice has been eroded during the 1990s, Giroux argues:

> Global media consolidation, coupled with the outbreak of a new war that encouraged hyper-patriotism and a rigid nationalism, resulted in a tightly controlled visual landscape – managed both by the Pentagon and by corporate-owned networks – that delivered a paucity of images representative of the widespread systemic violence. Selectively informed and cynically inclined, American civic life became more sanitized, controlled and regulated.[32]

If this is the case, then the confrontation offered by the contemporary zombie film acts as reminder: the silent majority cannot *always* be repressed. Indeed, the final shift in the portrayal of this cinematic figure of fear may be in the explicit reaffirmation of the responsibilities we as individuals and as part of a global society hold. The contemporary cinematic zombie is at once personal, national and global in its meaning, reflecting the changing historical, social, political and global structures that shape cinematic production. The new zombie refers to new fears of loss of individuality: an era of global epidemics and global media may well threaten the individual. In these texts, the only choice is to try to record a personal experience of disaster, as the final token of a lived experience. The zombie is our dark mirror for fear, and as those fears change, so will future representations of those creatures.

Notes

1 An extended discussion of these contexts, particularly the rise of fan-made film productions, is covered in my PhD thesis. In his chapter, 'Poverty Row for the MTV Generation', Russell makes a case for the fan productions of the 1990s to be considered in the same production context of the 'Poverty Row' studios of the 1940s, in that the limited budgets and time available for the producers of such texts is offset by the potential market for cheap filler material – in this case for the established video market. See Jamie Russell, *The Book of the Dead* (Godalming: FAB Press, 2005), p. 165.

2 Meghan Sutherland, 'Rigor/Mortis: The Industrial Life of Style in American Zombie Cinema', *Framework* 48:1 (Spring 2007): 65.

3 Rick Worland, *The Horror Film: An Introduction* (Oxford: Blackwell, 2007), pp. 113–14.

4 See Kim Newman, *Nightmare Movies: A Critical History of the Horror Movie From 1968* (London: Bloomsbury, 1988), pp. 65–71.

5 Worland, *The Horror Film*, pp. 107–08.

6 William Graebner, 'America's Poseidon Adventure: A Nation In Existential Despair', in Beth Bailey and David Farber (eds), *America in the Seventies* (Lawrence: University Press of Kansas, 2004), p. 168.

7 See Pete Boss, 'Vile Bodies and Bad Medicine', *Screen* 27:1 (January/ February 1986): 14–24; Noel Carroll, 'Nightmare and the Horror Film: The Symbolic Biology of Fantastic Beings', *Film Quarterly* 34:3 (Spring 1981): 16–25; Mark Jancovich, *Horror* (London: Batsford, 1992), pp. 112–17; Darryl Jones, *Horror: A Thematic History in Fiction and Film* (London: Arnold, 2002), pp. 175–80.

8 David Cronenberg in Chris Rodley (ed.), *Cronenberg on Cronenberg* (London: Faber and Faber, 1997), p. 60.

9 Jesse Stommel, 'Pity Poor Flesh', *Bright Lights Film Journal* 56 (May 2007): 6.

10 Harry M. Benshoff, 'The Monster and The Homosexual', in Mark Jancovich (ed.), *Horror: The Film Reader* (London: Routledge, 2002), p. 92.

11 David J. Skal, *The Monster Show* (New York: Faber and Faber, 1993), pp. 333–51; Worland, *The Horror Film,* pp. 111–12.

12 Skal, *The Monster Show*, p. 351.

13 Roberta McGrath, 'Medical Police', *Ten8* 14 (1984); Simon Watney, 'The Rhetoric of AIDS', *Screen* 25:1 (January/ February 1986): 81.

14 Jonathan Rigby, *English Gothic: A Century of Horror Cinema*, 3rd edn (London: Reynolds and Hearn Ltd, 2004), p. 286.

15 Callum Waddell, 'Chow Down on Dead Meat', *Fangoria* 244 (1 June 2005): 62.

16 Rigby, *English Gothic*, p. 285.

17 Alex Garland, *28 Days Later* (London: Faber and Faber, 2002), p. vii.

18 Cecilia Sayad, '28 Days Later', *Film Comment* 2003; www.filmlinc.com/fcm/28days.htm (accessed 11 January 2003); Kevin Lally, '28 Days Later', *Film Journal International* 106:7, July 2003: 37.

19 Benjamin Svetkey, 'Undead and Loving It', *Entertainment Weekly* 718 (7 November 2003): 48.

20 Leslie Felperin, 'Passport to Prosperity' *Variety* 393:3 (1 December 2003): 3. See also Carl DiOrio, 'Summer of Love for Speciality Labels', *Variety* 392:1 (18 August 2003): 9; Anthony Kaufman, 'Gotta Travel to the States', *Variety* 393:3 (1 December 2003): 3, 44.

21 See Gabriel Snyder, 'Zombie pic pair unearths U conundrum', *Variety* 393:11 (2 February 2004): 10; and Gregory Kirschling, 'Dead and Loving It', *Entertainment Weekly* 756 (19 March 2004): 34.

22 Tom Shone, 'This Time it's Personal', *Guardian*, 25 November 2005; http://film.guardian.co.uk/features/featurepages/0,4120,165008 5,00.html (accessed 10 December 2009).

23 Brian Lowry, 'Political anger finds "Homecoming" on TV', *Variety*, 29 November 2005; http://www.variety.com/article/VR1117933662.html?categoryid=1682&cs=1&query =Homecoming +Brian+Lowry (accessed 17 October 2007).

24 The film *Pathogen* (Emily Hagins, 2006) is widely reported as a positive example of community filmmaking, leading to other filmmakers documenting her work in the documentary film *Zombie Girl: The Movie* (Justin Johnson, Aaron Marshall and Erik Mauck, currently in post-production). See *I was a Teenage Horror Film Director: Emily Hagins*; http://www.pretty-scary.net/ modules.php?name=News&file=article&sid=680 (accessed 12 December 2007); Marrit Ingman, 'The Latest from Z Zeitgeist: Pathogen and Zombie Girl: The Movie', *Austin Chronicle*, 30 June 2006; http://www.austinchronicle.com/gyrobase/Issue/story?oid=oid %3 A380881 (accessed 12 December 2007).

25 Robin Wood, 'Fresh Meat', *Film Comment*, January/February 2008; http://filmlinc.com/fcm/jf08/deaddiary.htm (accessed 11 December 2009); Mark Kermode, 'DVD of the Week: Diary of the Dead', *Observer*, 22 June 2008; http://www.guardian.co.uk/film/2008/jun/22/dvdreviews.horror?gusrc=rss&feed=global (accessed 11 December 2009).

26 G. Romero in Mark Kermode, 'DVD of the Week'.

27 This was shown on the dedicated MySpace page created for the film. See http://www.myspace.com/diaryofthedead (accessed 15 December 2009).

28 George Romero, *Interview: Frightfest 2008* (Johanna Salomaki, 2008, Blaze Films Ltd.) in George Romero, *Diary of the Dead* (Artfire Films/Romero-Grunwald Productions; DVD Optimum Releasing Ltd, 2008).

29 Guillermo Del Toro's voice mocks the anti-immigration policies against Mexico, now pointless in the face of the returning dead, while Stephen King's eerily accurate impersonation of a fundamentalist preacher invokes the concept of a biblical apocalypse that Romero has briefly noted in previous films. Simon Pegg (of *Shaun of the Dead* (Edgar Wright, 2004), a reverential homage to zombie film) is used as a British news commentator heard on the radio. Pegg and Wright also featured as zombie extras in *Land of the Dead*.

30 See 'Reports of Missing and Deceased', Louisiana Department of Health and Hospitals (18 April 2006); http://www.dhh.louisiana.gov/offices/page.asp?ID=192&Detail=5248on (accessed 20 January 2008); Michelle Hunter, 'Deaths of evacuees push toll to 1,577', *New Orleans Times-Picayune*, 19 May 2006; http://www.nola.com/news/t-p/frontpage/index.ssf?/base/news-5/1148020620 117480.xml&coll=1 (accessed 20 January 2008).

31 Henry A. Giroux, 'Violence, Katrina, and the Biopolitics of Disposability', *Theory, Culture & Society* 24:7–8 (2007): 305.

32 Giroux, 'Violence, Katrina, and the Biopolitics of Disposability', p. 306.

8

'DEATH IS THE NEW PORNOGRAPHY!'

Gay Zombies, Homonormativity and Consuming Masculinity in Queer Horror

Darren Elliott-Smith

Queer representations of the undead in the moving image have long favoured the vampire, whose fluid depiction of sexuality has long been a site of queer identification.[1] Conversely, cinematic incarnations of the gay zombie have, until recently, remained few. While its undead siblings – the vampire, the intangible ghost and the figure of the golem (dead flesh reanimated via scientific means) – all emerge from a shared literary heritage,[2] the zombie is often considered to be a decidedly *non-literary* monster. The zombie, at least in relation to a contemporary understanding of the figure as a flesh-eating, reanimated rotting corpse, a shambling (or running) cadaver that spreads infection through bites or scratches and whose victims themselves become zombies after infection or death, *was* conceived in the cinema. Kyle Bishop concurs, suggesting that although zombies remain closely affiliated with the literary undead, their 'limited emotional depth, their inability to express or act on human desires and their primarily visual nature, make zombies ill-suited for the written word; zombies thrive best on screen'.[3] He argues that it is precisely due to the zombies' inability to express themselves, being bound to physical action, that they 'must be watched'.[4] This suggests both a compulsion to look at the figure of the zombie and a *wariness* of a monster that must be watched, kept at a remove for fear of integration or as protection against contamination. With the signs of horrific difference displayed on the surface of the monster's skin, difference can be acted upon (by avoidance or destruction). The zombie is a visibly 'outed' monster forced to inhabit its decaying flesh for eternity. The zombie can 'be watched', rendered visible and set apart in order to protect others from infection and conversion. The guardedness inherent in homosexual panic is also not far removed from this.

I want to reconsider the zombie as a perfect metaphor for the homosexual within the moving image, first by analysing the figure's potential for queer meaning then looking specifically at contemporary depictions of the gay zombie in the horror film before focusing mainly on the shambling, semi-articulate, gay zombie from Bruce LaBruce's melancholic zombie satire *Otto; or, Up With Dead People* (2008). Here my objective is to understand how the figure can be used both as a cipher for homosexuality and for sub-cultural critique within Western gay male culture.

Zombie Bottom Feeders

In relation to their cultural standing and symbolic sexual and economic power, as well as their potential for queer appropriation, the vampire remains a clear 'top' to the zombie's 'bottom'. Within the undead cohort, the zombie upstart is marginalised, outside the literary tradition, an uncharismatic and often comic creature whose features are often satirically deployed as a representation of 'mindless' conformity or consumption. In his study of the representation of the zombie in the moving image, Jamie Russell paints a very sorry picture of the figure, indeed referencing James Twitchell's understanding of the zombie as 'an utter cretin, a vampire with a lobotomy '.[5] Russell continues, that 'There are no aristocrats, blue bloods or celebrities among zombies ... just low-rent, anonymous monsters.'[6]

Russell asserts that, despite the zombie's close affinity with the moving image, it emerges from anthropological publications, the first being *The Magic Island* (1929), a study of Haitian voodoo cults by William Seabrook. His original 'discovery' of 'zombis' (sic) centred on a farmer who had apparently 'recruited' the undead as workers on his farm. The study clearly paved the way for early cinematic associations of the zombie with African and Afro-Caribbean magic threatening the West, and is played out in *White Zombie* (US, 1932) whose plot contains echoes of the slave trade, with its zombie 'master' and a revenge enacted upon its many white, Caucasian automaton zombies. In North American culture, with a history steeped in slavery and racial segregation, the zombie fast became a thinly veiled metaphor for the oppressed masses. In particular, it represents a loss of individual freedom and identity. As Wade Davis concludes,

> ... given the colonial history, the concept of enslavement implies that the peasant fears, and the zombi suffers, a fate that is literally worse than death – the loss of physical liberty that is slavery, and the sacrifice of personal autonomy implied by the loss of identity.[7]

Russell further conflates the fear of zombification with the fear, or perhaps the lure, of being rendered passive, mindless: 'Zombification – whether it's turning men into slaves or women into sex objects – is closely linked with themes of powerlessness and the loss of personal autonomy.'[8]

In George A. Romero's definitive series of zombie films, the zombie is identified with consumption rather than production. Once zombified, the 'slave's' fragile, rotting physicality and mindlessness becomes *counter*productive, developing into a compulsive flesh eater. In its ravenous corporeality, the zombie is arguably most closely affiliated with the cannibal. Romero's still ongoing, socially critical zombie films were indeed the first to conflate the figure with cannibalism in its ravenous corporeality. The impact of this new configuration was so effective that flesh eating was quickly established as a core trait of the cinematic zombie. Peter Dendle asserts that Romero's *Night of the Living Dead* (1968) (and the ensuing 'Dead' series, 1978–2008) 'liberat[ed the figure] from the shackles of a master, and [Romero] invested his zombies not with a function to serve, but rather a drive'.[9] Though Romero's zombies lose their individuality en masse, their capitalist cannibalism reveals a contradictory desire to regain individual subjectivity via consumption, but also, conversely, a desire to 'fit in' with the consumer community. Indeed, in the individual's aspiration for difference from others, a certain element of homogeneity is achieved, resulting in a clonish sameness. This same homogeneity is also integral to queer appropriations of the zombie. White male homosexual culture also encourages a sameness defined by materialism, being accepted into the 'scene' and the gym body image.

Zombie Sexuality: What's so Queer about the Zombie?

While the attractive vampire seduces, bites and renders passive its victims in order to satiate its desires, the zombie is a passive, sometimes pathetic creature that bears the visible scars of its own previous bodily penetration. The zombie manifests a somnambulistic, perpetually threatening and liminal sexuality that is bound to the corporeal and arguably has been treated with repugnance. In spite of the obvious analogies, the exposure of internal bodily spaces, bodily fluids and primal urges, it has remained largely an anti-erotic object. Gregory A. Waller concludes that zombies are not 'sexual beings' at all and that they rely on an even more basic feeding instinct (flesh rather than blood) than the vampire.[10]

The cycle of Italian, French and Spanish zombie films foregrounds the figure's conflation of sex with death. The soft-core nudity present in the zombie films of Jess Franco, Lucio Fulci and Jean Rollin from the 1970s are heavily influenced by the increasing availability and popularity of pornography at the time and similarly the aesthetic of the 'fantastique' which, as Russell puts it, is 'a sub-genre with a predilection for the erotic'.[11] In titles such as *Zombie Flesh Eaters* (Lucio Fulci, Italy, 1979) and *Zombie Holocaust* (Marino Girolami, Italy, 1980), it is the female body that is shown frequently in states of undress and under threat of attack by the shambling masses of the undead. In such films, it is not the zombie figure *per se* that is coded erotically. Rather, it is the sexually charged methods in which the zombie attacks, tears open victims and consumes flesh that are emphasised alongside the zombie's own body as essentially penetrable and penetrating, objectifying the corporeal in all its messy goriness. In this sense the zombie film's visualisation of the vulnerable body also reconfigures it as a site of eroticised, penetrable sexual wounds. Such films often feature zombies thrusting fists and sinking teeth into the fragile bodies of their victims, who, in turn, writhe in the implied orgasmic intensity of being turned inside out and devoured. As Russell points out, '[such films] create a disturbing link between physical pleasure and physical pain. These films frequently link sex with bodily trauma ... [at times] it seems as if bloody wounds and sexual orifices are on the verge of becoming interchangeable ...'[12]

Whereas the erotic pleasure of zombie attacks remain implicit in these European titles (for the most part, zombies do not 'have sex'), it is perhaps in queer horror's representation of the gay zombie that the erotic potential of the body as a penetrable/penetrating site of jouissance is explicitly realised. Gay zombie porn (and zombie porn *per se*) is first visualised in Vidkid Timo's *Night of the Living Dead* pastiche, *At Twilight Come the Flesh Eaters* (US, 1998), which juxtaposes a low-budget black and white porn parody of Romero's socio-political horror with behind-the-scenes sex between the porn film's crew and cast in colour. Unlike more explicit zombie-porn, *Flesh Eaters* does not feature the penetration of bodily wounds. Conversely, the hard-core straight zombie porn film *Porn of the Dead* (Rob Rotten, 2006) features explicit sex between porn stars and grotesquely made-up female zombies, who are sexually penetrated anally, vaginally and via wounds in their deteriorating flesh.[13]

Gay zombies uphold the figure's corporeal repugnance and its brain-dead stupidity, while allowing for a subcultural critique of gay masculine stereotypes. Queer narratives that embrace the zombie in order to revel in homosexuality's difference may also use the figure to critique the homogeneity and 'homonormativity' within homosexual subcultures. 'Homonormativity', in Lisa Duggan's formulation of the term, refers to 'a politics that does not contest dominant heteronormative assumptions and institutions, but upholds and sustains them, while promising the possibility of a demobilized gay constituency, and a gay culture anchored in domesticity and consumption'.[14]

Duggan continues that the process gives rise to the 'good gay subject', whereby relationships are built upon 'monogamy, devotion, maintaining privacy and propriety'.[15] The consequence is a hierarchy of 'worthiness', with those that identify as transgender, transsexual, bisexual or non-gendered deemed less worthy of equal rights than those in stable relationships that mirror structures of heterosexual marriage. Within the male homosexual community, homonormativity tends to a white, middle-class, youth-oriented clonishness that aspires to a hypermasculine body ideal. Conversely, gay zombie narratives often foreground differences *within* the amorphous horde, playing down the symbolism of infection (and its obvious connection with AIDS signifiers and the gay community) and instead focusing on sub-cultural tensions, critiquing stereotypes and highlighting the psychical trauma of 'fitting in'.

The infectiousness of the zombie also opens up the figure as a symbol of a quickly spreading epidemic of death, decay and queerness, which is passed from individual to individual in a viral fashion via a bite. The zombie's bite brings death, emaciation, decay and a desire to feed on the flesh of others. The concept of zombieism as sickness, with its signifiers of bodily wasting, weeping sores and signs of rot, clearly offers it as an AIDS allegory, alongside the vampire (the chief icon of queer infectiousness).[16] Like the vampire, the zombie's capability for 'unnatural reproduction' also opens the figure up to queer readings. As a reanimated corpse that continues to 'live', the zombie establishes an undead community via viral communication. It is via these alternative methods of unnatural reproduction (infectious bites or scratches) that the zombie figure threatens society's infrastructure. Via queer appropriation, the zombie who is simultaneously undead and decaying also offers an alternative to heterosexual reproductive futurism. In the very same body, the image of the crumbling, decaying body of the (homosexual) zombie is both a signifier of ageing and mortality – the eventual consequences of an anti-reproductivity that the gay man stereotypically represents, yet it continues uncannily to thrive.[17]

The zombie acts upon very primal instincts, eating to 'survive' even though it is already dead. Traditional zombies represent extreme lawlessness. They can be understood to be an embodiment of the 'id', ruled entirely by appetite. Their insatiable drive to cannibalise their victims can be read as a sublimation of an equivalent sexual drive. Such an 'unstoppable' drive calls to mind Leo Bersani's discussion of the homophobia stimulated by the AIDS crisis in 'Is the Rectum a Grave' (1987), where he states that it 'reinforces the heterosexual association of anal sex with a self-annihilation originally and primarily identified with the fantasmatic mystery of an insatiable, unstoppable female sexuality'.[18] The gay zombie may in fact represent the return of a repressed feminine appetite in the already annihilated gay man.

The slippage between homosexuality and cannibalism (and identification and desire) arguably finds its cinematic origins in Jonathan Demme's *The Silence of the Lambs* (1991). In her article, 'Oral Incorporations: *The Silence of the Lambs*' (1995), Diana Fuss discusses the film via Freud's *Totem and Taboo* (1913), developing his analysis of cannibalism to argue that, 'gay sex has always been cannibal murder'.[19] According to Fuss, Demme's film is 'all about the horrors of identification, identification as self mutilation, identification as decapitation, identification as oral cannibalistic incorporation'.[20] The central drive of the identification process is an introjective impulse to assimilate the object, to consume and become nourished by the very qualities that draw the cannibalistic subject to it initially. Compelled to repeat the act of identification/incorporation in order to compensate for inevitable disappointment, the subject is plunged into a continual cycle of destroying and assimilating the 'rival in whom the subject sees itself reflected'.[21] The (gay) cannibalistic subject consumes the 'Other', whom he erotically desires and disidentifies with. [22] It is via Freud and Fuss's understanding of oral incorporation and in this resexualisation of the monster's body that the zombie's potential for homosexual appropriation emerges. Gay zombie narratives can be said to show that the forlorn, isolated, nihilistic gay zombie is caught in a tension between exclusion *from* the communal (and from life itself) and a desire *for* the communal, a carnivorously motivated desire to identify with (and consume) others like himself.

'Zombie or Not, I Know a Show-Tune-Lovin' Friend of Dorothy when I see One!'

Gay zombie narratives often foreground the zombie's sexuality; for example, shorts such as *Gay Zombies!* (FronkandDego Films (FND Films), 2007) and *Flaming Gay Zombies* (Sadya Lashua and Aaron Mace, US, 2007) typically demonstrate elements of broad comedy and place the gay zombie in a context of homosexual panic. Both films display an excessive, stereotypically effeminate zombie behaviour (donning pink crop tops and clutching onto their Prada man-bags, even in death) which instils more fear in the victims than the prospect of actually being eaten. Alternatively, *Gay Zombie* (Michael Simon, US, 2007) features Miles (Brad Bulganin), a young gay male zombie who outs himself on the West Hollywood dating scene. His newfound living friends help him re-establish himself through 'makeovers' using caulk to fill in his rotting wounds while encouraging him to repress his cannibalistic impulses, that eventually overwhelm him, resulting in a flesh-eating rampage that is construed as cheating on his human boyfriend. *Creatures from the Pink Lagoon* (Chris Diana, US, 2006) is a 1950s 'creature-feature' pastiche which portrays a group of gay friends on holiday who are terrorised by homosexual zombies who emerge from a nearby lake having been infected by giant, atomic mutated mosquitoes. Only the film's promiscuous gays are susceptible to infection by the mutant mosquitoes and therefore to zombification, driving home its comic warning against cruising. With its comic fusion of parody, camp melodrama and musical, the film ridicules both effeminate *and* macho stereotypes of gay men, all of whom are miraculously cured upon hearing Judy Garland's voice, with the hero's proclamation that 'No homosexual, not even a flesh eating, walking dead homosexual can resist Judy Garland!'

Jeff Erbach's *The Nature of Nicholas* (2002), a low-budget coming of age, art-house horror, explicitly portrays zombieism as both a symbolic visualisation of gay shame and a monstrous projection of infectious homosexuality by oppressive heteronormative structures. The film centres upon the homoerotic relationship between two ten-year-old boys, shy Nicholas (Jeff Sutton), who develops a crush on his straight best friend Bobby (David Turnbull). After Nicolas kisses him, Bobby runs away in shame; the following day, Bobby's zombie doppelgänger visits Nicholas much to his delight and horror. With each visitation, Bobby begins to turn green and eventually rot. Eventually Nicholas conceals Zombie-Bobby as a play friend. While the ashamed Human-Bobby remains his friend, he shamefully demands that Nicolas let his zombie alter ego 'die'.

The Nature of Nicholas' zombie double motif clearly represents repressed homosexual desire and the shame demanded by heteronormativity. Melissa Carroll reads the figure both as a monstrous representation of heteronormative disgust and as a potentially subversive creation. The zombie in *Nicholas* is an obvious 'Other', representing the heterosexist fear of a queer infection that threatens a normative reproductive future promised by the figure of the child. But it also can function as a symbol of resistance whereby the boys embrace the critical potential of the zombie body:

> Their bodies are sites of discomfort that actually embrace the 'inhuman' in order to critique the figure of the human, which proves to be more monstrous than any perceivable threat.[23]

The zombie, with its own alternative methods of reproduction, rejects heterosexistly enforced identity and is thus a means of embracing difference. In this sense, gay zombie representation can also be used counterculturally, as a figure through which the queer subject can celebrate his marginalisation and simultaneously reject his 'monstrousness'.

Otto; or, Up With Dead People

In Bruce LaBruce's 'melancholic existential gay porno-zombie movie',[24] *Otto; or, Up With Dead People*, his zombie anti-hero represents a self-loathing, nihilistic, sexually indifferent, apolitical and dysfunctional gay male subjectivity desperately seeking hypermasculinity. In satirical style, the director takes on the politicised zombie metaphor and reworks it within the themes of his oeuvre: the marginalised subject who is fetishised by 'reactionary revolutionaries'; the eroticising and consumption of hypermasculine iconography; and the conflation of hard-core pornographic tropes with anti-capitalist proclamations.

LaBruce's film is a generic fusion of melodrama, music video, existential drama, fictional documentary, pornography, gore-saturated horror and satire. It dramatises the anxieties faced by Otto (Jey Crisfar) as he fails to assimilate into the horde and instead re-establishes his individuality and marginalisation. In *Otto*, the mob not only represents violent zombie-phobic humans, but also the harsh exclusivity of a zombie community (albeit a fake one) that also demands conformity. The conventional formula of the zombie narrative arguably pitches an Us (humans) vs Them (zombies) opposition, before revealing the zombies as the return of the repressed, as undead versions of ourselves in our human potential for monstrous violence. *Otto* transforms the binary into an Us (the film's gay 'fake zombie' actors) vs Us (gay 'authentic' zombies) opposition, pitting homosexuality against itself in a critique of gay subcultures. More importantly, LaBruce's narrative offers a critique of the banality of gay male subcultures, particularly those of the very homogenous club scene in Berlin, as being effectively 'dead'. LaBruce's self-reflexive presentation of the gay zombie highlights the figure as an agent of parody and pastiche where 'zombie drag' becomes yet another example of gender performance that offers the gay male subject hypermasculinity.

The eponymous main protagonist from La Bruce's *Otto* is unlike other horror film zombies in that he is not part of a consuming horde; instead, LaBruce sees Otto as the 'rebel', the 'outsider' and the solitary, marginalised individual: 'with Otto I intended to make ... more of a misfit, who didn't relate to the other zombies'.[25] Further still, Otto is different from the other gay zombies depicted in the film – he is a semi-articulate, mostly lucid creature whose undead confusion is portrayed as amnesia. Unlike the groaning, cannibalistic automata of the film's more stereotypically traditional zombies, he represents a newer generation that, according to the film, had,

> ... become somewhat more refined ... they had developed a limited ability to speak and more importantly to *reason*. It was a time where zombies had become, if not commonplace, but un-extraordinary ... the few zombies that had survived, managed to pass on intelligence to subsequent generations ...

The film questions the actual existence of real zombies by ambiguously presenting Otto as (possibly) the only authentic zombie among fictional undead actors, while never offering or discounting either a supernatural or rational explanation for his undead status. LaBruce also borrows Romero's stylistic use of colour and black and white from *Martin* (1977), to swap between an apparent reality and the fictional 'film-within-a-film' world by literally including the conceit of not one but two films being made within the overarching narrative. Hence the film's undecided title, *Otto; or, Up With Dead People*. Throughout LaBruce's film, we are unsure of which film we are watching: *Up With Dead People*, the 'political-porno-zombie-movie' fictional art film on the rising up of a horde of gay zombie insurgents (with its pretentious, art-house black and white aesthetic), or *Otto*, a documentary film on a troubled adolescent who is convinced he is a zombie (with its alternate colour, digital video style). The two eventually become interchangeable in LaBruce's overarching narrative. To make matters more complex, scenes from each of the films are often juxtaposed with one another, shown out of chronological order and both 'directed' by the film's fictional radical feminist filmmaker Medea Yarns (Katarina Klewinghaus). LaBruce interweaves Medea's films in fragmented form, presenting behind-the-scenes sections of the making of her films alongside scenes from the films themselves and including scenes from Otto's journey to Berlin existing outside of the 'mockumentary', 'behind the scenes' conceit.

LaBruce is a multiply dissident artist, with a Marxist-feminist, anti-capitalist stance on the commodification of the individual within capitalist heteronormativity and a gay scene he claims is 'bourgeois and dead'.[26] A profoundly political director, his works satirise homonormative as much as heteronormative cultures. He began making films during the emergence of New Queer Cinema in the early 1990s. As such, he has often been referred to as an *enfant terrible* of that movement whose works have never been regarded as positively as those of Gregg Araki, Todd Haynes and Tom Kalin. To an extent, LaBruce marginalises himself within the movement:

> You see I don't feel I have a lot in common with a bunch of rich kids who have degrees in semiotic theory, who make dry, academic films with overdetermined AIDS metaphors and Advocate men in them. I've never felt comfortable with the new 'queer' movement.[27]

LaBruce is also troubled by the reclaiming of 'queer' as an activist identity, which he considers a stumbling block in liberating homosexuals, viewing himself as estranged from gay/queer communities:

> [I] do not now feel, nor have I ever felt, part of any gay community ... if you didn't conform to the precise uniform and the Pavlovian behavioural patterns and the doctrinaire politics, you were treated [as] some kind of enemy.[28]

In this sense, LaBruce's representation of the equally marginalised Otto can be said to echo his own life experiences. LaBruce's intentions for the character of Otto were, from the outset, deliberately ambiguous, stating that,

> I wanted to make a zombie who was a misfit, a sissy and a plague ridden faggot. I deliberately leave it open to interpretation whether Otto is supposed to be a 'real' zombie or merely a screwed up, homeless, mentally ill kid with an eating disorder, who believes that he's dead ...[29]

Despite his wasted appearance, Otto is at a far remove from the typical abject zombie corpse. His look strikes one as more cultivated, stylised, more *deliberate* than that of the rotting corpse. By his own admission, Otto is a zombie who suffers an 'identity crisis'. In a direct-to-camera address, the eponymous anti-hero states:

> It's not easy being the undead – the living all seem like the same person to me and I don't think I like that person very much ... I was a zombie with an identity crisis and until I figured it out, I was stuck eating whatever non-human flesh was available.

Otto's definition of the 'living' at first can be understood to represent heteronormativity. It seems more likely, however, that the 'sameness' to which Otto (and LaBruce) refer to is that of conformist homosexual culture from which both feel alienated. Alongside his 'identity crisis', Otto is an amnesiac, with occasional flashbacks to what he refers to as 'the time before'. Throughout the narrative, he longs to rediscover his 'true self' and to reconnect with other people in order to determine what has brought him to this point. In one sense his journey as a neophyte zombie might be understood as the (re)discovery of his sexuality, yet from early in the narrative he seems drawn to other male zombies, with his homosexuality as a given. Together with his resolute declarations of his true zombieism, this would suggest that Otto is sure both of his sexuality *and* of being undead. It is his sense of not belonging and of his failure to fit in with the fake 'dead' subcultures offered to him in Berlin that causes him to question his identity.

In several direct-to-camera interviews, other characters discuss Otto's function as a *tabula rasa* (both for Medea and extra-diegetically for LaBruce). Actor Fritz Fritze (Marcel Schlutt), the revolutionary leader of gay zombies in Medea's film, discusses Otto as 'the "Hollow Man", the empty signifier, upon which she could project her political agenda'.

For LaBruce, too, Otto is a blank slate onto which he can project his own personal anxieties about alienating homosexual society. He represents Otto as the perfect victim, rejected by heteronormative and homosexual culture. Upon first meeting Medea, Otto is also cast as a 'fake-zombie'. At first he appears to fit in seamlessly into her zombie imitator-group. Medea comments on his appearance:

> In a way he fitted the typical porn profile – the lost boy, the damaged boy, numb, phlegmatic, insensate boy, willing to go to

> any extreme to feel something, to feel anything ... But there was something different about Otto, something more ... 'authentic' ...

Otto's 'authenticity', can also be read in terms of his *difference* not only from 'humans' but from the other zombie-actors. Largely represented as left-wing actors, Medea's 'zombies' are filming an avant-garde 'political porno zombie' which pastiches an uprising in the oppressed gay minorities. The presence of such 'actor-zombies' undermines the authenticity of all zombies within the film.

As with Romero's films, the zombies in *Up With Dead People* represent the once-consumed masses returning to consume 'the living', which LaBruce (via Medea) recasts, in terms of sexual politics, as conformist bourgeois homonormativity. LaBruce's new wave of zombies are gay men with an insatiable desire to eat and absorb men into their cohort. They are represented as commonplace in LaBruce's Berlin: the zombie, like the homosexual, has been so thoroughly assimilated into the dominant culture that it has taken on normative traits, become conventional and even banal. Like contemporary gay men within Western societies, these gay zombies are simultaneously tolerated and intolerable. Though they may be 'commonplace', Berlin is hardly a utopia for the undead. As Medea states, the gay zombie is considered even more abject to their oppressors, who then take to 'zombie-bashing' where the 'gay undead [are] hunted down and murdered even more ruthlessly than previous generations'.

In the film, Maximilian (Fritz's zombie lover played by Christophe Chemin) is attacked and killed by a gang of youths, and in the 'mockumentary' or agitprop documentary of *Otto*, the eponymous anti-hero is himself subject to both a 'stoning' and beating by similar youths. LaBruce's deliberate casting of largely Middle Eastern/Arabic actors as the 'stoning' children, and as Otto's assailants in the final zombie-bashing sequence, clearly references the 'real-world' homophobia of governments and religions in countries such as Iran and Saudi Arabia. The zombie-bashing is generally meted out by brown-skinned young men as exactors of threatening violence upon a largely white, male community of gay zombies. In this sense, Otto seemingly reverses the racial elements of the traditional Western zombie narrative which itself appropriated the folklore surrounding the Haitian 'zombi'. But Otto's inversion of the black–white binary does not subvert the dynamic. Although the zombie–

human opposition is switched, Otto's white zombie is still threatened by oppressed non-whites.

But zombie-phobia is exhibited not only by the religious right and certain ethnic groups, but also by almost all the non-zombies Otto comes across. In one scene, when he travels across Berlin on the U-Bahn, a succession of passengers of various sexual orientations and ethnicities enter the carriage. In reverse shots, their disgust is made clear. Most interestingly, two young gays enter the carriage, sit opposite Otto and bitchily mock him. LaBruce's presentation of the well-adjusted gay man ridiculing the marginalised homosexual directly references the director's own experiences of humiliation *within* the subculture.

Zombie Communities: Faking It and 'Passing'

Otto's apolitical indifference masks his longing to follow the 'smell of human density' and to be accepted into a community of others like himself. Otto's zombie drive is to seek out a like-minded community and to be accepted by others. In the film's opening sequence, he hitchhikes to Berlin, attracted by 'some overpowering smell ... the smell of flesh ... Berlin', only to be disappointed by what he finds. Through his film's fake zombies, LaBruce is referencing a fashionable trend within popular culture, which celebrates the figure of the zombie in events, theatrical performance, installation art and literary parodies.[30] If the zombie is adopted to highlight difference and revel in the pride of marginalisation, it also conversely evokes an assimilationist ethos that is essential to the figure. To wear zombie-drag en masse paradoxically declares both difference and conformity. Otto is considered by non-zombies to be indistinguishable from other gay zombies, but within a gay subculture that has largely adopted the zombie skinhead look, he is considered 'different' and further marginalised. As LaBruce describes gay cruising, 'it really is pretty much like night of the living dead. People are in a kind of somnambulist, zombie-like state; people are in a sexual trance almost. It's not really about the individual.'[31] If the homogenous gay club culture is depicted as 'dead', the truly dead Otto seems the *least* zombie-like of the film's characters (in his possession of speech, free will and autonomous thought).

In several sequences in LaBruce's film, Otto comes across, and is disappointed by, a succession of the counterfeit undead. In one scene he is picked up by a gay fake zombie outside a club ironically named *Flesh*, which is hosting a themed fancy dress 'Zombie Night'. He is cruised by another male 'zombie', presented as a classic skinhead with close-cropped hair, a black bomber jacket and a tight white T-shirt with red braces and Doctor Martens. He persuades Otto not to enter the club on the evidence that 'it's *so* dead'. Instead, he flatters Otto on his assumed 'costume' – 'you put so much effort into your ensemble ... really, really cool!' – before sniffing him, commenting, 'Wow! You even smell authentic!'

The comic misreadings of authentic and inauthentic zombie style become more explicit as the two head back to make love in the skinhead's apartment. As they kiss, blood begins to trickle from their interlocked mouths and the scene fades to black. A fade-up reveals the apartment now a scene of carnage with Otto having apparently eviscerated the skinhead. The white sheets, walls and posters are splashed in arterial spray, bloodied handprints and gore. Slowly the corpse of Otto's 'trick' then begins to move. Propping himself up on the bed, his entrails lying on his stomach, he proclaims, 'That was amazing ... can I see you again some time?' In this 'biting' satire on the deadness of gay clubbing culture in Berlin, Otto turns the tables on the city's 'meat-market' whereby the consumed 'twink' becomes the consumer.

Shaka McGlotten reads LaBruce's film alongside his own previous research on gay male online sociality, that also understands such communities as exhibiting a similar deadened, zombified existence, as a response to the effects of technologically influenced isolation, fractured gay subcultures and the disappearance of the communal. McGlotten's term 'dead and live life' characterises the narratives recounted by his online interviewees that criticise the normative templates offered to queers, 'the different ways we might feel more or less alive'.[32] For McGlotten, LaBruce's film offers an understanding of 'queer sociality which ... is animated by death, reflecting strange configurations of death-in-life'. He continues that Yarns and LaBruce's narratives are twin polemics that comprehend 'sites of death in life as potentially vital' for queer identification. Indeed, the film's ambiguity also works not only to question the authenticity of Otto's zombification, but also to draw parallels *between* the apparently living and dead. McGlotten suggests

24. The scene of evisceration with Otto as a ravenous 'bottom': *Otto; or, Up With Dead People.*

that zombies are anti-communal but only in the sense that they are establishing different ways of *un*living, that can challenge traditional heteronormative and homonormative ways of existence and of the communal. He suggests that zombies' sociality offers a queer alternative, as 'they do not possess the reflective self-awareness or empathetic identification as the hallmarks of meaningful intimate connection with ourself and others ... This, along with their boundary crossing reanimatedness, is part of what makes them inhuman.' LaBruce's zombie depicts not only the fear of loneliness, but how to *live* with it. McGlotten sees Otto as indifferently in control of his destiny; not really expressing a desire to connect with himself or others, his journey is a resolutely passive one that he defines as being motivated by 'soft-refusals'.[33] But how does this sit alongside Otto's zombie-like drive to seek out others like him? I would suggest that ironically McGlotten's reading of the zombie is not anti-communal but merely champions newer forms of the communal that critique the old, dead ways.

'Death is the New Pornography!': Sex as Anti-Communal

The original cuts of LaBruce's works also include hard-core gay sex, later excised under various theatrical and home entertainment release stipulations.[34] The performance of actual sex adds to LaBruce's low-budget, realist and exploitation aesthetic and effects a critique of the sanitised sex produced by North American gay porn studios such as Falcon Studios. For LaBruce, these porn studios perpetuate an unrealistic representation of gay sex, valorising a hypermasculine body image ideal whereby the body becomes an eroticised object in a capitalist mode of industrial production which, for LaBruce, is,

> ... innately fascist ... in that it has the same iconography as the Third Reich: the idea of the perfect body. It's body fascism. Their often fucking like pistons, very mechanical ... with its slick monolithic aesthetics, it's cold production line uniformity, and its easy propagandistic appropriation of the gay agenda.[35]

The eroticising of death is commonplace in *Otto*, as Medea declares that, 'Death is the new pornography'; sex has been supplanted by the death that has previously represented it. *Otto* replaces the female body as object of erotic spectacle, prevalent in earlier European soft-core zombie films, with that of the male, but further still explicitly links physical pleasure with physical trauma. For LaBruce's zombies, fucking and killing become literally interchangeable. The director also champions the sub-genre's queer expediency that 'zombie porn is practical: you can create your own orifice', and upholds its radical potential: 'I believe that zombie porn is the wave of the future, and that we will soon routinely see porous, corrupted flesh being penetrated by legions of lascivious zombies. So get ready for a revolutionary zombie porn extravaganza.'[36]

LaBruce's camera, like the European soft-core zombie film, opens the body. It sexualises the various orifices and inner 'piping' (the intestine, the vagina and now the anus) while simultaneously revealing the human subject as an empty shell that will nevertheless *do* for sex. Russell writes that the Italian zombie film exposed 'the body's inner mechanics to the audience's gaze ... the body's materiality and its status as an object ... a vision of the body's essential emptiness'.[37] Similarly, Peter Dendle suggests that sex between or with zombies symbolises an 'unapologetic revealing of humanity' in the exposure of one's physical innards.[38] The opening up of the body to externalise one's guts represents sharing one's inner feelings with others in an exchange of the self with another individual or within a community.

In one scene from *Otto*, anti-hero Fritz returns home to find his lover Maximilian dead, having shot himself in the head only later to be reanimated as a zombie. Rather than being repulsed, Fritz begins to passionately kiss Max who returns his kisses with an infecting bite. Fritz eventually reawakens fully zombified, but still horny, upon which Max proceeds to penetrate a hole in his undead lover's stomach with his penis, effectively fucking him into (and *in his*) immortality. Setting aside the male body's dual oral and anal orifices, an entirely new erotic entry point is ripped in Fritz's stomach – direct to the site of digestion. Consumption, digestion and assimilation seem to be the order of the day in the symbolism of this sequence which itself becomes a satire of gastric incorporation. If we understand the zombie's drive to consume living flesh as a literalising of desire for the love object, gut fucking is an extension of this desire while satirising the (gay) zombie's penchant for 'unnatural reproduction'. Literally planting seed into his partner's stomach, Maximilian bypasses the mouth and/or anus, and there is a particular emphasis in the scene on the nourishing potential in the act of gut-fucking. The frequent scenes of 'reanimation' and 'recruitment' in LaBruce's film represent zombies as both incredibly potent and fertile. This symbolic impregnation of Fritz, taking Max into his stomach, is a comic literalising of the zombie's unnatural reproduction.

Yet given the potential for undead sex to strengthen relations and increase a sense of the communal between gay zombies (however radical or destructive its intentions) within narratives like *Otto*, for LaBruce, sex between zombies, while eroticising the internal in a 'frenzy of the visible',[39] ultimately proves to be alienating.[40] After the final wrap of '*Up With Dead People*', Otto's romanticised love-making with Fritz in his crisp clean bed sheets seems to promise a redemption of some sort, a reconnection with masculinity and gay male community. His zombie-like pallor, scars and bruises seem to disappear in the healing white light of Fritz's bedroom, and for a moment Otto appears 'normal'. However, the morning after reveals the promise of redemption to be false. Fritz wakes to find a note on his pillow, on which is sketched a gravestone reading 'Otto: RIP'. In the scenes that follow, Otto is shown to kill himself. Shown out of context, this sequence is presented as his actual suicide, in which he pours petrol onto himself in a wasteland on the city's outskirts, and sets himself on fire. Eventually Medea enters the frame to throw a bucket of water over what the spectator now sees is a burning dummy. In reality, having not killed himself, Otto continues to seek an identity and leaves Berlin to journey north. In the film's final shots he is shown hitchhiking on a country highway, speaking in voice-over on his decision:

> I really didn't know what my destination was ...
> But something told me to head north ...
> The cold doesn't bother me, in fact, I find it comforting,
> It preserves my flesh ...
> Maybe I'll find more of my kind up there and learn to enjoy the company. Maybe I would discover a whole new way of death ...

LaBruce's film suggests that death is neither an end nor answer. Otto instead continues in a limbo-like state, never knowing others like him, never knowing where to go, unable to separate reality from fantasy, never experiencing the 'suicidal ecstasy'[41] connoted in the combination of sex and death.

In *Otto*, McGlotten rightly states that there is little evidence of Leo Bersani's melodramatic 'shattering of the self', nor is there a clear referencing of Lee Edelman's anti-futural 'death drive'. Instead, he sees in Otto a passive indifference to such polemics (as to Medea's political posturing in the film). But this apathy seems to achieve empowerment. Otto is able to 'enact a freedom from the responsibilities and obligations that are the ordinary stuff of life',[42] to ape heterosexual 'coupledom', to seek out one's soul mate, to indulge in gay male promiscuity. He reads Otto as a powerful 'fantasy/model of an agency that is empowered as it is automatized', seeing it as a more useful approach to zombie theory that has in the past, for him, only operated as a metaphor for racial and political difference, infection, consumerism or the savage of the proletarian drone.

Otto's final lonely journey is seen by McGlotten as 'speculatively optimistic' in its refusal of 'self-immolation', living on as if in limbo. His conclusion that Otto's search for 'a whole new way of death' can be seen as a radicalised acceptance of one's own indifference towards life and being inspired to live it anyway, seems perhaps too flaccidly optimistic.[43] If Otto's final search is presented as utopian fantasy, given LaBruce's cynical tone and the film's overt nihilism, I would suggest that this, too, is a futile act. Otto's zombified status (whether the result of an actual

25. The rainbow as a queer symbol halos Otto: *Otto; or, Up With Dead People.*

or symbolic suicide) can be seen as an act of self-divestiture. However, the drive to devalue the self becomes meaningless in the (hypocritically capitalist) economic exchange of Otto by Medea who revalues him as her muse. We can read Otto's journey in two ways: as a symbolic suicide or a journey of discovery into the unknown, both of which will eventually prove unsatisfying. Otto ironically continues: 'At one point I did consider ending it all, like at the end of Medea's movie. But how do you kill yourself, if you are already dead?'

In this final shot, by a rural roadside of saturated yellow fields and blue skies, a rainbow appears behind Otto's head. Framed in this way by the most venerable of queer symbols, Otto's words take on a new resonance. LaBruce's ironic rainbow in the film's final shot simply resets Otto on an indifferent drive (or on 'Auto', as McGlotten fittingly puns) to connect with others like himself, fulfilling societal demands for the communal but facing ultimate disappointment.

Notes

1 The critical analysis of the inherent homosexuality of the vampire myth is undertaken in such articles as Richard Dyer's 'It's in his kiss! Homosexuality as Vampirism and Vampirism as Homosexuality' in *The Culture of Queers* (London and New York: Routledge, 2002), pp. 70–89, and Ellis Hanson, 'Undead', in D. Fuss (ed.), *Inside/Out: Lesbian Theories, Gay Theories* (London and New York: Routledge, 1991), pp. 324–40.

2 See, for instance, Sheridan Le Fanu's *Carmilla* (1872) or Anne Rice's *Interview with the Vampire* (1976) and Poppy Z. Brite's *His Mouth with Taste of Wormwood* (1995) and *Lost Souls* (1997), all of which feature homosexual vampires.

3 Kyle Bishop, 'Raising the Dead: Unearthing the NonLiterary Origins of Zombie', *Cinema in Journal of Popular Film and Television* 33 (Winter 2006): 196.

4 Bishop: 'Raising the Dead', p. 196.
5 Kyle James Twitchell, *Dreadful Pleasures: An Anatomy of Modern Horror* (New York: Oxford University Press, 1987), p. 15.
6 Kyle Russell, *Book of the Dead: The Complete History of Zombie Cinema* (Godalming: FAB Press, 2005), pp. 7–8.
7 Wade Davis, *The Serpent and the Rainbow* (New York: Simon and Schuster, 1985), p. 8.
8 Russell, *Book of the Dead*, p. 24.
9 Peter Dendle, *The Zombie Movie Encyclopedia* (Jefferson, NC: McFarland and Company, 2000), p. 6.
10 Gregory. A. Waller, *The Living and the Undead: From Stoker's Dracula to Romero's Dawn of the Dead* (Champaign, IL: University of Illinois Press, 1986), p. 280.
11 Russell, *Book of the Dead*, p. 88.
12 Russell, *Book of the Dead*, p. 131.
13 See Steve Jones, 'Porn of the Dead: Necrophilia, Feminism and Gendering the Undead', in Christopher Moreman and Corey James Rushton (eds), *Zombies Are Us: Essays on the Humanity of the Walking Dead* (Jefferson, NC: McFarland and Company, 2011), pp. 40–61, for a wider reading of *Porn of the Dead.*
14 Lisa Duggan, *The Twilight of Equality?: Neoliberalism, Cultural Politics, and the Attack on Democracy* (Boston: Beacon Press, 2003), p. 179.
15 Duggan, *The Twilight of Equality?*, p. 179.
16 Ellis Hanson considers the figure of the vampire to be the utmost in monstrous metaphors for the spread of AIDS within the gay community; Hanson, 'Undead', pp. 324–26. The metaphor of the AIDS patient as the dead or 'living corpse' has been acerbically rendered in zombie films such as, *I, Zombie*: *A Chronicle of Pain* (Andrew Parkinson, UK, 1998), in which the infection and decay of zombieism is directly paralleled with sexually transmitted disease.
17 For example, Todd Haynes' *Poison* (US, 1991) features a section entitled 'Horror', a black and white 1950s mad-scientist parody which parodies the 1950s McCarthyist fear of the unseen threat of secret communism and veiled homosexuality.
18 Leo Bersani, 'Is the Rectum a Grave?', *AIDS: Cultural Analysis/Cultural Activism* 43 (Winter 1987): 222.
19 Diana Fuss, 'Oral Incorporations: *The Silence of the Lambs*', in *Identification Papers: Readings on Psychoanalysis, Sexuality and Culture* (New York: Routledge, 1995), p. 84.
20 Fuss, 'Oral Incorporations', p. 92.
21 Fuss, 'Oral Incorporations', p. 92.
22 Jose Munoz defines disidentification as a practice by which subjects outside of a racial or sexual majority negotiate with the dominant culture by transforming, reworking and appropriating ideological impositions from the mainstream. In terms of gay male identification, the subject simultaneously recognises himself in the image of a hypermasculine ideal (symbolised in its purest form in the straight male), but also recognises that it is different from his homosexual self. From *Disidentifications: Queers of Color and the Performance of Politics* (Minneapolis: University of Minnesota Press, 1999).
23 Melissa Carroll, 'Homophobic Zombification: Queer Pustules of Resistance', presented at the 6th Interdisciplinary Conference on Monsters and Monstrosity at Oxford University, 2008; http://www.inter-disciplinary.net/at-the-interface/evil/monsters-and-the-monstrous/project-archives/6th/session-5b-monsters-of-sexuality/ (accessed 11 June 2010).

24 Taken from Bruce LaBruce's website; http://www.brucelabruce.com/ (accessed 11 June 2010).

25 Personal interview with LaBruce by Darren Elliott-Smith, April 2008.

26 Taken from an interview with LaBruce by Jop Van Bennekom from *Butt* magazine 12 (2004): 8–17; http://www.buttmagazine.com/?p=161 (accessed 11 June 2010).

27 Bruce LaBruce, *The Reluctant Pornographer* (New York: Gutter Press, 1997), p. 14.

28 LaBruce, *The Reluctant Pornographer*, pp. 13–14.

29 Taken from an interview with LaBruce by Ernest Hardy, 'Zombie Deep Throat' (2010), cited online; http://ernestardy.blogspot.com/2010/01/zombie-deep-throat.html (accessed 11 June 2010).

30 These include social website *Crawl of the Dead* (http://www.crawlofthedead.com (accessed 14 June 2010)), which advertises zombie pub crawls, festivals and marches across the world, including Iowa's 'City Zombie March', the 'Zombie Walk' in London and Canada, and the World Zombie Day held in London in October 2008. In art exhibitions, undead still-life and performance art is a regular feature. LaBruce himself recently exhibited his 'Untitled Hardcore Zombie' at the Soho Theatre in London and at Peres Projects Los Angeles in 2009. Contemporary zombie also extends to literary appropriation in Seth Grahame-Smith's *Pride and Prejudice and Zombies* (2009), spawning a series of parodic sequels and prequels (*Sense and Sensibility and Sea Monsters* (2010), *Pride and Prejudice and Zombies: Dawn of the Dreadfuls* (2011)).

31 Taken from an interview with LaBruce in 'Rotten to the Core', Michelle Castillo, *New York Press*, 26 May 2010; http://nypress.com/rotten-to-the-core/ (accessed 11 June 2010).

32 Shaka McGlotten, 'Like, Dead and Live Life: Zombies, Queers, and Online Sociality', in Stephanie Boluk and Wylie Lenz (eds), *Generation Zombie: Essays on the Living Dead in Modern Culture* (Jefferson, NC: MacFarland and Company, 2011), p. 182.

33 What McGlotten means by 'soft refusals' is not necessarily a collapse into complete apathy, but rather than the radical queer polemics of Bersani and Lee Edelman, he views Otto's attitude to be 'going with the flow', a 'whatever ...' state of being, or 'another way of conceiving zombie desire not only as deadening drive toward repetition compulsion or explosive *jouissance*, but as desubjectivized way of being "in the flow" of desire'; McGlotten 'Like, Dead and Live Life', p. 185.

34 See, for instance, *No Skin Off My Ass* (1993), *Hustler White* (1996), *Skin Gang* (1999), *The Raspberry Reich* (2004) and *Super 8½* (1994), which feature actual sex scenes between LaBruce and his on-screen love interests. Most were produced and financed by hard-core porn producers with whom LaBruce contracted to release alternative soft-core, theatrical and DVD cuts of their original explicit versions.

35 Matthew Hays, *The View from Here: Interviews with Gay and Lesbian Directors* (Vancouver: Arsenal Pulp Press, 2007), p. 185.

36 Taken from a person interview with LaBruce by D. Elliott-Smith at the London Lesbian and Gay Film Festival, April 2008.

37 Russell, *Book of the Dead*, p. 136.

38 Dendle, *The Zombie Movie Encyclopedia*, p. 6.

39 Here I refer to Linda Williams' phrase which states that the frenzy of the visible further covers up the true artificiality of pornography. In this sense the zombie film's externalising of the body's interior can be read as a similar attempt to authenticate human subjectivity via corporeal exposure. Linda Williams, *Hardcore: Power, Pleasure and the Frenzy of the Visible* (Berkeley and Los Angeles: University of California Press, 1989).

40 *LA Zombie* (LaBruce, GE/CA, 2010) continues the director's fascination with the pornography genre and the monstrous icon of the zombie. The film features a gay alien zombie (gay porn star François Sagat) who encounters various disconnected characters who die, resulting in a necrophilic sex scene between the zombie and corpse. Sagat's zombie proceeds to either penetrate their dead bodies (via various bodily wounds) with an enlarged scorpion-stinger-tipped penis or masturbates over them, ejaculating black alien semen, which has life-giving qualities. Unlike the zombies in *Otto* who are screwed into immortality and continue to remain shambling, rotting zombies, there is clearly a more redemptive element to the undead sex from *LA Zombie* in that the dying and the undead are actually brought back to life or restored in an intact human form.

41 Bersani, 'Is the Rectum a Grave?', p. 210.

42 McGlotten, 'Dead and Live Life', p. 185.

43 McGlotten, 'Dead and Live Life', p. 188.

Part 3

HYBRID BLOODLINES

9

FROM MEXICO TO HOLLYWOOD

Guillermo Del Toro's Treatment of the Undead and the Making of a New Cult Icon

Costas Constandinides

Guillermo Del Toro's border crossing habits classify him both as an 'obedient' and 'disobedient' storyteller. Jenifer Orme in her article 'Narrative Desire and Disobedience in *Pan's Labyrinth*' focuses on 'the refusal of characters to submit to the narrative desires of others'.[1] Orme also notes that the film itself is disobedient as it refuses to 'satisfy audience desires and conventional generic expectations'.[2] Even though Del Toro's work outside Hollywood may reinforce Orme's observation, the fact that Del Toro is complying with the demands of a transnational cinema which is in a direct dialogic relationship with the generic conventions of Hollywood should not be neglected. This relationship is of course one of the reasons Del Toro receives invitations to work in Hollywood. With critically acclaimed titles like *Pan's Labyrinth* (2006) and Hollywood blockbusters like *Blade II* (2002) and the *Hellboy* films (2004 and 2008), Del Toro's treatment of, and interest in, the fantastic cannot be left unnoticed. The Hollywood projects he has worked on and his ability to maintain a diverse approach to the fantastic seal his status as a visionary and a film fan enthusiast.

According to Mike Wayne, 'Hollywood remains a key interlocutor in an unavoidable, unequal but, nonetheless, often productive cultural dialogue.'[3] Wayne notes that Hollywood is the core of popular cinema, thus when a film produced outside Hollywood 'articulates some relationship to popular culture, it at one and the same time strikes up a dialogue'[4] with the dominant paradigms of Hollywood cinema. Wayne proposes two types of engagement: 1) emulation, where international cinema 'adopts the cultural model of the Hollywood film, its narrative strategies, its generic markers and its use of stars';[5] and 2) translation, which 'also seeks some engagement with popular culture as defined by Hollywood, but here emulation gives way to a reworking of such cultural materials, making them "other" to what they once were'.[6] The existing literature on Del Toro makes special note of the fact that the director does not reject Hollywood's narratives and 'unhomely' iconography; on the contrary, his non-Hollywood films are closer to Wayne's second model of engagement with popular culture, which is translation. Del Toro reworks cultural materials shaped by popular horror cinema and places them in a more liberating ideological context, which allows him to focus on the humanness of the characters, while decorating these codes with more exotic trappings.

Del Toro's disobedience is then a mythical notion since his films are carefully constructed in such a way that the de-familiarization of the generic conventions does not lead to aggressive alienating devices, but instead offers different levels of engagement, which are aimed at a wider audience. The emulation of Hollywood codes invites the viewers to identify the cultural materials that influenced his cinema, and the translation of these codes invites the viewers to communicate with the ideologically informed elements of the film. The existing literature on the work of Del Toro very effectively describes his cinema as a hybrid form; this description stems from comparative examinations between Del Toro's work and films or literary works that are usually treated as urtexts of a specific genre or sub-genre. According to Antonio Lazaro-Reboll, 'Del Toro's filmic production is clearly an example of the dynamic process of cross-cultural horror exchange, since it borrows from Hollywood and non-Hollywood filmmaking practices, partaking of diverse international horror traditions, or what could be labeled as transnational horror.'[7] Orme, on the other hand, situates Del Toro's work in a dialectic engagement with literary and filmic fairy-tale traditions.[8] She focuses on Del Toro's employment of the disobedient act in *Pan's Labyrinth*, both a narrative device to set the story in motion and an ideologically informed act against the narrative desires of the central character's stepfather, the fascist Captain Vidal.[9] Orme writes that a film like *Pan's Labyrinth* 'announces its fealty to the fairy tale in the alignment of its heroine with well-known fairy-tale heroines like Snow White, Lewis Carroll's Alice (*Alice in Wonderland*, 1865), and Dorothy of MGM's *The Wizard of Oz* (1939)'.[10] The existing literature on Del Toro's films produced outside Hollywood is of course valuable; however, it seems that it neglects the fact that Del Toro's treatment of the undead not only echoes or reworks the traditions of the fairy tale, the vampire myth and the ghost story, but also pre-echoes and echoes his own ways of telling a story.

The main aim of this chapter is to revisit Del Toro's first feature film, *Cronos* (1993); the chief reason I chose this film to talk about Del Toro's *auteurist* aspirations is because I personally think it is his only film produced outside Hollywood that slightly deviates from the conventions of classical narration. Thus, I discuss *Cronos* in relation to the rest of his work produced outside Hollywood since the narratives in *The Devil's Backbone* (2001) and *Pan's Labyrinth* activate recurring patterns that are already present in *Cronos*, but have been neglected due to the ambiguous role of Aurora (Tamara Shanath), the granddaughter of the central vampiric character, Jesus Gris (Federico Luppi). While in the case of *The Devil's Backbone* and *Pan's Labyrinth*, the alignment that Del Toro establishes between the viewer and the young protagonists (Carlos (Fernando Tielve), the boy in *The Devil's Backbone*, and Ofelia (Ivana Baquero), the girl in *Pan's Labyrinth*) is straightforward, the reading of the role of Aurora in *Cronos* becomes a rather complex task. Her silence is never explained Hollywood-style in the film and one of the interesting questions that this silence triggers is to what extent silence itself activates the fantasy in the film as a form of trauma. Hence, one of the narrative acts that I intend to explore is the 'unrepresentable'[11] absence of Aurora's parents; this unrepresentable narrative invites us to ask key questions that have not been addressed in previous analyses of *Cronos*. Who is telling the story in the film? Who is imagining this indeterminate undead body of the grandfather?

Another character that this chapter revisits is Ron Perlman's role as Angel De la Guardia. The aim of this brief discussion is to compare his role in *Cronos* to his previous acting roles, even though a first reading of his performance in *Cronos* may not invite such a comparison because it is one of those rare times that Perlman portrays a character that is not monstrous or deformed in appearance. However, he has a desire to surgically improve the shape of his nose, which on another level works as a witty subtext. Therefore, I argue that Del Toro establishes Ron Perlman as a cult icon by building a character whose body works as an in-between text. Although Perlman's body does not straightforwardly refer back to his previous roles, the obsession he has with his nose, his sometimes impulsive behaviour and the cartoonish-like misfortunes he experiences with his nose work as a subtle and humorous reference to his previous roles as a deviant body. While Del Toro is very careful not to turn Perlman's presence in the film into a caricature act, it seems that there is this underlying desire to engage with Ron Perlman's previous work, and this comes out as a formless meta-cinematic act, which almost feels like Ron Perlman's presence in the film should be credited as 'Ron Perlman as himself'.

While the discussion of the role of Aurora and of the body of Ron Perlman seem to limit the scope that the title of this chapter sets, I will not neglect to address issues relevant to the ways Del Toro treats the undead, specifically the mythology of the vampire, both in Hollywood and outside Hollywood, by comparing *Cronos* to *Blade II*. A first viewing of these films is quite sufficient to observe that Del Toro seems to be committed to the supernatural and the fantastic. He always creates an engaging cinematic imagery, which is the result of meta-cinematic and intertextual practices of telling the story. The term meta-cinematic is used in the same way it is understood in Bruce Isaac's book *Toward a New Film Aesthetic* (2008); one of the main arguments in Isaac's book is that the term 'meta-cinema' acquires a new meaning when discussed in relation to the images produced by contemporary popular cinema. Cinematic images no longer reproduce reality, but they perform cinematic moments through quotation and generic play. This process 'draws attention to itself (cinematic image) as a component of a manufactured media'.[12] *Cronos* draws attention to itself as a constructed space on a number of levels and therefore this directorial approach allows for a multilevel interpretation of the role of each character in the film. For example, Ron Perlman's presence draws attention to itself through the very fact that he is not portraying a physically grotesque character; Del Toro is aware of this 'domestication' of Ron Perlman's body and seems to activate a comic dialectic between Perlman's role in the film and his previous roles.

From this collision between Del Toro's obedient and disobedient film rhetoric emerges a stylistic conflict. The director's Mexican and Spanish films seem to be enriched by the integration of magical realist elements, whereas in the case of his Hollywood films the result is simply movie magic. The magical realist element may work as an indication that vampirism in *Cronos* is a metaphor for something more humane and basic rather than something subliminal or sublime. The vampire in *Cronos*, I argue, is a metaphor for illness rather than a reinvention of the mythology of the undead. In order to support this argument, I draw on Havi Carel's interpretation of the body in Cronenberg's *The Fly* (1986) in her article 'A Phenomenology of Tragedy: Illness and Body Betrayal in *The Fly*'. Carel's main argument is that the monstrous in the film is a 'metaphor of illness':

> Seth's physical corruption as he becomes more and more monstrous is, in fact, a depiction of illness, and elicits disgust in the viewer that is *identical* to the disgust elicited by physical corruption brought about by illness. The external deformation of Seth as he becomes more and more fly-like, shown so spectacularly in the film, is a representation of the internal destruction and physiological chaos caused by disease.[13]

Interestingly, Carel develops her argument based on Cronenberg's own reading of the film. For example, she begins her essay with the following quote, which she borrows from Rodley's *Cronenberg on Cronenberg* (1992): 'We've all got the disease – the disease of being finite.'[14] The presence (grandmother's obsession with newspaper obituaries) and absence of death (unrepresentable absence of the parents) in the early stages of the film *Cronos* creates a tension that is communicated to Aurora even though the warmth of the house and the antique shop may suggest otherwise. Carel notes in her analysis of *The Fly* that there are references to cancer: 'I suggest that *The Fly* is one of the most complete cinematic portrayals of a cancerous process, from mutation to death, in all its tragic horror. As such, *The Fly* is a phenomenological study of illness, depicting in minute detail aspects of the changes brought about by illness.'[15] Similarly, *Cronos* contains a number of references to cancer and therefore death is imminent in the film as the deterioration of the body is a representation of an internal chaos that is caused by the imminence and repression of death as a narrative. The reason Del Toro names his vampiric character Jesus relates to the idea that he carries a psychological burden and physically suffers in an attempt to contain/control death and master Aurora's trauma.

26. Near-identical arrival of the protagonists in *The Devil's Backbone* ...

While Del Toro's trilogy *Cronos*, *The Devil's Backbone* and *Pan's Labyrinth* raises interesting questions about who is telling the story, his Hollywood products seem to obediently follow the conventions determined by the financially-driven logic of the industry; thus, in *Blade II* and the *Hellboy* films, questions like who is telling or shaping the story and for whom the story is told do not activate the same level of engagement with the text when compared to Del Toro's trilogy produced outside Hollywood. Even though Del Toro's trilogy is not a trilogy in the narrow sense of the term, there are recurring elements in his films that allow for such a labelling. These elements are the child as a narrative of restoration or healing and the absence of both parents, or one parent. The introduction of the main child characters in *The Devil's Backbone* and *Pan's Labyrinth* is almost identical. The stories are set amidst the Spanish Civil War and both the boy in the first film and the girl in the second film are transported by a car to a new space through a wasteland in the first film and through a ruinous landscape in *Pan's Labyrinth*. Their arrival in their new 'homes' activates a narrative of refusal to accept their new reality. In these two films, the foreign dimension or the magical realist element is the result of a more or less predictable narrative, since the story is also linked to an ideological dimension and to the realities of war, which haunt the exchange between inner self and the limits of the external

27. ... and *Pan's Labyrinth*.

space. These conflicts are communicated in a manner that can be easily understood by a wider audience; the child being an ideal character to initiate a shift from the historically specific to a culturally fluid project since it does not symbolise a fixed ideological cause. Lazaro-Reboll's study of Del Toro's *The Devil's Backbone* underlines that 'plot, story, and characterization contribute to a transnational comprehension of the historical background for audiences, and lend themselves to a universal symbolic reading'.[16] Lazaro-Reboll concludes that Del Toro carefully translates his material 'into American generic forms, providing therefore a familiar template and a narrative resolution which resituate the film in American film-going culture'.[17] These choices limit the scope of interpretational schemas that viewers and critics may apply in order to understand the film; in *Cronos*, however, the disintegration of normality is not informed by the consequences of war.

Film Synopsis

Cronos begins with an omniscient voice-over narration about a device that was invented by an alchemist in the sixteenth century, without providing a logical, religious or even scientific account in the manner that a Hollywood film might do about the live matter or insect inside the device; however, it clearly states that the purpose of this device, named Cronos, was to give eternal life to its beholder. After the accidental death of the alchemist in 1937, the only information provided about the device is that it was hidden in the bottom of an archangel statuette. Many years have passed since the day of the alchemist's death, and the same statuette appears in the antique shop of the main character, Jesus Gris (Federico Luppi). Jesus becomes suspicious about the content of the statuette after a strange visit by a man who expressed an interest in the object. Jesus discovers the Cronos device and he starts playing with it in an attempt to work out what it does, but to his great surprise the undead object penetrates his flesh with mechanically operated needles, which look like the legs of an insect. The powerful industrialist De la Guardia (Claudio Brook) is aware of the existence and power of the Cronos device and he is persistently searching for it and sends his nephew Angel De la Guardia to purchase the statuette from Gris's shop. Angel buys the statuette but Jesus keeps the device and he is gradually possessed by it. The device rewards him with youthful energy; however, he develops a thirst for blood. De la Guardia's nephew is instructed by his uncle to harass Jesus, and the latter's refusal to give the device to De la Guardia brings about his temporary death at the hands of the nephew. Jesus wakes up from his temporary death, and with Aurora as his disobedient side-kick they sneak into De la Guardia's factory in order to find the instructions on how to use the device. The De la Guardias try to kill Jesus unsuccessfully and Aurora keeps her grandfather alive by placing the device on his body. Jesus momentarily desires the blood of Aurora, but she prevents him with her voice, which 'tames' Jesus' bestial otherness. Jesus refuses to subordinate himself to the desires of the undead device and destroys it. The destruction of the device signifies his acceptance of death and Aurora's voice her integration into social reality and her understanding of the permanence of death.

The Unrepresentable in *Cronos*

The development of the notion of the unrepresentable in *Cronos* is also based on William Peat's 2009 article 'The Labyrinth of Good Intentions: Transmitting Repressed Trauma via Fairy Tales'. Peat notes that 'several authors claim that fairy tales are indeed beneficial to the well-being of children'[18] and he cites Bruno Bettelheim's view that fairy tales can alleviate the psychological and emotional problems that children experience.[19] Peat also cites Postman's take on Bettelheim's opinion: Postman states that within the context of the fairy tale the narrative of evil can be manifested in a beneficial form as it 'permits children to integrate [evil] without trauma'.[20] Peat reads Ofelia's escape into the liminal magical space that she created as an act of liberation from the limitations of the physical world and the narrative desires of her fascist stepfather Captain Vidal. He also argues that Del Toro invites the viewer to 'witness a child's attempt to reconcile the collision of a harsh, real world with her fairy tale perception of life. Ofelia, the main character of Del Toro's story, uses the fairy tale landscape to transport her consciousness to another place in an attempt to face her fears by believing in something beyond her reality.'[21]

Aurora's silence in *Cronos* indicates that she experiences an emotionally or psychologically tense experience due to the absence of her parents. Her grandfather attempts to heal this tension by writing letters to her, supposedly sent by her parents, but the reality is that her parents are dead. The fact that her grandmother is obsessed with death and her grandfather is depicted as an atemporal character, a fairy tale-like affectionate figure, signifies that Del Toro's treatment of the vampire myth is, consciously or otherwise, a projection of Aurora's perception of time and Aurora's development of mechanisms to defend herself from a form of separation anxiety or death anxiety (she does not know that her parents are dead, maybe because she cannot comprehend the notion of death, but her silence indicates that she went through a traumatic experience). Roger Clark and Keith McDonald's reading of *Pan's Labyrinth* reinforces my argument regarding Del Toro's systematic use of recurrent themes and patterns in his films produced outside Hollywood, as their description of Ofelia's condition in the film can be used to describe Aurora's role in *Cronos*: 'Stranded in a world which makes little sense to her and where her continued safety is at risk, Ofelia gains access to a transformative world in which fantasy acts both as an escape and also as a means of making sense of her situation.'[22] Similarly, Aurora gains access to a transformative world not because she happened to be there when Jesus was threatened and at the same time tempted by the device. Aurora is not an onlooker; on the contrary, the invasive presence of the object acts as a means of making sense of her situation, just as 'the pervasive presence of timepieces, locks, keys and uniformed soldiers'[23] force Ofelia to escape to a different world.

Since Aurora cannot speak and since Del Toro withholds information about her parents from the viewers, I argue that this tension is transmitted externally as a perverse fairy tale; therefore, similarly to *The Devil's Backbone* and *Pan's Labyrinth*, the child, in this case Aurora, is creating the supernatural elements of the story due to an 'unrepresentable' event that disrupted the normality of her upbringing. Slavoj Žižek's psychoanalytic interpretation of the role of the birds in Hitchcock's film of the same title (1963) is useful here as he talks about a disintegration of reality triggered by the mother's (Jessica Tandy) inner space, where the intrusion of the love interest (Tippi Hedren) of her son (Rod Taylor) is seen as a threat (Sophie Fiennes, *The Pervert's Guide to Cinema*, 2006). According to Žižek, the disintegration of reality is the result of a disturbance of the individual's installation/integration into social reality. I would like to isolate this part of Žižek's reading of *The Birds* to argue that *Cronos*'s unhomely dimension is an explosion of Aurora's incapacity to fit into the social reality. This incapacity, which transforms into a tension, is the result of the unspeakable reality of her parents' death. The grandfather does not 'allow' Aurora to communicate her anxieties by explaining the reality to her. He himself approaches Aurora when he does not know how to explain his vampiric condition to his wife and then he allows his granddaughter to care for him and protect him when his body becomes a liminal space: a decaying space that externalises a mental state between madness and dementia. Jesus Gris's carnivalesque and stitched body after his resurrection is both an ode to King Lear and Frankenstein's monster. Jesus Gris's condition forces Aurora to become an adult so as to ease her grandfather's horrifying experience. Aurora has to take on the role of the wife and the daughter to take care of her grandfather and this process equips her with the maturity to face death at the end of the film. Simultaneously, Jesus Gris is abandoned by his biomechanical 'creator', and wanders the streets after the 're-animation' scene in the cremation parlour without being able to comprehend his condition.

The Vampire, the Clown and the Bleeding Nose

Del Toro creates a narrative that plays with familiar codes and cinematic moments, but at the same time he suspends the existing interpretational patterns in the viewers' perception of vampire films by portraying an agonising, yet humane and perversely poetic process of transformation. The fact that Del Toro denies a glamorous representation of the vampire suggests that the aim of the film is not to challenge the cinematic image and mythology of the vampire, but to explore a psychological state of bodily transformation which is closer to humanness rather than a condition beyond life. This is achieved through a combination of traditions and genres including melodrama, expressionism and magical realism. Del Toro's approach raises questions that may initially seem mundane; nonetheless, they become interesting due to the encounter that the main character has with the world of the living (Aurora) after becoming undead.

Cronos is a name associated with Greek mythology, either referring to chronos, the personification of time, or to the Titan Cronus; in the film, Cronos is the name of a clockwork device invented by an alchemist. This name, along with the names of the characters, invites the viewer to make certain associations which are relevant to the grand narrative of Christianity and to Greek mythology. Cronus was the leader of the generation of Titans who were divine descendants of Ouranos, the sky. Cronus deposed and castrated Ouranos and was later overthrown by his sons Zeus, Hades and Poseidon. Oedipal conflicts, hubris and retribution, then, are very powerful narrative acts in Del Toro's films as the characters tend to challenge their limits of power. The image of the vampire is not a collage of charm, eroticism, style and raw energy or aggression; on the contrary, it is an image that is unglamorous: an experiment that went wrong. Since the image of the vampire in the film in question is not really the image we are familiar with, the word 'undead' may become problematic.

One of the moments that reinforces the concluding remark of the previous paragraph is when Jesus Gris instinctively follows a man, whose nose is bleeding, to the toilet during a New Year's party. A medium long shot frames Jesus taking the stairs and then the camera moves continuously with a crane shot and stops to frame the mezzanine level, where the nose bleeder and then Jesus head to the toilets. During this action the camera frames a clown who is dressed as a clock and then follows the famous scene, where Jesus licks a drop of blood from the floor. The subtle element of the clown somehow interrupts the logical flow of narrative and visual information and draws attention to itself in a way that communicates that the film's space and time is made inconsistent; the fact that the clown decorates an event that is not usually decorated with clowns invites a number of readings. Clark and McDonald write that what strikes them about *Pan's Labyrinth* 'is not so much the ways in which the real and fantasy worlds are interconnected by magical portals, but the way in which these realms are revealed as being part of one chaotic, interdependent environment. From the outset, when Ofelia sees a nymph at the outskirts of the forest, it is made clear that the fantasy world is not automatically an alternative to the strife of the real.'[24] Similarly, the clown may be an indication that the transformative world that Aurora and her grandfather experience is not beyond life, but is formed by unwitting transmissions of their inner space in an attempt to speak about death.

In addition, Jesus can see his reflection in the mirror, a choice which suggests that the vampire did not lose his connection to reality; he is not beyond life. Thus, fast healing and the thirst for blood is the result of the bodily fluids exchanged between the insect in the device and Jesus Gris. The transformation is not supernatural but biological. The viewer is denied the familiarity and scopic pleasures of the vampire genre and she is invited to engage with intellectual pleasures that derive from this peculiar treatment of the undead. Del Toro attempts to introduce elements of the fairy tale in the film, which dress the relationship Jesus has with his granddaughter Aurora. These choices seem to pre-echo Del Toro's trademarks outside Hollywood, which are the relationship between a child and a 'foreign' body or space and a loose reworking of the tradition of magical realism.

Interestingly, the clown theme is repeated in different ways later in the film, and these choices create an ambiguous and polysemic portrayal of the vampire narrative. The sophistication and subtle humour of the film deny both the pleasures of parody and superficial action, but at the same time the film makes clever references to the early stage and Hollywood representation of the vampire, specifically Count Dracula. The Count was usually coded as a suave trickster in a tuxedo and in this scene the main character is similarly wearing a tuxedo – due to the occasion, of course – but it nevertheless reminds us of that early image. In the very same scene, Del Toro's vampire seems confident, goes on the hunt and everything seems to be leading to a conventional feeding scene; however, Del Toro disappoints the fans of vampire films. We see a vampire who does not know how to approach his victim, an inept and disorientated character, unlike the dynamic and eroticised moments of feeding in conventional vampire films. The slapstick and comic asides that follow do not function in a conventional manner, but instead they aim to build a character, that is frail and who goes through an involuntary process of transformation. Del Toro's deconstruction of the arrogant vampiric anti-hero continues in the cremation parlour scene where the 'cosmetologist' of the parlour dresses and embalms the body of Jesus; the final result is a clown-like painted face. In general, the infamous coffin moment in every vampire film is demythologised here and treated in a playful manner, thus Del Toro breaks away from the specific mythology by translating the conventional iconography that is usually associated with vampire films.

In the final moments of the film, Jesus confronts Angel on the roof of De la Guardia's factory. Ron Perlman's character expresses an interest in cosmetic surgery throughout the film as he wants to fix his nose. In this scene, the mise-en-scene is fascinating because it is reminiscent of the arrangement of elements in the aforementioned scene where Jesus follows the nose bleeder to the toilets during the New Year party. Perlman is bleeding from his nose while confronting Jesus on the roof of the factory with a huge clock amid the imposing De la Guardia sign. The lighting effect is cold and bluish and Perlman's make-up seems to be intentionally ambiguous; he appears as both monstrous and clownish, thus adding to Del Toro's witty treatment of Perlman's contribution to the history of cinematic monstrous bodies. Perlman's performance in *Cronos* may seem minor, but it is one of his few well-known film performances where he appears without prosthetics. I would argue that Del Toro's treatment of Perlman's character is informed by the actor's previous iconic roles and therefore there is a nuance of a meta-cinematic act in the way the character is obsessed with cosmetic surgery. Therefore the body of the actor performs the character and simultaneously performs his image as a cult icon. Del Toro appears to be mimicking Tarantino's casting practices; the latter selects actors that have been associated with subcultural or exploitation films in order to redefine the cultural value of these traditions. This self-reflexive use of an actor's cultural load is realised here through Perlman's trans-cinematic performance, and Del Toro seems to be the first filmmaker who understands how to use Perlman's body in a clever manner so as to highlight this narrative possibility that his body carries.

The clown make-up motif, along with the elements of the fairy tale, can be read as an attempt to blend the mythology of the vampire with the tradition of magical realism. Lois Parkinson Zamora and Wendy B. Faris write that within the 'limits' of magical realism, 'the supernatural is not a simple or obvious matter, but it is an ordinary matter, an everyday occurrence – admitted, accepted, and integrated into the rationality and materiality of ... realism. Magic is no longer quixotic madness, but normative and normalizing. It is a simple matter of the most complicated sort.'[25] According to Parkinson Zamora and Faris, the fundamental difference between realism and magical realism is that the first model 'intends its version of the world as a singular version',[26] an objective depiction of social realities, in other words 'realism functions ideologically and hegemonically. Magical realism also functions ideologically but ... less hegemonically, for its program is not centralizing but eccentric: it creates space for interactions of diversity.'[27] While there have been interpretations based on an ideological reading of the film *Cronos*, which place emphasis on the film as a form of resistance against capitalism,[28] the eccentric and chaotic space of the film states an intention to subvert, but at the same time interact, with the monologic iconography of Hollywood Gothic as a form of hegemonic and conservative discourse. Aurora does not seem to question the condition of Jesus, and the supernatural is incorporated within the limits of her perception as a normal experience. The eccentric is manifested through the ambiguous use of the clown theme. The clown theme essentially creates a sense of nostalgia for early forms of entertainment and play; at the same time, it communicates a refusal to connect the representation of the vampire or the 'unhomely' in the film to monstrosity and aggression.

The fairy tale, along with magical realism, are further manifested in the scene where Aurora offers her toy chest as a bed 'chamber' or sleeping casket to her undead grandfather. The stitched body of Jesus amidst Aurora's toys blurs the distinction between life, death and artificiality, but these are amongst the few moments of the film where space and colour coding signify human warmth. Aurora welcomes the foreign body of her grandfather in her private space and the latter starts to open up to her and asks her whether she remembers her father, even though he does not say anything about their absence. Aurora perceives the realistic and the supernatural as one chaotic, yet liberating space, which is essentially a representation of Jesus' and of her own internal struggle to master death.

The *Blade* Connection

The storyline of *Blade II* reloads the Oedipal conflict in the evidently influential story of *Frankenstein*. The vampire overlord Damaskinos (Thomas Kretschmann) is a conventional Gothic patriarch who aspires to create an indestructible vampire body to exterminate his arch enemy, Blade (Wesley Snipes). Through genetic experimentation, Damaskinos produces a more powerful, yet monstrous, vampire, Nomak (Luke Goss). Nomak feeds uncontrollably and in turn produces a new breed of vampires (The Reapers), destructible only when exposed to sunlight. Later in the film it is revealed that Nomak is Damaskinos' son, who seeks retribution for his abominable condition. Nomak starts a vengeful war against the 'pure' race of vampires. Blade joins forces with the enemy, to eliminate Nomak and his followers. Before the final titanic fight sequence between Blade and Nomak, the latter kills his uncaring and malignant father; Damaskinos' fall is brought on by his own act of hubris. The film then, similarly to other science fiction predecessors, rearticulates the prosaic questions that emerge from scientific 'arrogance'. Nomak's hybrid body, like Frankenstein's creature and like Jesus Gris, is intentionally abominable and foreign, unlike the 'pure' vampires of the *Blade* trilogy; it projects a loss of continuity and it is a product of the exploration of the limits of an already liminal body: in other words, Nomak is a post-vampire or bio-vampire. Damaskinos' body, on the other hand, functions as meta-cinematic text: his bold head, bent posture, clawed hands and slightly pointed ears are an ode to Murnau's *Nosferatu*. Interestingly, Del Toro's vampires are not products of divine retribution, but are associated with industrial iconography and genetic engineering. These bodies are products of 'illegitimate' science; they are not invaders or primitive monsters, but imperfect bio-organisms.

While scholarly commentaries on Del Toro's work have successfully outlined the intertextual narrative practices visible in his work, they fail to identify the stylistic recurrent patterns and the consistency of his themes in his trilogy produced outside Hollywood. A transformed Gothic sensibility informs *Cronos* and reinforces this chaotic atmosphere that Aurora's trauma unleashes. It may be argued that *Cronos* is a neo-Gothic film, but Del Toro does not mimic American cinema's reworking of the Gothic iconography; its transformation from the Old World decadent iconography to the intimidating qualities of the remnants of post-industrial landscapes and neglected urban landscapes. Del Toro incorporates the factory as a locus of hegemony to communicate a resistance-effect message against the invasion of transnational capitalism and not to simply play with the Gothic trappings that contemporary Hollywood recycles. On the other hand, for the purposes of the *Blade* sequel, Del Toro obeys the monologic and hegemonic discourse of Hollywood and offers interpretational accessibility through a basic intertextual vampire narrative.

On another level, *Cronos* may operate today as a form of resistance to the present vampire and zombie boom. Perhaps the *Twilight*-effect itself aided the maturing process of my point of view on *Cronos*. Hence, the less developed rhetoric that – regardless of my reading of Aurora's role, Perlman's body and Jesus' vampiric behaviour – the film as film breaks away from stagnant narrative and stylistic conventions without rejecting the traditions of the cinema of the undead. On the contrary, the film is a celebration of these traditions and a welcoming invitation to other filmmakers to offer their own translations of the central paradigm of vampire or zombie mythology. Indeed, film directors like Park Chan-Wook (*Thirst*, 2009), Bruce LaBruce (*Otto; or, Up With Dead People*, 2008) and Bruce McDonald (*Pontypool*, 2008) have produced their own takes on these mythologies; and while products like the *Twilight* saga and *True Blood* have triggered a newfound scholarly interest in the undead, maybe our scholarly search for new 'blood' should also be directed towards international cinema or transnational horror cinema so as to discover new interpretational pleasures of the cinema of the undead.

Notes

1 Jennifer Orme, 'Narrative Desire and Disobedience in *Pan's Labyrinth*', *Marvels & Tales: Journal of Fairy-Tale Studies* 24:2 (2010): 219.
2 Orme, 'Narrative Desire and Disobedience', p. 219.
3 Mike Wayne, *The Politics of Contemporary European Cinema: Histories, Borders, Diasporas* (Bristol: Intellect, 2002), p. 73.
4 Wayne, *The Politics of Contemporary European Cinema*, p. 73.
5 Wayne, *The Politics of Contemporary European Cinema*, p. 73.
6 Wayne, *The Politics of Contemporary European Cinema*, pp. 73–74.
7 Antonio Lázaro-Reboll, 'The Transnational Reception of *El espinazo del diablo* (Guillermo Del Toro 2001)', *Hispanic Research Journal* 8:8 (2007): 46.
8 Orme, 'Narrative Desire and Disobedience'.
9 Orme, 'Narrative Desire and Disobedience'.
10 Orme, 'Narrative Desire and Disobedience', p. 220.
11 Knoepflmacher states that traumas are 'fictive deflections from an unsettling past that has become unrepresentable'; U. C. Knoepflmacher, 'The Hansel and Gretel Syndrome: Survivorship Fantasies and Parental Desertion', *Children's Literature* 23 (2005): 176–77.
12 Bruce Isaacs, *Toward a New Film Aesthetic* (New York: Continuum, 2008), p. 137.
13 Havi Carel, 'A Phenomenology of Tragedy: Illness and Body Betrayal in *The Fly*', *Journal of Media Arts Culture* 4:2 (2007); http://scan.net.au/scan/journal/display.php?journal_id=95 (accessed 24 October 2011).
14 David Cronenberg in Chris Rodley (ed.), *Cronenberg on Cronenberg* (London: Faber & Faber, 1992), p.128.
15 Carel, 'A Phenomenology of Tragedy'.
16 Lázaro-Reboll, 'The Transnational Reception of *El espinazo del diablo*', p. 42.
17 Lázaro-Reboll, 'The Transnational Reception of *El espinazo del diablo*', p. 43.
18 William Peat Jr, 'The Labyrinth of Good Intentions: Transmitting Repressed Trauma via Fairy Tales', *The Looking Glass: New Perspectives on Children's Literature* 13:1 (2009); http://www.lib.latrobe.edu.au/ojs/index.php/tlg/article/view/132/127 (accessed 24 October 2011).
19 Bruno Bettelheim, *The Uses of Enchantment: The Meaning and Importance of Fairy Tales* (New York: Knopf, 1976).
20 Neil Postman, *The Disappearance of Childhood* (New York: Vintage, 1994), p. 94.
21 Peat Jr, 'The Labyrinth of Good Intentions'.
22 Roger Clark and Keith McDonald, '"A Constant Transit of Finding": Fantasy as Realisation in *Pan's Labyrinth*', *Children's Literature in Education* 40 (2010): 56.
23 Clark and McDonald, '"A Constant Transit of Finding"', p. 54.
24 Clark and McDonald, '"A Constant Transit of Finding"', p. 56.
25 Lois Parkinson Zamora and Wendy B. Faris, 'Introduction: Daiquiri Birds and Flaubertian Parrot(ie)s', in Lois Parkinson Zamora and Wendy B. Faris (eds), *Magical Realism: Theory, History, Community* (Durham, NC: Duke University Press, 1995), p. 3.
26 Parkinson Zamora and Faris, 'Introduction', p. 3.
27 Parkinson Zamora and Faris, 'Introduction', p. 3.
28 See John Kraniauskas, '*Cronos* and the Political Economy of Vampirism: Notes on a Historical Constellation', in Francis Barker, Peter Hulme and Margaret Iversen (eds), *Cannibalism and The Colonial World* (Cambridge: Cambridge University Press, 1998), pp. 142–57.

10

'NOLLYWOOD, OUR NOLLYWOOD'

Resisting the Vampires

Nicola Woodham

Far from being products of folk belief or a clear-cut representation of the extractions of a dominant power, vampire stories articulate relationships and offer historians a way into the disorderly terrain of life and experience in colonial societies.

Luise White[1]

We need look no further than civil society and the visual arts scene in Nigeria to realize the consequences of donor dependency. Our artists have no time or interest in producing work for impoverished Nigerians who cannot afford to buy their overpriced uber-abstractionist works. The Nollywood filmmaker in contrast makes films for the masses. The masses are his bread and butter. Without the danfo driver in Ajegunle or the market woman in Mushin, his films would not sell and he would go out of business. The Nigerian visual artist on the other hand does not need his fellow Nigerians to survive as long as s(he) has enough Western expatriates patronizing him.

Anonymous[2]

The bus is a Mercedes, but for Divine it's much more than that. 'What's inside that bus is Nollywood,' he says, 'my entire film, everything inside that thing.' The thing slows down and comes to a stop next to him, and then his film squeezes itself out through a sliding door: 15 young actors and assistants, loaded onto the bus at Winnies and booked for two weeks. It also contains an HD camera, a cameraman, a director, two plastic bowls filled with

> cassava porridge and spicy chicken, three lights, a microphone, an Adidas bag full of costumes, a few bottles of Guinness and the generator. And three stars. 'It all comes to $38,000,' says Mr. Divine, pointing out that 'That's the trick, making films with next to nothing.' Mr. Divine, the head of Divine Touch Productions Limited, has a real name: Emeka Ejofor.
>
> Dialika Krahe[3]

Nollywood is the video film industry largely based in Nigeria[4] that grew out of a landscape with few resources for investment in locally produced cinema. An aridity resulting from restrictive economic policies can be attributed to the World Bank and the International Monetary Fund, their Structural Adjustment Programmes (beginning in the 1980s) depleting the standard of living via the reduction of social expenditure. Up until then, the definitive cinema of Africa was Francophone African cinema,[5] largely funded from foreign investors and distributers. It was in the early 1990s, however, that some self-funding entrepreneurs in Nigeria began the production of hugely popular feature-length video films.[6] One such direct-to-video film is *Living In Bondage* (1992), directed by Chris Obi Rapu and produced by Kenneth Nnebue. This thriller paved the way for future Nollywood directors with its dramatic story of ritual murder and vengeful haunting. Themes of greed, jealousy and occult oppression proved popular and as technology progressed more groups of producers invested in more readily available digital video equipment to make low-budget films to distribute at an affordable price on VCD (video compact disc). Distribution is controlled by central markets, for example the Onitsha Market in Lagos, but pirating has a huge impact on the availability of films.[7] Many movies are seen on pirated copies. To date, the US$250 million industry generates over 1,000 films a year,[8] in a range of genres from action movies to supernatural films. Nollywood has its own awards ceremony, the African Movie Academy Awards, and annual film festivals. Hence, the Nollywood pioneers created an enormous opportunity to tell stories about Nigerian life by Nigerian filmmakers and actors. These bold films could be criticised for being melodramatic, as we are pulled into sometimes epic, emotional journeys with scenes of graphic sex and violence. The style can be abrasive with sometimes distorted sound and loose narrative threads, issues that are recognised by producers and are gradually being addressed.

Production values vary, but what always comes across is the drive of producers who want to make an average $20,000 stretch to cover costs. The video films have many different audiences. Onookome provides a detailed account of the 'street audiences', who include standing audiences, who view videos playing at video and music stalls, and 'video parlour' audiences, who pay a small fee to view a film, usually in a small room with television and video player set up.[9] Also, there is much talk of new cinemas being built in Lagos, such as the 'Silverbird' cinemas, but arguably these show mainly foreign imports at a high cost. Nollywood films are notably consumed in the diaspora via markets (such as London's Ridley Road market in Dalston) or via the internet. For example, Nollywood Love Channel on YouTube is the first to buy licenses for Nollywood films, thus effecting some return for the filmmakers.[10] Nollywood producers have shown that a video film industry can grow outside the usual structures for production, where digital technologies can ease the financial pressures of cinefilm production and for distribution and reception.

This activity is long awaited, and seeks to amend an imbalance. While filmmaking cultures thrived across the developed world, countries colonised by the British were denied cinematic autonomy to a large extent. Africa was being documented in film from the 1930s onward, but films such as those made by the Colonial Film Unit (established in 1939) portrayed Nigerians as 'other' and uncivilised. These developmental and educational films were 'about' the African populace and narrators addressed a white Western audience. This filmmaking existed in parallel with Hollywood films that misrepresented African religions and ways of life. While a counter voice existed in Nigerian television, that thrived from before independence and via feature film producers such as Segun Olusa, Francis Oladele and Ola Balogun, who were making films in the 1970s, it is Nollywood that has put Anglophone African cinema on the map.[11]

Undoubtedly, the producers use a film language that was consolidated in the Hollywood studio film era of the 1930s and 1940s and often the films do follow the three-act paradigm. Notably, the USA has monopolised film distribution in Nigeria, and foreign imports abound. However, on a political level these comparisons still suggest a hierarchy that is not useful to the Nollywood project. Indeed, it was this ambivalent relationship with Hollywood that drew my attention to Nollywood films. One of the starting points for my research into the Nollywood occult films I was examining was the concept of the 'voodoo construct' coined by artist and writer John Cussans.[12] In his paper, Cussans uses examples from popular films to comment on the voodoo construct; motifs that make up the construct include the voodoo witch doctor, voodoo curse and voodoo doll. As I see it, the voodoo construct provides a way of looking at how Yoruba-derived religions have been rationalised and adapted for use in modes of Western consumption, such as mainstream cinema. For me, after seeing semblances of these motifs reappear in Nollywood occult-themed video films, I wanted to think about the significance of these motifs in the context of contemporary Nigerian cinema.

Notably, the films I was looking at were produced as part of evangelical propaganda, and to some extent the producers slipped into the shoes of Hollywood directors as they, too, were involved in a demonisation of animistic beliefs. My research led me to conduct several interviews with two Nollywood directors, Teco Benson and Prince Emanuele Sam Uzochukwu, as I wanted to find out about their influences and ask whether they set out to challenge stereotypes that abound in Hollywood voodoo and to reclaim them for stories that take in a contemporary approach to religion. The directors wanted to talk about Nollywood and to step out of the shadow of Hollywood and I found myself needing to shift emphasis away from such comparisons. It became more important to consider the conditions of the production of the films in more detail and the history of film production in Sub-Saharan Africa and to look at the position of these occult motifs specifically within Nigerian popular video film. The strange hybrid, the Nollywood vampire, remains, and it is he and she that sheds light on the complex relationship between production, distribution and consumption of the video films discussed below.

I first presented my interviews with the directors alongside an analysis of two films in 2009, at the Cine-Excess III conference 'Beyond Life: The Undead in Global Cult Media'. At the time, I was keen to highlight that the Nollywood filmmakers were currently aiming to give a boost to the Nigerian economy by finding international investment for their export, but I have subsequently revised this view. Putting distribution in the hands of the government and external investors is not necessarily going to ensure a return for the country. I initially resisted making a textual analysis of the films, feeling that writing about films that are clearly a response to the lack of self-representation via the media in Africa was not my place as a Western film writer. I was wary of practising a form of intellectual theft by attempting to analyse the films without first-hand experience of the Nigerian condition. But I am now more concerned that this might lead to a certain kind of political reticence. Since then, it has become important to look at the vampiric impact of neoliberal capitalism on Nigeria and the possible use of the vampire motif as a tool for commenting on and creating rumours about social anxieties particular to contemporary Nigeria. I am also indebted to the Nollywood directors I interviewed at the time for their frank insights about their work. What I present here is textual analysis informed by anthropological and film theory. The film I will focus on is *Armageddon King (1* and *2)* (Ralph Nwadike, 2003). This film can be described as an example of Nigerian evangelical horror where the horror derives from dramatic depictions of the occult and its perpetrators, whether in the form of a Christian Satan or a folkloric vampire or sorcerer. The climax of the film involves an epic face-off with the forces of evil, conducted by an evangelical pastor who aims to establish cosmic and earthly equilibrium. This video film provides an indication of the social and moral anxieties and concerns of Nigerian filmmakers working in the Nollywood industry at the time of writing and the way these anxieties can be combated with religious faith. As I see it, this is done by taking familiar stories that have a grounding in folklore and combining them with contemporary scenarios set in mostly urban Nigerian locales to make them relevant to today's Nollywood audiences.

In the first part of this chapter I will analyse the significance and function of a key incarnation of the undead, the vampire, and look at how this is used to comment on the current moral and political atmosphere of Nigeria. In the second part, I will look at the use of special effects to suggest spiritual power and energy. I shall also consider the comments made by Nollywood directors I interviewed about the role of faith in the films, and their own moral agendas. The dynamic between these two sections is a victory of one over the other, evil overridden by good, social malaise erased by faith in the power of religion.

Vampires and 419 Culture

In *Armageddon King 1* and *2* (Ralph Nwadike, 2003), a member of a vampire coven, Zaza (Rita Nwanko), falls in love with a police detective (Emmanuel Ehumadu). She begins to ask questions when she discovers that her skin doesn't burn up in daylight, like her sisters'. She discovers that she has not yet been fully transformed into a vampire. Eventually, there is a battle between an evangelical pastor and the head of the coven, Cabal, who is defeated ... but is he? Cabal seems to still be alive amidst the flames he is burning in.

While I don't want to suggest that these narratives are a direct reflection of society, I do think the filmmakers use fiction to make subversive comments about financial inequality in Nigeria. Indeed, the people who populate the narratives of these films are caricatured versions of the rich and the poor. In *Armageddon King 1* and *2* the vampire motif is used more as a symbol to criticise a vampiric social dynamic of the rich utilising their power to make money out of other people's labour rather than as a reference to actual current beliefs. This metaphorical quality ascribed to the vampire figure resonates throughout literary and film history, from Sheridan Le Fanu's Countess Karnstein in *Carmilla* (1872) to the urban yuppies that populate *The Hunger* (Tony Scott, 1983).

In *Armageddon King 1* and *2*, the images are slippery, and metaphors merge and blend. A point of interest is the set-up of the vampire 'colony', as it is called by the vampire characters in the film. First off, we have a brilliant reappearance by Alex Usifo Amaigbo, who played Beelzebub in *End of the Wicked* (Benson, 1999) among many roles. He has a growling voice and regal demeanour as Cabal, the leader of the coven. Here, the vampire sect have a 'cover' as prostitutes and pimps. The vampire women go out and lure clients into dark corners, where they get more than they bargained for and become prey for these girls who are literally 'surviving on the street'. Cabal is part-paternal, part-lewd in his treatment of the girls and fits the bill as a kind of 'uber pimp'. The black uniforms and trilby hats pulled over the faces of the men in the colony add to this gangster image, and more particularly 419 men – 419 refers to the part of the Nigerian Criminal Code that relates to fraudulent crime and is used as a short cut to suggest a culture of fast wealth, usually made by fraudulent means.[13] Thus, the vampire motif has a slippery, metonymic quality within this narrative. The colony

28. Nollywood vampires: *Armageddon King 1.*

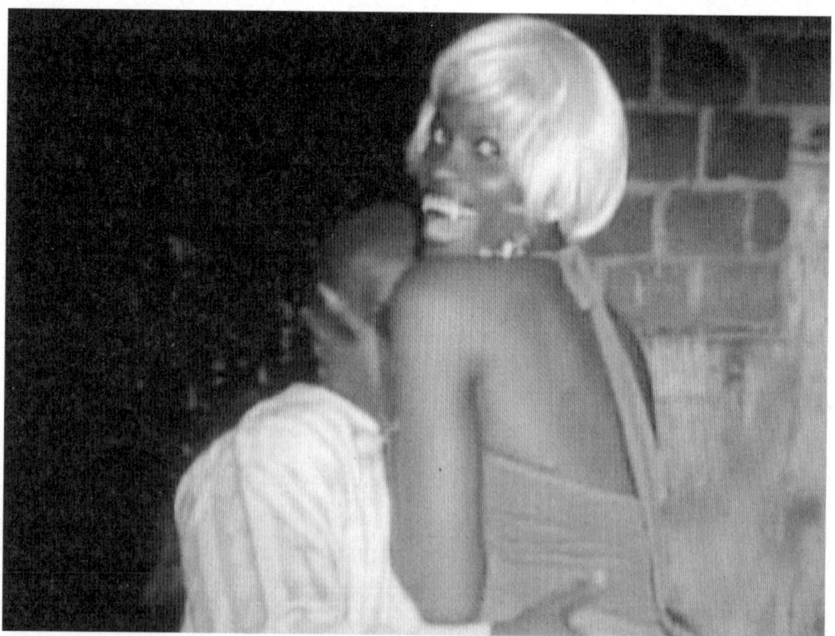

29. Vampires and 419 culture: *Armageddon King 1.*

survive as pimps and hookers but they also serve, I think, to comment on corruption in contemporary Nigeria. These vampires/419 men are not let off the hook at the end and are characteristic of a broader picture of unscrupulousness that the film paints. Later on in the film, as detectives try to solve the numerous murder cases, it is also revealed that vampires have infiltrated the local police force, who have been ordered to arrest anyone and everyone to solve the crimes, even innocent citizens. So the story puts together an image of a Nigerian town where the local criminals are as lawless as the police.

The naming of the vampire sect as a 'colony' is surely another indication that the vampire motif is being used to resonate with the idea of a fear of invisible societies operating within visible society. This suggests bad memories of colonisation by the British and at the same time picks up on a current popular concern amongst the film directors and their audiences about the danger of people 'working on their own' and not pulling together as part of a unified society. The leader's name, Cabal, also carries echoes of secret political privileges. Here, names and characterisation within the narrative are multi-suggestive, poetic and allow for an unpacking that points to folklore and current political and moral anxieties. This poetic slippage or hybridisation of motifs and themes is a feature that characterises the films as a whole. This is part of the filmmakers' agenda to create recognisable situations that resonate with Nigerian concerns. They allude in a loose, caricatured way to current issues and concerns for the makers. These producers depict the nature of a malaise, where people are using other people and benefiting from financial inequality in a vampiric way.

I would suggest that it is no coincidence that the vampire motif is used to specifically talk about economic injustice. It is not just a narrative device, nor is the backdrop of corruption based on financial disproportion just an interesting foil to the presentation of the power of faith. There is a tradition of linking the vampire with economic drainage or using someone's labour for another's gain in Sub-Saharan Africa storytelling and rumours. The function of vampire tales has been discussed in anthropological and historical studies. Luise White in her detailed study of vampire tales, *Speaking With Vampires: Rumour and History in Colonial Africa* (2000), looks at the way vampire stories were used as a way to discuss fears about colonialist theft and power in East and Central Africa during the colonial period. Here, vampires are real people, in known society, not supernatural beasts in hiding. She writes extensively about the way these tales circle around the truth; they are rumours and hard to pin down. They sound fantastic; in one story that White registers, colonialists and their employees who have imposed new administrative procedures and social control on traditional ways of life become blood-sucking monsters, who hide their victims in pits. White prioritises the study of rumours in the form of vampire stories as a vital source of information about people's attitudes to colonialist inequality. She interviewed over 130 participants.

> The result [of her research] is not a history of fears and fantasies, but a history of African cultural and intellectual life under colonial rule, and a substantial revision of the history of urban property in Nairobi, of wage labour in Northern Rhodesia and the Belgian Congo, of systems of sleeping-sickness control in colonial Northern Rhodesia, and of royal politics and nationalism in colonial Uganda.[14]

Also, Brad Weiss's ethnography of the Haya of Tanzania shows that rumours of blood-stealing and selling continue in contemporary East Africa; the Haya use these rumours to explain rapid accumulation of wealth. These rumours express connections between bodies and commodities, semantic value and economic transactions, rural livelihoods and urban travels as well as local 'experience' and global 'events'.[15] Even though Sub-Saharan Africa is no longer under colonial rule, arguably these tales are still used to talk about social inequalities.

In *Armageddon King 1* and *2*, the vampire motif is used to suggest corruption and economic inequality in a metaphorical way. But also the idea of the 'vampire' as a being that literally sucks the life out of one person for their own gain is a useful one here for the directors who want to talk about corruption and people holding power over people. So the vampire motif is useful for tracing a trajectory that began with colonialists pillaging primary sources from Sub-Saharan Africa and insisting that Sub-Saharan Africa take on the Western capitalist modes of production. The use of the motif then becomes useful as a means to comment on the failures of the industrialised society that was set in place during the period of colonialism of Sub-Saharan Africa by Great Britain – the failure of oil companies and state governors to distribute the profits from oil extraction to the people of the Niger Delta, for example. Arguably the extreme financial inequality in Sub-Saharan Africa can largely be traced back to the shift in value of pre-industrialised modes of production, from production for sustenance with a patron–client economic structure to the values of neoliberal individual-based free-market economies. The vampire image allows for a comment on both colonialism and its legacy: the value of personal wealth and consumerism, profiteering, pressure to compete in market trading and exporting, and various forms of corruption that endeavour to sidestep any obligation to fairly distribute wealth.

Daniel Jordan Smith has looked at the dynamic between Nigerians' attitude to 'fast wealth' and their attitude to social responsibility. He points out that Sub-Saharan Africa houses both patron–clientist economic structures and neoliberal market economic structures. It's a social ideal and many do still uphold the idea that any gain should not be coveted by the individual but shared out, mainly by a patron or by the head of the family. This is still a form of inequality, but it is based on obligation and seen as more reliable that neoliberal individualism. Many Nigerians still hope that they, too, will have a share of the 'national cake' if they bolster economic growth and compete on the global markets.[16]

The relationship between shifts in modes of production and belief in the supernatural is an interesting one. The vampire motif, which in Nigeria is closely associated with sorcery and witchcraft, allows directors to comment on problems that arise when societies that have been based on patron–clientism and kinship shift to capitalist market economies. Anthropologist Peter Geschiere notes that rather than a reduction of witchcraft beliefs occurring as a result of industrialisation and 'development', there is an increase in supernatural motifs used in rumour and storytelling in Sub-Saharan Africa since colonialism, and an increase in witchcraft accusations. Daniel Jordan Smith, in response to Geschiere,[17] has looked at the rise of supernatural motifs used in rumour and storytelling in Sub-Saharan Africa since colonialism:

> Nigerian stories of satanic rituals and occult practices in the pursuit of wealth also point to tensions and ambivalence as people experience the entanglements of class and kinship. Nigerians recognise that, in the present period of rapid social change, individual desires increasingly conflict with widely shared values

> of social obligation. In both popular Nigerian discourse and in anthropological literature, diverse practices of the occult have been glossed as 'witchcraft'. Witchcraft accusations have been widely linked to tensions produced in kinship relations marked by the volatile mixture of intimacy and inequality ... With increasing urbanisation, the penetration of a capitalist market economy, and post-independence opportunities for the Nigerian elite to enrich itself by looting the state, inequality has reached unprecedented levels.[18]

The function of the supernatural in societies, including Sub-Saharan Africa, is complex. It can be argued that this form of magical thinking is a way to explain the unknown or the new. Silvia Federici comments on Michael Taussig's classical work *The Devil and Commodity Fetishism in South America* (1980) in her book *Caliban and the Witch* (2004). She writes:

> ... the author maintains that devil-beliefs arise in those historical periods when one mode of production is being supplanted by another. In such periods not only are the material conditions of life radically transformed, but so are the metaphysical underpinnings of the social order – for instance, the conception of how value is created, what generates life and growth, what is 'natural' and what is antagonistic to established customs and social relations.[19]

The vampire then, unprovable and existing in the realm of rumour, is a fitting figure for these metaphysical explorations and any discourse around them; especially when the ontological status of the new mode of production, here capitalist market economy, is in flux. As a system that more and more relies on virtual layers of debt, it becomes more abstract, while the real impact of shrinking market growth is materially felt. The vampire is also the being who sucks the life out of an individual, the act of consumption defining him/her. First, he or she is the producer, profiteering on the life blood (labour of others), and second, a tragic consumer who is caught up in the endlessness of the cycle of desire, feeding and the return of desire that mimics the state of the neoliberal capitalist consumer.

These anthropological studies are useful for understanding some of the moral dilemmas that are current to Sub-Saharan Africa. Given that the producers do mention that the portrayal of contemporary moral issues are on their agendas, I think this is illuminating. Also, when we consider the reception of the films, and audience studies that look at how the films function as part of a dialogue amongst viewers who create a counter voice in response to financial inequality, I think it is relevant to consider the actual conditions for production of the films and how the content of the films resonates with this.

As discussed, the ontological status of vampires is difficult to define – they exist in the realm of rumour. These video films also function in the realm of rumour in the way they are received and viewed. Often they are passed from hand to hand, stories are told and retold between viewings and during viewings. The occult tales are gossiped about, the inequalities are discussed, the social messages are repeated, and in the process the world is 'put to rights'. This verbal speculation around the viewing of these video films is the subject of a paper by Onookome Okome, 'Nollywood: Spectatorship, Audience and the Sites of Consumption' (2007), who sees this disorderly discussion about the films as a force in itself.[20] This uncontrolled dialogue of solidarity, during and around film viewings, is a vital form of mobilisation against inequalities, economic and social. Nollywood dramas about vampires take up their place as part of rumour and are used to make sense of moral and social anxieties. In this way their distribution and their actual current position in the 'independent' mode of production is what gives them their potential and power. This independent mode of production is one that exists as a parasite of market economy modes and can feed from its donor mode while potentially subverting it from within.

The Power of Faith in *Armageddon King 1* and 2

If *Armageddon King 1* and *2* allow for a reflection upon financial inequality, then they also allow for a reflection on the importance of collective action that can rebalance this. Nwadike builds up a picture of power and greed, but this is a means to an end, not the end in itself. In the discussions I had with two filmmakers in April 2008, it was this portrayal of African-centred morality in Nollywood video films that was given as one of the main motivations for making them. I interviewed Teco Benson (*End of the Wicked*, 1999; *Mission to Nowhere*, 2008) and producer and writer Prince Emanuele Sam Uzochukwu from Sam Civic Investment Productions (*Rising Moon*, 2005, directed by Andy Nwakalor). As Teco Benson pointed out:

> [W]e don't want the cinema to work on Western influence. This time we actually try to tell our stories from our perspectives. Because before the advent of Nollywood we saw African people from the perspective of the Westerners. We saw films which were being released in Hollywood. But the democratisation of the media is an opportunity to tell our stories from our perspectives. African stories for African people. African people can identify with the stories, they love them.

He went on to say that the films were important in that they were an opportunity to portray an African, rather than a Western, morality. 'People are beginning to wake up to the reality of life, they are having the self-esteem to accept themselves the way they are. We have a culture which is a lot to do with morality and respect for elders. The Western culture that we have seen in Hollywood films has destroyed our culture.' When I asked him if he thought that Nollywood filmmakers were consciously challenging or reconfiguring Western stereotypes, he replied, 'We are trying to portray people the way we are, we don't believe in confrontation.' Indeed, the making of these video films is part of building a filmmaking culture that attempts to rebalance the effects of non-Africa-centred or non-Africa-funded films that were previously made in Nigeria, or simply to jump-start an industry that had to overcome obstacles in the past.

There are a number of reasons for the lack of films to come out of Nigeria before the emergence of Nollywood. One reason is the agenda of the Colonial Film Unit. While documentary and educational films were prioritised, drama and feature filmmaking were not. Tom Rice points out that one type of such filmmaking was that produced by the Colonial Film Unit in Nigeria in the 1940s and 1950s, which left a legacy that needed to be erased. Quoting Ikechukwu Obiayahe, he argues that the legacy of colonial cinema within independent Nigeria was hugely restrictive and continued to prioritise traditional forms of documentary and developmental film.[21] Even at the end of the colonial era in the late 1950s, films produced by the Nigerian Film Unit used British camera-operators with local filmmakers still in assistant roles:

> Nigeria's moves towards independence were still represented and conceived by British, rather than local, filmmakers. Furthermore, while the film was supposedly intended for local audiences on the mobile cinema circuit, in its mode of address and content, it serves primarily to introduce northern Nigeria to an international audience. Colonial influences and interests remain at the fore.[22]

This idea of the 'mode of address' is key, and places a Nigerian audience off-centre, and more seriously, assumed in many instances that Nigerian audiences were incapable of complex film interpretation, a depressing moment in film history that revealed the racism underlying the Colonial Film Unit.

Any Nigerian-funded and produced filmmaking in the independent era was also limited by the monopolisation of American distributers. This meant that any possibility of growing African production and distribution was limited. With imports came the Hollywood misrepresentation of Africa, but beyond that, stories that were entertaining but not familiar to an African audience. Both filmmakers in the interviews said that Hollywood had influenced them, and they had watched a lot of 'foreign movies', mainly from the USA. Benson said that he had access to foreign films via VHS cassette which he watched at home, and told me that anything that was screening in Hollywood was available on cassette. He explained that Nigerian cinemas failed due to lack of government investment and the majority of people not being able to afford to go. Uzochukwu was a fan of the same movies. But both went on to emphasise that they wanted to use these Western genre films as a springboard for African concerns. Uzochukwu said he made his films using stories which were 'familiar to him'. He even said he didn't watch other Nollywood films because he didn't want anything to sway his thought – he was interested in making films which 'touch people'.

Therefore, even though there is an acknowledgement of Hollywood films evident in Nollywood hits, with their Western production methods, use of traditional production roles and classic film language, these are seen by the producers as tools to allow African tales and motifs to come through. If Hollywood is beneficial for any part of the Nollywood project, it is in the way filmmakers reconfigure all sorts of combinations of Hollywood signifiers to create rich films that defy genre classification. *Armageddon King 1* and *2* are part crime thriller, part occult horror and part religious epic. This bricolage technique can also be noted in the treatment of faith in the films. In this section, I want to look closely at some of the special effects techniques that are used to engage the audience. While access to budgets for special effects is limited, Nollywood filmmakers have created a style with the use of low-budget effects and limited effects software packages. Full use has been made of special effects to manifest the unseen; particularly, it can be argued, in portraying the transferral or draining of spiritual energy.

The special effects in *Armageddon King* 2 use superimposition and chroma-key to create dramatic manifestations of the devil and vampiric energy as it draws life out of its victims. At one point, a vampire on his hunt attacks his victim by splitting into three floating heads and attaching a lightning fork from each to his victim. Like a quivering ghost-busting spider, he zaps his prey. Also, the colony is visited by their supreme beings, who appear in diamonds of silvery light above the colony shrine. The effect is just an illustration of a drawing of the horned ones superimposed on some layers of colour, but animated to great effect. The deep voice and looming position are impressive.

At the end of the film there is a face-off between Cabal and a pastor in an evangelist church. The idea of two belief systems colliding and battling for supremacy takes shape in shrouds of glowing light around the characters. It is joined by orchestral, library, ripped music. Typical of Nollywood is the lightning-bolt effect, where tendrils of light exude and lock onto the fighters. This lightning-bolt motif is a symbol of the passage of energy, produced from low-budget technology; the effects are not slick but they provide a sense of spectacle. But beyond the spectacle, the bolt is a spectre of the history of the passage of energy, transfusions and draining within post-colonial cultures. The effects in this scene are in tune with the tone of evangelist sermons: repetitive, incantatory, fervent and relentless. When all is done and good defeats evil, the light subsides, and evil Cabal rolls over on the floor, dead. Normality resumes. Just as the vampiric tales Luise White wrote about were poetic and creative, so too these videos are propelled with creative flair.

Filmmakers have for a long time embraced the use of effects to suggest alternate realities. For Nollywood filmmakers, I think this strategy has a special significance as Nigerian belief systems are multifaceted and video allows for a clear depiction of different realities via the use of different effects in each one. Hollywood techniques are reconfigured and formulas are hybridised to form the new Nigerian cinema that is generated from these low-budget video films.

With regard to *Armageddon King 1* and *2*, what's exciting about films like these are not just their Western popular culture references, or an analysis of the positive effect of their low-production values. The revelation is the pure fact that something as overfamiliar and rehashed in Western popular culture as the vampire story just hasn't ever been made before on video from this homemade Nigerian perspective , although, as I have argued, the vampire motif is well used as part of Sub-Saharan African folklore as told orally or in literature. Up until now, technology simply wasn't in the hands of Nigerian creatives to comment on the immoral act of 'sucking another's blood', of taking energy unfairly from another, of draining the pot, of not putting in what you take out, especially in terms of material wealth and human compassion.

What came across from both filmmakers is the level of personal investment that has been involved in dedicating their lives to making films. For both, their personal efforts are inextricable from their interest in seeing Africa develop on a national level. This resonates with the opinion of an anonymous forum poster on the internet forum *Nigerian Village Square, A Market Place for Ideas*:

> Nollywood is our very own child of circumstances. It evolved in the milieu of the collapse of the cinema infrastructure/network in the 1980s plus the state of insecurity in major urban centres which drove would be cinema-goers from the cinema halls, abandoning them to be taken over by Pentecostal churches. The traditional Hollywood movie production and distribution marketing model of cinema release followed by video cassette/ DVD release was turned on its head by Nollywood with direct release to video cassette and nowadays VCD or DVD. This was not deliberate; it was a response to the prevailing circumstances. Over time, this has become a new and revolutionary mode of film production freeing the African filmmaker from the historical

> constraints of seeking funds from governments local or foreign to make films.[23]

For Nollywood to grow in the conventional economic sense, many producers and government representatives believe that the government should intervene and assist with more legislation to fight piracy, and external funding (India's EXIM Bank has shown interest in funding films) to fund films and to market them abroad. This may work as a short-term solution, but the underlying issue remains. If Nollywood is to compete in global market economies, does it just end up feeding the source of financial inequality that so many of its films set out to lament, and in some cases subvert? One option for producers is to keep distribution independent and use online platforms and subscription fees as a way to avoid state intervention and to keep profits for themselves.[24] An ideal distribution strategy that exists within a neoliberal economy will always have shortfalls.

Notes

1 Luise White, *Speaking With Vampires: Rumour and History in Colonial Africa* (Berkley: University of California Press, 2000), p. 10.

2 Anonymous, 'Nollywood, Our Nollywood', *Nigerian Village Square* (forum) (2006); www.nigeriavillagesquare.com (accessed 17 July 2011).

3 Dialika Krahe, 'Nollywood's Film Industry Second only to Bollywood in Scale', Spiegel Online International (2010); http://www.spiegel.de/international/world/0,1518,690344-3,00.html (accessed 17 July 2011).

4 'Nollywood' is largely based in Nigeria, but the term also refers to films made in other Sub-Saharan African countries such as Ghana.

5 Okome Onookome, 'Nollywood: Spectatorship, Audience and the Sites of Consumption', *Postcolonial Text* 3:2 (2007): 1–21.

6 Onookame posits that this new culture of recording onto VHS stems from the use of VHS tapes to record and sell documentation of local theatre productions. The popularity of these Yoruban spoken performances on tape paved the way for the production of video films. Eventually these films were made in 'English and Pidgin English, and the main themes that engaged early Yoruba video producers changed from the mythological world of the Yoruba pantheon into the "ghettoized" world of the new urban world that Lagos represented'.

7 Johnathan Haynes, 'Video Boom: Nigeria and Ghana', *Post Colonial Text* 3:2 (2007): 1–10. 'The basic structures of the video business are similar in Nigeria and Ghana. The marketer/distributors, based in Opera Square in Accra and in Idumota Market in Lagos, with other Nigerian centers in the Igbo cities of Onitsha and Aba and the Hausa city of Kano, have effective control of the market. They are the main

source of capital, as banks and other formal sector institutions are wary of the film business.'

8 Unesco Institute for Statistics, *Information Sheet Number 1: Analysis of the UIS International Survey on Feature Film Statistics* (UNESCO, 2009).

9 Onookome, 'Nollywood: Spectatorship, Audience and the Sites of Consumption', pp. 1–21.

10 Interview with Jason Chukwuma Njoku, founder of Nollywood Love Channel on YouTube; http://www.youtube.com/watch?v=PXVP9gjro1M (accessed 19 July 2011).

11 Manthia Diawara, *African Cinema, Politics and Culture* (Bloomington: Indiana University Press, 1992).

12 In a talk entitled 'Voodoo Terror: (Mis)Representations of Vodu and Western Cultural Anxieties' (presented for 'Feels Like Voodoo Spirit – Haitian Art, Culture, Religion, The October Gallery', London, 14 October 2000).

13 See Daniel Jordan Smith, 'Ritual killing, 419, and fast wealth: inequality and the popular imagination in southeastern Nigeria', *American Ethnologist* 28:4 (November 2001): 803–26.

14 White, *Speaking With Vampires*, p. 6.

15 Brad Weiss cited in David Samper, 'Gossip and Rumour', in Philip M. Peek and Kwesi Yankah (eds), *African Folklore An Encyclopedia* (London and New York: Routledge, 2004), pp. 152–53.

16 Jordan Smith, 'Ritual killing, 419', p. 807.

17 Peter Geschiere, *The Modernity of Witchcraft: Politics and the Occult in Postcolonial Africa* (Charlottesville: University of Virginia Press, 1997).

18 Jordan Smith, 'Ritual killing, 419', p. 819.

19 Silvia Federici, *Caliban and the Witch Women, the Body and Primitive Accumulation* (New York: Autonomedia, 2004), p. 170.

20 Oonokome: 'Nollywood: Spectatorship, Audience and the Sites of Consumption', pp. 1–21.

21 Ikeckucwu Obiaya, 'A Break with the Past: The Nigerian Video-film Industry in the Context of Colonial Filmmaking', *Film History: An International Journal* 23:2 (2011): 149–46.

22 Tom Rice, Nigerian Film Unit (2010); http://www.colonialfilm.org.uk/production-company/nigerian-film-unit (accessed 15 November 2011).

23 Anonymous, 'Nollywood, Our Nollywood'.

24 Femi Odugbemi, 'The Future of Film Distribution in Nigeria', *Nigerian Films.com* (2010); http://www.nigeriafilms.com/news (accessed 15 November 2011).

11

THE ULTIMATE SUPER-HAPPY-ZOMBIE-ROMANCE-MURDER-MYSTERY-FAMILY-COMEDY-KARAOKE-DISASTER-MOVIE-PART-ANIMATED-REMAKE-ALL-SINGING-ALL-DANCING-MUSICAL-SPECTACULAR-EXTRAVAGANZA

Miike Takashi's *The Happiness of the Katakuris* as 'Cult' Hybrid

Steve Rawle

The Happiness of the Katakuris (*Katakuri-ke no kôfuku*) was just one of seven Miike Takashi films produced in 2001. Coming in close proximity to key Miike works like *Ichi the Killer* (*Koroshiya Ichi*, 2001), *Visitor Q* (*Bijitā Q*, 2001) and *Dead or Alive: Final* (2002), *Katakuris* is a surprising, startling experience, even for audiences familiar with Miike's work. The conventional promotion of Miike's work situates his cinema within a rhetoric of excess and violent, sometimes misogynistic, content.[1] The audience had been primed for a Miike whose work was shocking, disgusting, aggressive, agitational and, above all, very violent, often with a sexual overtone. But *Katakuris* does little of this; there is no overt violence, chastened sexuality, no shocking excess, and it's not extreme. This is a film that won't test the limits of the hardest of male filmgoers, as the press around extreme movies would have us believe, unless, of course, the film were simply too happy, too deliriously upbeat and too musical for your average (assumed), 'discursively constructed' Asia Extreme viewer.[2]

This chapter will explore *The Happiness of the Katakuris* not, as critics would dub it, as a 'zombie musical', but as a hybrid generic experience typical of cult cinema. By examining the film's critical reception, which generally struggles to grasp the hybridity of the film's intermingling of generic traditions or attempts to explain it via recourse to the organising logic of the *auteur*, the chapter will argue that *Katakuris* provides a more transgressive and hybridised cult experience than its reception, and promotion, has tended to endorse. In addition, the argument will position the film in close proximity to key social and economic circumstances that help historicise the thematic and narrative concerns of the film (those not necessarily shared by its source material). Subsequent discussion will also set the film in the context of recent Japanese cinema in the generic referents upon which it draws, namely the musical and the zombie-horror film. While *Katakuris* can be seen as a hybrid experience, it is not an isolated occurrence in Japanese cinema, although it might be seen as something of a forerunner of some generic traditions (certainly those eventually reaching the West).

Eastern Star's 2008 DVD release of *The Happiness of the Katakuris* promotes the hybrid zombie-musical pleasures of the cult text. Above a wavy psychedelic title banner, there is a strap line that proudly pronounces '*The Sound of Music* meets *Dawn of the Dead*'.[3] The images also support this positioning of the film: below the title, the six members of the Katakuri family are shown running and dancing through a green field, mountains in the background. Above the mountains is superimposed a transparency of the film's sequence in which bodies rise from the grave and dance. This is echoed in the UK Tartan Asia Extreme release (2003), the strap line here, above the same image of the family, 'The hills are alive with the sound of screaming!' Once more, this promotes the transgressive quality of the film's main generic referents, alluding to lyrics from *The Sound of Music*, once a mainstream blockbuster, now a text appropriated by cult audiences. Below the title of Tartan's release reads a tagline that again promotes the transgressive quality of the film's combination of disparate elements: 'Love. Music. Horror. Volcanoes. Cinema was never meant to be like this!' Both releases here promote the film's two main pleasures: the transgression of generic norms (although with a skewed prominence given to two main supporting generic strains, the musical and the horror film), and the role of the *auteur* in organising this (both designs put Miike's

30. Film poster for *The Happiness of the Katakuris.*

name above the title of the film: Takashi Miike's *The Happiness of the Katakuris*).[4] Largely, as I will explore later in the chapter, these are the two main critical and popular responses to the film's cult hybridity, although that hybridity is often ungraspable, and, again dictated by the promotional efforts of Eastern Star and Tartan, dictated by the promotional efforts of the distributors in the West. It is worth noting, however, that this is not echoed in the Japanese releases: one of the Japanese posters simply places a photograph of the family, captured in ironic musical performance pose (this was also the main image in the Hong Kong marketing) over a simple green field background under the bold title (in *romanji*, but without the wavy psychedelia of the Western distribution). Other posters included a mocked-up cover for a karaoke single, complete with disc poking out of the top, referring to one of the musical sequences in the film. The variances here point significantly to differences in popular pleasures for different audiences, nationally and regionally, and the promotion of the cult film experience in low-budget Japanese cinema, something that will also be seen in other Japanese films drawing on zombie film traditions.

A brief synopsis of the film is required at this point. *The Happiness of the Katakuris* concerns itself with a representative Japanese family set upon by hard times. Masao (Sawada Kenji) is a shoe salesman who is made redundant in the economic recession of the 1990s. When he learns of plans to build a new road, he decides to set up a guest house in the countryside to take advantage of the new opportunity. There he moves with his family, his wife Terue (Matsuzaka Keiko), white-collar criminal son Masayuki (Takeda Shinji), recently-divorced daughter Shizue (Nishida Naomi), her daughter, and the film's narrator, Yurie (Miyazaki Tamaki), Masao's father Jinpei (Tanba Tetsurô) and their dog Poochi. When the road fails to emerge, the family find themselves at odds, and when a guest finally arrives, he does so to commit suicide. Upon finding the body, the family decide to bury it nearby in order to protect the family (because Masayuki is suspected). Fortunately, another guest, a famous sumo wrestler, and his young schoolgirl girlfriend, soon arrive. However, he dies during sex and smothers the girl. Again, the family decide to bury the bodies. Meanwhile, Shizue has become involved with a conman, Richâdo Sagawa (Imawano Kiyoshiro), who claims to be the nephew of the Queen and a member of the British and US armed forces. When Jinpei confronts Richâdo, the hustler falls to his death in a cliff-top fight (which is rendered in claymation). When an escaped killer on the run arrives, pursued by police, the family panic, and decide to relocate the bodies. This is interrupted, however, by a nearby volcanic eruption (again in claymation) that solves all the family problems (even though we're informed of Jinpei's death soon after); the family are united by working together, and the guest house is relocated to a more useful locale. The film is also liberally interwoven with musical numbers, mostly upbeat ironic rock numbers, including one karaoke ballad, and the film is shot in multiple, sometimes conflicting, styles. From an *auteurist* perspective, however, the film avoids the nihilistic determinism that is so often associated with Miike's work, and, although it was released in Tartan's Asia Extreme range, can't be conventionally pigeonholed as 'extreme'.

Cult *Katakuris*: Transgressing the Boundaries of Genre

Katakuris is undoubtedly a shocking film in its transgression of conventional generic and stylistic standards, especially when one considers the popular reputation of its *auteur*. Unlike the earlier *Visitor Q*, which covers very similar thematic territory with lashings of lactating nipples, incest, necrophilia and rape, *Katakuris* aggressively and surprisingly transgresses the boundaries of genre and style, combining multiple genre codes and styles, becoming a hybrid[5] of:

1. Family Comedy
2. Disaster Movie
3. Horror Film
4. Murder Mystery
5. Claymation
6. Karaoke Video
7. Musical

Notions of hybridity are at the heart of conventional scholarship surrounding cult cinema and their attendant taste cultures. Umberto Eco's textual notion of the cult film, in his seminal analysis of *Casablanca* (Michael Curtiz, 1942), prioritises the formal dimensions of hybridity that are exemplified by *The Happiness of the Katakuris*: as he alleges, 'in order to transform a work into a cult object one must be able to break, dislocate and unhinge it so that one can remember only parts of it, irrespective of their original relationship with the whole'.[6] The cult film[7] has hybridity built into its very make-up, as may be exemplified by other cult films, such as *The Rocky Horror Picture Show* (Jim Sharman, 1975), which similarly casts the musical in the context of the science fiction pulp narrative that affectionately lampoons the cinema of the 1950s. Where a film like *Rocky Horror* diverges from Eco's placement of the cult film is in its historical circumstances, that the film is considered a cult film not because of its textual features but because of its adoption by Midnight Movie cultures, and by a hard-core audience of aficionados who *use* rather than consume the text. While Miike's film has attracted some audience participation features (examined later in this chapter), it is clear that the film is not in the same league of cult cinema activity as

Rocky Horror, despite its audience using the film to promote specific cinephile tastes.

While Eco's conception of the cult film presents a textual hybridity that is 'cultural', Jeffrey Sconce, in his seminal article on paracinematic taste cultures, positions marginal taste cultures in opposition to more mainstream taste. His Bourdieu-inspired thinking envisions cult cinema communities' attachment to paracinematic texts outside the mainstream, often outside their initial historical circumstances, as presenting 'a direct challenge to the values of aesthete film culture and a general affront to the "refined" sensibility of the parent taste culture. It is a calculated strategy of shock and confrontation.'[8] One of the most observable phenomena of audiences' adoption of cult Asian cinema is an oppositional stance toward Hollywood cinema's perceived redundancy, paucity of ideas and creativity. The cult Asian cinema text is thereby adopted as a signifier of cultural difference, one that uses that text to announce an oppositional cultural taste that adopts the more marginal text in order to reject the mainstream 'parent taste culture'.[9] Miike's work is not necessarily totally divorced from mainstream cinema, as the recent success of *13 Assassins* (2010) in Japan demonstrates, representing a mainstream breakthrough for Miike that has been a long time coming in his home nation, despite the relative cult success of some of his films in the West. Where the adoption of Asian cinema is more problematic is where audiences see cult cinema *as* mainstream tastes, or as emblematic of traditional or mainstream cinema, essentially that 'all Japanese cinema is like this'. An amateur film critic posting video blogs on YouTube, Bad Movie Guy, in a review of *Katakuris* presents the film in just such terms, calling it in the process a 'masterpiece'. The description of the film, though, promotes such a conception of Japanese cinema, which could certainly be described in Orientalist terms: 'A Japanese horror/musical/ comedy! That's right, only in Japan could a movie like The Happiness Of The [sic] Katakuris get made!'[10] The reviewer's conceptualisation of Japanese cinema is derived from the experience of films like *Katakuris*, which determines the film as typical of a cinema that is routinely 'crazy' or 'weird'.

Ernest Mathijs and Xavier Mendik, in their introduction to *The Cult Film Reader*, offer a deconstruction of the different conceptions of 'cult' that are invoked to designate and define a cult film text or experience. At a macro level, they identify four textual and cultural elements that construct or define cult cinema: anatomy (its textual features); consumption (reception); political economy (exhibition and ownership); and cultural status (the film's contemporary location).[11] For the purposes of this discussion, I am concerned with two of these: anatomy and cultural status. Under the heading of anatomy, Mathijs and Mendik offer eight further categories that come to determine the cult film text's anatomy: 'innovation' (on a level of form and in the context of film history); 'badness' (otherness, oppositional tastes or the rejection of conventions); 'transgression' (the destruction of moral, stylistic or political barriers, in terms of 'crudeness' or 'inventiveness'); 'genre' (within genre norms or in defiance of them); 'intertextuality' (quotation, cannibalisation or playfulness); 'loose ends' (narrative openness, either due to complexity or ineptitude); 'nostalgia' (the idealisation of the past); and simple 'gore' ('yukkie stuff').[12] Determining the 'cultural status of cult film' involves four further categories: 'strangeness' (what is assumed to be ordinary to one culture becomes 'strange' once it crosses national boundaries); 'allegory' (the assumption of metaphor to lend 'cultural weight'); 'cultural sensitivities' (a problematic category between exploitation of culturally sensitive issues – including misogyny and non-Western ethnicities – or a commentary or subversion of them); and 'politics' (the cult film's ideological dimension, drawing on the previous attitudes toward exploitation or subversion).[13] Several of these categories help to determine the textual anatomy of *Katakuris*, as well as its cultural status. While it might be difficult to position the film as innovative in the sense of Mathijs and Mendik's examples, which include works by Godard and Buñuel, it certainly invokes tropes of 'badness', especially through its use of performance, particularly musical performance, irony and a rejection of conventions. The film is rooted in its generic hybridity, where multiple genres are intertextually referenced or culled from a transnational economy; nostalgia is textually evoked, while gore is present, although minimal. The cultural positioning of the film, especially its perceived 'strangeness' in popular and professional criticism, and the context of Japan, politically, socially and ideologically, will be explored throughout the following discussion as a means of situating the film's contemporary themes and metaphorical allegory, even where the film tends to transgress logic, the boundaries of genre and national/transnational meaning.

In addition to the cult reading of the film, however, hybridity points to other national and transnational dimensions of meaning. As Joyce E. Boss has argued, responding to the general inadequacy of what she sees as the 'too easy and potentially meaningless' theorisation of the consequences of hybridity, 'recognizable instances of hybridity – in characters, genres, texts, and such – call our attention to larger unresolved social issues involving identity and power'.[14] Like other Miike work, *Katakuris* engages with this aspect of globalisation.[15] Therefore, we might see this extended into its inclusion of the undead, the past, and slippages into nostalgia and a general lack of clearly signified borders between genres, styles, tones, logics, politics and time-spaces. Likewise, this implicates the borderlessness of transnationalism that implicates issues of social identity and 'nation' in the work.

Although the film might be considered as typical of Miike's body of work (typical in its lack of typicality, in that it transgresses the expectations of the Miike branding), it is also a remake of Kim Ji-Woon's popular Korean black comedy, *The Quiet Family* (*Joyonghan Gajok*, 1998), although it bears little similarity to that film. Although Kim's film is broadly comedic, the tone and style of the film is unified, and certainly contained by a more consistent and stabilising logic of narration and characterisation than Miike's reinterpretation of the work (which, it has to be noted, is not just down to individual stylistic choices on the part of the makers, but also down to budgetary limitations).[16] Like Kim's film, Miike's focuses on attempts to reunite and protect the family unit, although *The Quiet Family* prioritises the family's complicity in covering up and keeping quiet together. Where the two films share an important point of connection is in their shared use of the female narrator. As Anthony C. Y. Leong notes, 'the events depicted may be apocryphal, being the product of an overactive imagination'.[17] Similarly, this is echoed by Tom Mes' argument that Miike 'employs a visual style derived from a child's own creative expressions'.[18] Miike doesn't use the device to call attention to the potentially subjective nature of the events depicted (as he does in *Audition* (*Ŏdishon*, 1999), for instance), but to justify logically a stylistic and generic treatment that defies external logic. Yurie witnesses rather than participates in the narrative's events, although she narrates from a position of adulthood rather than from childhood, which may call into question processes of memory (or the subjective creation of memory) and nostalgia (one of the key elements Mes detects in Miike's work),[19] as well as potentially accounting for the more outlandish treatments of the narratives, such as the musical numbers, the emergence of zombies and the ludicrous deus ex machina that resolves the story and brings happiness to all.

Culturally Positioning the Cult Text

The role of happiness in *Katakuris* is an important consideration for the film within Miike's oeuvre. Some critics have dismissed Miike's work as nihilistic, or symptomatic of a generation indoctrinated into consumerism with few limits to transgress and no political agenda.[20] And, similar to *Visitor Q*, this is framed in a film that focuses on the damaging fallout from the 1990s' complex recession that put an end to the economic miracle and the bubble economy of the 1980s. Katakuri Masao, the head of family, fits the key demographic of many workers laid off between 1993 and 2000, where major enterprises targeted gradual staff reduction in the range of 15 to 30 per cent. Senior staff were targeted in particular – Katakuri-san is presented to us as a senior shoe salesman, a typical salaryman subject to the 'senior staff shock' (*kanri shoku*). White-collar workers in particular were subject to this phenomenon, especially senior staff between 45 and 50, where redundancies were prioritised for workers near the top of salary scales. Between 1993 and 2000, net job losses totalled 1,870,000, with 'senior staff shock' accounting for 225,000 jobs losses in 1993 alone.[21] Jean-Marie Bouissou refers to this period as the end of the Japanese Model, a serious and aggressive threat to traditional stability and economic progress. *The Happiness of the Katakuris* taps directly into this economic and social situation for its scenario, in relocating the film to Japan, drawing on similar contextual circumstances to *Visitor Q*. Katakuri-san in particular represents those senior figures made redundant in the period following 1993. Rather than suggesting a nihilistic and abnegating loss of social cohesion and destruction, the film works to promote happiness, as, despite the challenges the family must overcome, the Katakuris are reunited, deliberately by Masao as a process of recovery, although that recovery engages with the traumas of death, the suspicion of murder by his son, and a killer on the loose. Again, like *Visitor Q*, but unlike the resolution of

Dead or Alive (*Dead or Alive: Hanzaisha*, 1999), where the world is literally destroyed for its rootless protagonists, the engagement with exceptional circumstances helps the family find partial restoration and recovery from the political and social circumstances that threaten prior stability.[22]

Explorations of 1990s Japanese cinema have tended to see the recession as playing a key determining role in establishing social and political themes. In addition to this, the Kobe earthquake and sarin gas subway attacks of 1995 have helped to develop a picture of Japanese trauma that extends beyond the economic to all sectors of family and public life. This is a traditional matrix of despair that others have identified in Japanese culture. Colette Balmain sees 'the syntax of despair, emptiness and isolation ... expressed thematically and formally by Japanese horror cinema' in a cycle of 'devastation and renewal' that she traces back to the seventeenth century.[23] Into this 'syntax' of contemporary despair, *Katakuris* makes its appearance. The film is also contemporary with key examples of the J-Horror, where Balmain properly locates the syntax at its most pronounced. But whereas the J-Horror cycle engaged with the destruction and emptiness of modernity, Miike's response takes a different path.[24]

'The rise of new media, DVD in particular,' Mitsuyo Wada-Marciano has written, 'has altered the trajectory of cultural flow worldwide toward a decentralized model of multiplied venues that are less beholden to the theatrical screen.'[25] Talking specifically about the rise of the phenomenon that came to be called J-Horror, Wada-Marciano argues that the loose movement's growth was facilitated by the rise of DVD as a popular media for home consumption. 'The timing of its appearance was fortuitous, since the genre has both a sufficient mass of existing narrative content in novels, manga comics, and television programs, and speed in generating new content, whether shot on film or video, to meet the demand of the growing DVD market.'[26] While not specifically a part of the J-Horror phenomenon, despite its close proximity in timing and the inclusion of some generic horror content, *Katakuris* benefits heavily from this shifting market condition. Again, as Wada-Marciano argues, due to 'the genre's affinity with the DVD format, J-horror has extended its reach through an enormous amount of works and broadened its parameters'.[27] Like earlier works to which Wada-Marciano refers, such as *Onibaba* (*Onibaba'a*, Shindo Kaneto,

1964) or *Ugetsu* (*Ugetsu monogatari*, Mizoguchi Kenji, 1953), *The Happiness of the Katakuris* has been subsumed into the mass of cinema being released as or in proximity with J-Horror (partly due to its collocation with the Asia Extreme marketing), mostly due to Miike's *Audition* being identified as part of the genre, and due to the proximity of the film to the overriding themes and social connections made by J-Horror to which Balmain referred. Therefore, the film tends to be described in a very limited generic range by critics.

As a sampling of reviews demonstrates, professional and amateur critics have tended to pigeonhole the film as a 'zombie musical', preferring to highlight the generic horror qualities of the film and its cross-fertilisation with what may seem to be its polar opposite, the musical. For instance, in response to a call for recommendations on a horror film website, a respondent who recommends the film simply and forcefully promotes it: 'It's a zombie musical from Japan!'[28] Another blogger, calling themselves Gaijin Otaku Gundan, in response to the film's appearance on Jonathan Ross's short *Asian Invasion* series, calls it simply a '[d]eliriously funny zombie musical'.[29] In both cases here, there is a tendency for the reviewer, either through the identification of Japan or through the established *otaku* credentials, to promote a cultural positioning of Japan that emphasises cultural difference (highlighting the film's 'strangeness', to return to Mathijs and Mendik's taxanomy of the cult text, while also revelling in its generic transgression), or demonstrates the countercultural capital of the viewer through their immersion within the Other culture. It is not simply enough that the film's pleasures can be established through the quasi-generic hybridity of the 'zombie musical' (although this is limited to just one scene in the film), but that it is 'a zombie musical from Japan!' Japan here becomes a signifier of *otaku* cool, of difference where the, as previously mentioned, 'only in Japan' argument is emphasised.[30]

Other critics have tended to emphasise this generic categorisation, once more demonstrating an ungraspable hybridity of the film's generic construction. In *Asia Pacific Arts*, the magazine of UCLA's Asia Institute, the film is described as 'a pioneer in a groundbreaking new genre: the zombie musical'.[31] Mark Schilling, the film critic of the *Japan Times*, simply calls it 'the first Japanese zombie musical'.[32] Scott Morris, reviewing in *The Oneliner*, pronounced the film to be 'perhaps the best example of a zombie musical in existence',[33] while Nick Dawson in *Empire* claimed that Miike 'bizarrely, uses the medium of zombie musical to show the charmingly shambolic way in which he embraces good-old family values – a feat that has to be commended'.[34] The *New York Sun*'s Grady Hendrix comes closest to grasping the hybridity of the film, however, when describing it as a 'low-budget zombie/musical/hotel management/black comedy'.[35] Although the 'zombie musical' distinction is central to the promotion of the film's marginal and sub-cultural appeal, there is a tendency in the critical response to the film to promote both the generic positioning of the film in the novel cult category of the zombie musical (despite its very marginal presence in this film) and to stress the film's main pleasures within the transgression of generic norms, although the actual instance of transgression is much more substantial than the single zombie musical scene suggests. In sampling reviews like these, however, there is also a tendency to assume the Otherness of Japan, the unique cult exoticness of its cinema and the appeal of a cinema that is assumed to be of a paradoxical homogenised heterogeneity ('only in Japan').

As previously mentioned, this was certainly something primed by the marketing of the film, and the '*Sound of Music* meets *Dawn of the Dead*' sound bite. While there are superficial similarities to both movies, namely the green grassy hills on which the film ends and the appearance of zombies in one scene, the marketing was reductive and more or less pre-empted the critical response that saw this as a 'zombie musical'. The attempt to position the film within the boundaries of a single genre ignores its cult sensibilities, its transgression of genre boundaries and the sheer lunacy of its camp appeal. Curiously, though, the initial US marketing by Vitagraph films did not play up this generic category, tending instead to highlight the entertainment of the film, its musicality, but with the 'terrormonger' Miike as a stabilising referent to promote the transgressive quality of that entertainment.

In one of the few serious, if brief, analyses of the film, Ian Conrich still cannot help but highlight the 'zombie musical' part:

> Takashi Miike's absurd melange of ideas that focuses on the challenges met by a family attempting to run a mountainside chalet, in film [sic] that is in places inspired by *The Sound of Music*. A guest at the chalet who successfully commits suicide becomes

> the subject of a musical number performed by the hotel owners upon their discovery of the body. Later, the corpse, accompanied by several other unfortunate dead and buried visitors to the chalet, returns from the grave to perform a group zombie musical number.[36]

Conrich hits on a much more productive line of critical enquiry, however, when he attributes the film to a line of cult musicals that includes *The Rocky Horror Picture Show*, *Joe's Apartment* (John Payson, 1996), *Cannibal! The Musical* (Trey Parker, 1993) and Troma's *Poultrygeist: Attack of the Chicken Zombies!* (aka *Poultrygeist: Night of the Chicken Dead*, Lloyd Kaufman, 2006). Later examples might also include *Repo! The Genetic Opera* (Darren Lyn Bousman, 2008), a camp rock opera about a future in which human organs are available on payment plans, and are repossessed accordingly. In these films, rightly located as cult musicals, both through their reception, cultural placement and textual features, Conrich notes that 'musical performance in each cult film needs to be placed in a context where, most commonly, the programmatic text can be seen as a violation of conventions'.[37] So, while Conrich doesn't devote a great deal of time and space to a detailed analysis of *Katakuris*, he does locate it within a rather limited body of cult musicals that display a recurring textual feature, if not always a consistent cult reception. The film hasn't spawned the cult midnight movie performances between film and audience that we see with *Rocky Horror* or *The Sound of Music*, although there are rules for '*The Happiness of the Katakuris' Drinking Game*'![38]

Although Conrich argues that the cult musical sees the programmatic text as 'a violation of conventions',[39] Miike's film does fall under musical convention when we consider its, to use Richard Dyer's term, 'utopian sensibility'.[40] Dyer argues that the desire for utopian resolution in entertainment, generally located in the musical, responds to social conditions at the time, that 'entertainment *works* ... to [address] specific inadequacies in society'. Entertainment broadly 'is not just what show business, or "they", force on the rest of us, it is not just the expression of eternal needs – it responds to real needs *created by society*'.[41] The musical is a specific expression of this form of response to the social needs of the times in which the text is produced. *The*

Happiness of the Katakuris therefore responds very strongly to generic convention in this respect, just as we might see the transgression of sexual norms in *Rocky Horror* doing so. The social and economic circumstances outlined above constitute a response to inadequacy, the 'senior staff shock', and the need, not for desperate action to restore previous norms, as in *Visitor Q*, but for utopian resolution. As Dyer notes, the usual separation of narrative from number in the musical is where the narrative figures a sense of utopian recovery, rather than just the numbers. He argues that this 'gives a historical dimension to a musical, that is, it shows people making utopia rather than just showing them from time to time finding themselves in it'.[42] In this sense, while the generic categorisation and structure of the film is transgressive of the norms of the musical, there is a shared focus on utopia and the development of utopian structures and sites. The final musical number of the film, having survived the volcanic explosion, is entitled 'That's Happiness!' The family, now united through the events of the narrative, find utopia from despair when the guest house is uprooted and located fortuitously in an idyllic countryside location, perfect for business. Although the number informs us of the death of Jinpei, the tone remains upbeat, ironic and uninhibited. So, while Masao took the family to the guest house to find utopia, only the restorative transformation of the film's narrative can determine the form that utopia will take. Other sequences in which the family seek utopia turn out to be either frustrated (the discovery of the death of the first guest) or false (Shizue's romance with the conman Sagawa). The binary that Dyer locates in the musical between scarcity and abundance is realised in this final sequence, conforming very clearly with the generic conventions of the musical.

Despite this, there is a knowing referentiality about the film and its invocation of the super-happiness of the musical. There is certainly, partly due to the film's filtering through a child's imagination (although remembered *a posteriori*), a camp aesthetic at play, where the film quotes from other film genres, defies logic (the totally redundant opening of the film in the restaurant in which a claymation creature steals a woman's uvula) or slips between genres. At times the tone is ironic and the style highlights the artificiality of the scenario. This is evident in two of the musical numbers: first, when the family discover the first guest's body, the number is an over-the-top overwrought rock

31. The zombie dance in *The Happiness of the Katakuris.*

number, with aggressive non-naturalistic lighting, canted angles and highly codified gestural performances; and second, in the romantic ballad between Masao and Terue, which is conceived as a karaoke video, complete with lyrics at the bottom of the screen. As Susan Sontag argued, camp thrives on the synthetic, the quoted and the simply outrageous. '[T]he essence of camp,' she contends, 'is its love of the unnatural: of artifice and exaggeration.'[43] As Tom Mes frequently contends in *Agitator: The Films of Takashi Miike*, Miike's aesthetic is founded on exaggeration, of style and representational content, an aesthetic that here flows over into camp. Steven Cohan alleges that the musical's camp reputation is a consequence of the genre's 'formal concerns correspond[ing] with (in the sense of paralleling but also addressing) the dialectical operations of camp as an ironic engagement with the incongruities of the dominant culture's representational systems and hierarchal value codings'.[44] This is rendered here on the level of excess, the use of formal artifice, and the invocation of incongruity, incoherence and changes in tone, both formally and sentimentally. While elements of these may also be seen in other Miike films, the ironic deployment of tone, specifically happiness, creates this engagement with the incongruities of dominant styles. In this, 'the other meaning is not simply being "projected" onto the film', as Cohan describes the textuality of camp, but 'has ... a textual materiality of its own'.[45] In this respect, *The Happiness of the Katakuris* prefigures the ironic deployment of the musical in later Japanese films such as *Memories of Matsuko* (*Kiraware Matsuko no isshô*, Nakashima Tetsuya, 2006) or even the mass dance number that concludes Kitano Takeshi's *Zatôichi* (2003).

Katakuris and the Japanese Zombie Movie

As Balmain notes in *Introduction to Japanese Horror Film*, the Japanese zombie film is a relatively recent manifestation: she locates the beginning of the cycle with the enormous global success of the *Resident Evil* video game (originally known as *Biohazard* (*Baiohazādo*) in Japan, 1996). The original game, set in an American city called Raccoon City, followed the exploits of the Raccoon City police department's Special Tactics and Rescue Service (S.T.A.R.S.). It sets a template for the transnational adoption of a Western model of the zombie movie,[46] derived from classic American zombie films, such as *Night of the Living Dead* (George A. Romero, 1968) and *Dawn of the Dead* (Romero, 1978), where the undead are cannibalistic infected humans. As Balmain notes, the 'shuffling zombie in the Japanese zombie film tend to be recycled revenants of the zombie films of the 1970s'.[47]

Wild Zero (Takeuchi Tetsuro, 2000), a forerunner of *The Happiness of the Katakuris* as cult musical (rock 'n' roll) zombie comedy, invokes a self-conscious intertextuality to refer to its generic roots. Trapped in a warehouse filled with heavy artillery, the film's heroes, led by rock band Guitar Wolf (its members Guitar Wolf, Bass Wolf and Drum Wolf), refer explicitly to *Night of the Living Dead* in dialogue. Although this is intended to position the film specifically in terms of its transnational generic referent, the characters end up squabbling about who has or hasn't seen the film. Like *Katakuris*, the film is generically transgressive, combining its musical roots (performances are framed as gigs by Guitar Wolf) with a science-fiction-horror-comedy-romance plot. At the heart of the zombie hordes roaming the Asahi countryside is an alien invasion (Guitar Wolf defeats the invading alien menace by slicing their spaceship in half with his guitar). Leung Wing-fai has argued that the film is 'importing genre, exporting cult'. In a similar fashion to Balmain, Leung contends that the zombie genre is 'trans-cult(ural)';[48] its adoption is 'the result of cultural borrowing from American popular culture and an eclectic mix of generic influences'.[49]

Wild Zero, like other recent Japanese films that revolve around or include zombie tropes, such as *Katakuris*, *Junk* (*Junk: Shiryô-gari*, Muroga Atsushi, 2000), *Versus* (Kitamura Ryûhei, 2000), *Stacy: Attack of the Schoolgirl Zombies* (*Stacy*, Tomomatsu Naoyuki, 2001), *Tokyo Zombie* (*Tôkyô zonbi*, Satô Sakichi, 2005),[50] *Zombie Self-Defense Force* (*Zonbi jieitai*, Tomomatsu Naoyuki, 2006), *Samurai Zombie* (*Yoroi: Samurai zonbi*, Sakaguchi Tak, 2008), *Big Tits Zombie* (*Kyonyû doragon: Onsen zonbi vs sutorippâ 5*, Nakano Takao, 2010),[51] adopts the generic figure of the zombie intertextually as a transnational referent. Whereas the American zombie film transforms the undead zombie figure from Haitian mythology via Romero's films into a symbol of capitalist consumerism, the Japanese zombie movie invokes the figure of the zombie as part of its generic melange (as a revenant rather than a symbol of consumerism). Traditionally, Asian horror films have explored different undead traditions: *yūrei*, the ghostly avengers more specifically linked to J-Horror films like *Ring* (*Ringu*, Nakata Hideo, 1998) or *Ju-on: The Grudge* (*Ju-on*, Shimizu Takashi, 2003); *jiangshi* (*kyonshī*), the hopping vampire, more specifically associated with Hong Kong films like *Mr. Vampire* (*Jiang shi xian sheng*, Ricky Lau, 1985); or *yōkai* such as *nukekubi*, creatures who appear human by day, but whose heads detach at night and feed on human prey (although not strictly undead, these creatures conform to the human consumption shared by undead traditions established in the West that include zombies and vampires, many of which have been imported by Asian texts in cinema, anime and *manga*).[52] The zombie films tend to be highly intertextual, sometimes invoking tropes from 1950s science fiction – both *Wild Zero* and *Zombie Self-Defense Force* feature flying saucers – or explicitly reference more recent trends in global cult cinema, as in *Big Tits Zombie*, which refers heavily to Robert Rodriguez's parodic *Planet Terror* (2007), pastiching its degraded colour-scheme, film scratches, right down to its pole-dancing opening credit sequence.

Rather than referring to more local traditions, Japanese zombie films quote from a global tradition of genre filmmaking. As such, the Japanese zombie film, steeped in knowing intertextuality, camp and transnational meaning, can be situated close to larger trends in recent Japanese culture, such as what Douglas McGray dubbed 'Japan's Gross National Cool',[53] or what Christine R. Yano has referred to as (drawing on McGray) 'the soft power of pink globalization'.[54] Examining the sometimes angry response to Hello Kitty in international discourse, Yano contends that, 'Hello Kitty enacts the transgressiveness of kitsch ... pandering emotionalism and lower-cultural tastes.'[55] Similarly, we might see something comparable occurring in the adoption of the zombie film in Japanese cinema, although without 'pandering emotionalism'. The Japanese zombie film, including *The Happiness of the Katakuris*, pertains toward cult, kitsch and certainly to 'lower-cultural tastes'. However, there is less of a tendency toward readoption by Western mainstreams with the Japanese zombie film, which, despite the recent fascination and growth in production of zombie films internationally, has tended to happen at more marginal levels, at the fringes, often with audiences of Japanese cult cinema or zombie cinema more generally. Hence, the reception of *Katakuris* tends to promote an Other conception of Japan in its 'Only in Japan!' discourse or the recognition of the film generically as the 'zombie musical'. There is no specific backlash, as Yano locates with Hello Kitty, although the films mentioned above adopt tropes, styles or generic iconography of the zombie film – the zombie as mass, infected or as a metaphor of consumerism – encompassing the super flat aesthetic of the 'Gross National Cool' and the re-exportable cult cinema that does not threaten the hegemonic superiority of American cinema economically or stylistically. Rather, the Japanese zombie film fits within existing discourses of a global cult cinema, especially where the 'strangeness' or ideological positioning of the cinema sits between exploitation (through its adoption) and subversion (through its combination with other elements in its hybridity).

Returning to Familiar Ground: Reducing Hybridity to the *Auteur*

Despite this cult textual material and the cultural context of the film, aspects of the critical reception of *Katakuris* tended not to see this as an obvious cult film. Rather, we tend to see Miike offered as the stabilising critical referent, as a means of locating the transgressive pleasure of the film – rather than an 'unhinged' film, we find an 'unhinged' filmmaker. Reviews often use the term *auteur* in relation to Miike, promoting the authorial interpretation of the work, rather than a generic one. So, like the 'discursive' formation of the Extreme viewer, we tend to have discursively formed cultures of taste around the *auteur*. The 'calculated strategy of shock and confrontation'[56] then belongs to Miike, not to this transgressive film, so even though we find the film deviating from conventional notions of genre and style, the cult *auteur* precedes the reception of the film.

Sampling reviews as before, we find the film constructed along taste lines, not in the limited generic terms of before, but specifically in terms of Miike. As one reviewer notes, the film is 'more freaky shit from Japanese auteur Takashi Miike'.[57] Other reviews do likewise, locating the strangeness and subversiveness of the film in terms of Miike's oeuvre. 'Cult Japanese director Takashi Miike subverts genre cinema with this hilariously entertaining Frankenstein's monster mash of horror movie and musical,' is Film4's recommendation,[58] while others also promote the familiarity of the *auteur*'s previous work. As one critic writes, 'For those familiar with more of [Miike's] work ... this is business as usual.'[59] Janice Page of the *Boston Globe* also has recourse to the figure of the cult *auteur*, but adds a stabilising recent Western referent: 'If you thought "Sweeney Todd" presented the gruesome side of hospitality, wait till you see bed-and-breakfast tragedies spun out by a splatter auteur.'[60] So, where other examples of the film's reception point to an ungraspability of hybridity in the film, others highlight the film's cult credentials via reference to the *auteur* as a means of organising that reception. While it is perhaps to be expected in most criticism, where *auteurism* is a default position in popular discourse, the *auteur* here comes allied with a promotion of the cult work's strangeness, its defiance of generic categorisation, and cultural sensibilities. These are contextualised using a homogenising reference to Miike's other work, although *Katakuris* cannot simply be likened to the style, violence and 'splatter' of those other works.[61]

The Happiness of the Katakuris draws on a number of generic and cult cinema traditions. The film hybridises a series of genres, tones and stylistic criteria in a manner that transgresses taste, form and transnational politics. As this chapter has attempted to show, this hybridity has often been collapsed into other critical conceptions. While some reviews, professional and amateur, have grasped the hybridity of the film's approach to genre and style, as well as its camp aesthetic, there has been a tendency to define the film either by the more familiar work of the *auteur*, as a simple hybrid, the 'zombie musical', or as a 'strange' product typical of Japanese cinema ('only in Japan!'). While each of these is problematic, this chapter has demonstrated the discourses behind such critical receptions, and has articulated the ways in which the reception conforms to other criteria of cult film reception and textual defiance of conventions. *The Happiness of the Katakuris* is typical of both cult cinema textuality and is in accordance with recent Japanese zombie films, where those films adopt and transform tropes from international genre cinema in a hybridity that is typical of recent Japanese zombie cinema, where *Katakuris* is an example of both a national genre cinema outside the mainstream, and a transnational cult cinema where the notion of 'nation' is received quite differently.

Notes

1 The issues surrounding the problematic promotion of Asia Extreme cinema has been well covered by a variety of scholars, including this author: Oliver Dew, '"Asia Extreme": Japanese cinema and British Hype', *New Cinemas* 5:1 (2007): 53–73; Daniel Martin, 'Japan's Blair Witch: Restraint, Maturity, and Generic Canons in the British Critical Reception of Ring', *Cinema Journal* 48:3 (2009): 35–51; Chi-Yun Shin, 'Art of branding: Tartan "Asia Extreme" films', *Jump Cut: A Review of Contemporary Media* 50 (2008); http://www.ejumpcut.org/currentissue/TartanDist/2.html (accessed 5 July 2011); Steven Rawle, 'From The Black Society to The Isle: Miike Takashi and Kim Ki-Duk at the intersection of Asia Extreme', *Journal of Japanese and Korean Cinema* 1:2 (2009): 167–84.

2 Dew, '"Asia Extreme"', p. 60.

3 This quote also appears on the back of the Tartan Asia Extreme DVD release, although attributed to its original source in *The Independent*.

4 The Westernised marketing here is using the Western system of name order with given name before family name, while the rest of the chapter retains the Japanese format of family name first, followed by the given name, hence Miike appears as both Miike Takashi and as the Westernised Takashi Miike.

5 Although the film hybridises these normally disconnected genres and styles, it assumes no dimensions of taste categories to their relationship or hierarchisation in the film. While there are several dimensions to the hybridity, including irony, playfulness and budgetary concerns, the film does not privilege one form over another.

6 Umberto Eco, 'Casablanca: Cult Movies and Intertextual Collage', in *Faith in Fakes: Travels in Hyperreality*, trans. William Weaver (Reading: Vintage, 1986), p. 198.

7 It has to be pointed out, however, that Eco's notion of cult is closer to 'cultural', emphasised in his choice of *Casablanca*, as well as his argument regarding the collection of 'cultural topoi' in the cult work. However, his initial positioning of hybridity within the cult film's textual construction is important to retain here, not least to position the critical framework of this analysis.
8 Jeffrey Sconce, '"Trashing" the Academy: Taste, Excess and an Emerging Politics of Cinematic Style', *Screen* 36:4 (1995): 376.
9 I'm indebted to unpublished work by Emma Pett on helping contextualise these assumptions.
10 Bad Movie Guy, 'Bad Movie Guy.com Presents *The Happiness Of The Katakuris*', YouTube, 2009; http://www.youtube.com/watch?v=UpUCALTUyGg (accessed 5 July 2011).
11 Ernest Mathijs and Xavier Mendik, 'Editorial Introduction: What is Cult Film?', in E. Mathijs and X. Mendik (eds), *The Cult Film Reader* (Maidenhead: Open University Press, 2008), p. 1.
12 Mathijs and Mendik, 'Editorial Introduction', pp. 2–4.
13 Mathijs and Mendik, 'Editorial Introduction', pp. 8–10.
14 Joyce E. Boss, 'Hybridity and Negotiated Identity in Japanese Popular Culture', in W. M. Tsutsui and M. Ito (eds), *In Godzilla's Footsteps: Japanese Pop Culture Icons on the Global Stage* (New York and Basingstoke: Palgrave Macmillan, 2006), p. 104.
15 Aaron Gerow has located Miike's work within a metaphorical framework that places his work, thematically and stylistically, within a series of concepts that prioritise hybridity and centrelessness, a lack of firm foundations; these include: 'in-betweenness', 'rootlessness', 'homelessness', 'liminal', 'nomadic' and 'wandering'. While Gerow is more concerned with the existentialism of Miike's characters (fitting with Boss's expanded conception of hybridity), the lack of a coherent stylistic signature and a rootlessness of his films' politics, this 'homelessness' does extend into the generic roots of Miike's work, the frequent difficulty of identifying a single generic strand in his work. For Gerow, these concepts extend into the overarching structure of Miike's body of work, but in *The Happiness of the Katakuris* this is located within the single work which slips easily and often without motivation between generic and stylistic standards. The rootlessness of *Katakuris* is embedded in the single film. Aaron Gerow, 'The Homelessness of Style and Problems of Studying Miike Takashi', *Canadian Journal of Film Studies* 18:1 (2009): 26–37.
16 Tom Mes, *Agitator: The Cinema of Takashi Miike* (Godalming: FAB, 2004), p. 254.
17 Anthony C. Y. Leong, *Korean Cinema: The New Hong Kong: A Guidebook for the Latest Korean New Wave* (Victoria: Trafford, 2003), p. 97.
18 Mes, *Agitator: The Cinema of Takashi Miike*, p. 254.
19 Mes, *Agitator: The Cinema of Takashi Miike*, pp. 29–30.
20 Isolde Standish, *A New History of Japanese Cinema: A Century of Narrative Film* (London and New York: Continuum, 2005), p. 332.
21 Jean-Marie Bouissou, *Japan: The Burden of Success* (London: Hurst & Co, 2002), pp. 257–58.
22 Bouissou argues that paths to recovery were more stable in Japan than those in the West. Despite significant unemployment and the growth of 'cardboard cities' of homeless people, the effects on social stability were less damaging, Bouissou contends, than they have been in the West: 'Social cohesion was therefore less affected, the crime rate and the proportion of poor people among the population remained very low, and no Japanese

town ever witnessed police chasing after rioting demonstrators.' Bouissou, *Japan: The Burden of Success*, p. 275.

23 Colette Balmain, 'Inside the Well of Loneliness: Towards a Definition of the Japanese Horror Film', *Electronic Journal of Contemporary Japanese Studies* (2006); http://www.japanesestudies.org.uk/discussionpapers/2006/Balmain.html (accessed 29 April 2009).

24 *Visitor Q* fits very comfortably into this cycle of work; its aggressive reworking of the traditional structure of patriarchy is achieved by confronting the audience in every conceivable way with excessive content; the film itself is rough, cheap and shot on digital video, giving it a 'fast' and bright aesthetic by which to confront the viewer. With aggressive, exaggerated content, including the rape of a murdered female body, and a protracted opening sequence in which the patriarch of the family, it is eventually learned, has incestuous sex with his teenage daughter, the narrative confronts the nature of patriarchy in the post-bubble economy Japan. The 'syntax of despair' is experienced on a personal level, as the head of the family desperately attempts to assert his diminished masculinity, linked to the loss of his professional identity, upon those around him. The corollary of these attempts is humiliation, including a degrading anal rape by microphone at the hands of group of teenagers he attempts to film for a documentary on youth violence. In response to this, however, he attempts to exploit his bullied son as subject material, neglecting his fatherly responsibility toward him. Although *Visitor Q's* response is at times misogynistic (especially regarding the role of the daughter) and conservatively restores the matriarchal centre of the home, although transformed, the film frequently transgresses 'good' taste in terms of representational content, but not in generic terms in which, as a family drama-comedy, it is entirely consistent.

25 Mitsuyo Wada-Marciano, 'J-Horror: New Media's Impact on Contemporary Japanese Horror Cinema', in J. Choi and M. Wada-Marciano (eds), *Horror to the Extreme: Changing Boundaries in Asian Cinema* (Aberdeen, HK: Hong Kong University Press, 2009), pp. 27–28.

26 Wada-Marciano, 'J-Horror', pp. 25–26.

27 Wada-Marciano, 'J-Horror', p. 33.

28 Darkwish, 'Comment: Your Brains ... er ... Movie Recommendations ... Needed', *Neatorama* (2008); http://www.neatorama.com/2008/05/14/your-brains-er-movie-recommendations-needed/ (accessed 7 July 2011).

29 Gaijin Otaku Gundan, 'BBC 4: Jonathan Ross' Asian Invasion – Japan', *Gaijin Otaku Gundan – My Life With The J-Geek Cult*, 12 January 2006; http://gogblog.wordpress.com/2006/01/12/bbc-4-presents-jonathan-ross-asian-invasion-pt-1-%E2%80%93-japan/ (accessed 7 July 2011).

30 This tendency can also be seen in a video post on the evocatively titled WTF Cinema, a blog that reviews marginal, shocking and irreverent cinema. One episode is devoted to *The Happiness of the Katakuris*, in which the reviewer presents his inability to interpret or present a coherent sense of the film. He prefaces the review, however, by introducing the viewer to Japan, the country that brought us 'tentacle rape, catgirls and bukkake' as a means of contextualising the film as a 'typical' product of this weird, morally problematic country. Mad Centaur Productions, 'WTF Cinema Episode 7 – Happiness of the Katakuris', *Mad Centaur Productions*, 16 June 2011; http://blip.tv/jeffcentaur/wtf-cinema-episode-7-happiness-of-the-katakuris-5282534 (accessed 7 July 2011).

31 Shirely Hsu, 'There's Something About Asian Horror ... Maybe It's the Schoolgirl Zombies', *ASA* (1 August 2003); http://www.asiaarts.ucla.edu/030801/20030801_horror.html (accessed 7 July 2011).

32 Mark Schilling, '"Funuke Domo, Kanashimi no Ai o Misero": A sparkling desperate housewife', *Japan Times Online*, 13 July 2007; http://search.japantimes.co.jp/cgi-bin/ff20070713a3.html (accessed 29 April 2009). As later discussion in this chapter suggests, Schilling is incorrect in this judgement.
33 Scott Morris, 'The Happiness Of The Katakuris: Both funny ha-ha and funny peculiar. Think The Sound Of Music meets Wallace & Gromit with added zombies', *The Oneliner* (19 May 2003); http://www.theoneliner.com/film120.html (accessed 29 April 2009).
34 Nick Dawson, 'The Happiness of the Katakuris', *Empire* (n.d.); http://www.empireonline.com/reviews/reviewcomplete.asp?FID=9001 (accessed 29 April 2009). Dawson here seems to be confusing a genre with a medium.
35 Grady Hendrix, 'Takashi Miike's Crime Wave', *New York Sun*, 26 August 2008; http://www.nysun.com/arts/takashi-miikes-crime-wave/84573/ (accessed 29 April 2009).
36 Ian Conrich, 'Musical Performance and the Cult Film Experience', in I. Conrich and E. Tincknell (eds), *Film's Musical Moments* (Edinburgh: Edinburgh University Press, 2006), p. 129.
37 Conrich, 'Musical Performance', p. 129.
38 Anonymous, '"The Happiness of the Katakuris" Drinking Game!', *Lazydork.com* (n.d.); http://www.lazydork.com/movies/happinesskata.htm (accessed 29 April 2009).
39 Here Conrich is prefiguring Mathijs and Mendik's deconstruction of the textual and political economies of the cult film in their work.
40 Richard Dyer, 'Entertainment and Utopia', in *Only Entertainment* (London: Routledge, 1992), p. 26.
41 Dyer, 'Entertainment and Utopia', p. 26.
42 Dyer, 'Entertainment and Utopia', p 31. Dyer is cautious here to point out that the process of utopian transformation is still one controlled by and focused almost solely on men, of men 'making history'. *The Happiness of the Katakuris* also falls into this pitfall at times, where the patriarchal leadership of Masao is challenged, but never fully undermined. The recovery of utopia at the end of the film is a confirmation of his desire for utopia, rather than a consequence of his agency, although his plan does come to fruition.
43 Susan Sontag, 'Notes on Camp', in *A Susan Sontag Reader* (Harmond: Penguin, 1983), p. 105.
44 Steven Cohan, *Incongruous Entertainment: Camp, Cultural Value, and the MGM Musical* (Durham, NC, and London: Duke University Press, 2005), p. 45.
45 Cohan, *Incongruous Entertainment*, p. 23.
46 The Japanese version of *Resident Evil*, *Biohazard*, was also in English.
47 Colette Balmain, *Introduction to Japanese Horror Film* (Edinburgh: Edinburgh University Press, 2008), p. 115.
48 Leung Wing-fai, 'Importing Genre, Exporting Cult: The Japanese Zom-Com', *Asian Cinema* 22:1 (2011): 110.
49 Leung: 'Importing Genre, Exporting Cult', p. 119.
50 Based on a manga by Hanakuma Yusaku, *Tokyo Zombie* was marketed in the UK by Manga as 'The Japanese *Shaun of the Dead*', although the film bears little resemblance to Edgar Wright's 'zom-rom-com' (see Kelly L. Smith, '"Shaun Of The Dead": The World's First Rom-Zom-Com (Romantic Zombie Comedy)? Film somehow incorporates a love triangle, zombies, music, slackers and vinyl-records-as-lethal-weapons', *MTV News*, 22 September 2004; http://www.mtv.com/news/articles/1491298/shaun-first-

romantic-zombie-comedy.jhtml (accessed 7 July 2011)). While the adoption of the analogy prioritises a sense of hybridity, the homogenisation of transnational hybridity is problematic in this respect, where the analogy is used to familiarise the viewer to the film. If the film does resemble its British counterpart, it is through a buddy-comedy dynamic to the first half of the film. In the US, the tagline 'Premium of the Dead' was used; while this still invokes a generic referent to locate the film within its adoption of the zombie film, the analogy is obviously much less specific and therefore less misleading.

51 Nakano's work has long sat in the *pinku*, video sex comedy tradition, and *Big Tits Zombie* (although the film's title is more correctly *Big Tits Dragon*) is no different, although the film is adapted from a manga by Mikamoto Rei.

52 Susan J. Napier has explored how the vampire myth functions in the context of modernity's questioning of traditions of femininity in Japan and in the West. Napier argues that *shōjō* identity is challenged in a number of manga, including *Vampire Princess*, which, she argues, 'shows a provocative ambivalence toward femininity and tradition' ('Vampires, Psychic Girls, Flying Women and Sailor Scouts: Four faces of the young female in Japanese popular culture', in D. P. Martinez (ed.), *The Worlds of Japanese Popular Culture: Gender, Shifting Boundaries and Global Cultures* (Cambridge and New York: Cambridge University Press, 1998), p. 98). The vampire tradition, especially the drinking of blood, is explicitly linked to femininity in this equation, something which cannot often be said of the zombie film, which rarely locates the monster as a gendered Other, but as a semiotic signifier of global capital.

53 Douglas McGray, 'Japan's Gross National Cool', *Foreign Policy* (2002); http://www.douglasmcgray.com/grossnationalcool.pdf (accessed 5 July 2011).

54 Christine R. Yano, 'Monstering the Japanese Cute: Pink Globalization and its Critics Abroad', in W. M. Tsutsui and M. Ito (eds), *In Godzilla's Footsteps: Japanese Pop Culture Icons on the Global Stage* (New York and Basingstoke: Palgrave Macmillan, 2006), p. 164.

55 Yano, 'Monstering the Japanese Cute', p. 164.

56 Dew's categorisation of the formation of the 'typical' Extreme viewer makes it difficult to see how a cult musical could at all be placed with this typology. Noting a 'heightened marginality' – a category that fits *Katakuris* well in terms of its transgressive stylisation, its cultural content and critical disreputability – Dew sees films by Miike, like *Audition* and *Ichi the Killer* (the stabilising referents for Miike's authorship), positioned for the pleasure of a viewer constructed discursively, where 'the extreme nature of the film texts is emphasised in order to authenticate them as "outlaw" vis-à-vis mainstream taste, and literally dangerous' (Dew, '"Asia Extreme"', p. 60). Where *Katakuris* fits into this discourse is in its adherence to notions of taste. It is not through a simple opposition to good taste that the film cements its placement outside conventional or mainstream taste cultures (as with *Visitor Q*, or Miike's more 'sickening' violent work), but simply through the possibilities of allowing viewers to articulate their own placement within oppositional taste cultures.

57 Ed Gonzalez, 'The Happiness of the Katakuris Film Review', *Slant Magazine*, 19 August 2002; http://www.slantmagazine.com/film/review/the-happiness-of-the-katakuris/413 (accessed 29 April 2009). This review also highlights the hybridity of the film, by referring to it as 'probably the film best equipped to fill that black-camp-karaoke-musical-horror-claymé-domestic-dramedy void in your DVD library'.

58 Film4, 'The Happiness of the Katakuris (2001)', Film4.com (n.d.); http://www.film4.com/reviews/2001/the-happiness-of-the-katakuris (accessed 29 April 2009).

59 Jeremy Heilman, 'The Happiness of the Katakuris (Takeshi [sic] Miike) 2001', Movie Martyr.com, 29 August 2002; http://www.moviemartyr.com/2001/katakuris.htm (accessed 29 April 2009).

60 Janice Page, 'The Happiness of the Katakuris', *Boston Globe*, 25 October 2002; http://ae.boston.com/movies/display?display=movie&id=1741 (accessed 29 April 2009).

61 This assumes that those works were the more accessible Miike films at the time, including in particular *Audition* and *Ichi the Killer*.

12

AMANDO DE OSSARIO'S 'BLIND DEAD' QUARTET AND THE CULTURAL POLITICS OF SPANISH HORROR

Andy Willis

In this chapter I will consider an often overlooked contribution to the cinema of the undead, Spanish director Amando de Ossario's 'Blind Dead' quartet of films which all feature the spectre of resurrected medieval Knights Templar: *La noche del terror ciego/Tombs of the Blind Dead* (1972), *El ataque de los muertos sin ojos/Return of the Living Dead* (1973), *El buque maldito/The Horror of the Zombies* (1974) and *La noche de las gaviotas/Night of the Seagulls* (1975). Whilst far from a coherent sequential series of films, these works offer the opportunity to look at the way in which their take on the idea of the resurrected undead can be read in relation to very specific socio-political contexts; in this instance, a Spain moving towards the end of the dictatorship of General Franco who had been in power since the end of that country's Civil War in 1939. In order to do this, I will consider the films' cautious interaction with Catholicism and their representation of the then contemporary modern world and its encroaching liberal values. I will argue that the creation of the Blind Templars can be read as both a clear response to Spain's strict censorship regime and an increasing anxiety as the country moved towards a state of increased social flux. I will therefore be reading the quartet in the social and cultural context of this changing Spain of the 1970s, a period of great political upheaval and unease about the potential for rapid social change driven by the more open-minded values witnessed in operation across other parts of Western Europe. However, as I offer these readings I am also very conscious that my interpretations are based on some slightly troublesome foundations which in turn offer another important context for any attempted analysis of the films. That is, the fact that there has been a variety of versions of the quartet in existence since they were made, many appearing in diverse cuts that introduce varying levels of sex and violence for different territories, making any absolute assertion of meaning enormously elusive.

Versions that Rise from the Grave: Problems of Reading the Blind Dead

Since their theatrical release in the 1970s, the Blind Dead quartet have become more widely available to international audiences via initially VCR and more recently DVD reissues. As many of these versions were promoted as being more 'authentic' than previous incarnations, this proliferation provides one of the major problems for anyone hoping to definitively read de Ossario's work. As these films, like many other European genre works of the period, were released in different versions designed for a number of countries around the world, depending upon their levels of censorship, any conception of what an 'authentic' version might in fact be is difficult to arrive at. However, whilst this elusiveness may be the case, the search for authentic versions of films such as this quartet has remained something that has concerned horror film fans. Such enthusiasts' search for what they may see as a more 'authentic' product informs Mark Jancovich's influential discussion of the ways in which certain groups of horror film fans distinguish themselves from broader consumers of the genre. For him, this often revolves around films that show extreme violence:

> [M]any of these horror fans privilege as 'real' and 'authentic' those films of violent 'excess' whose circulation is usually restricted (and often secret and/or illegal), and they do so specifically to define their own opposition to, or distinction from, what they define as inauthentic commercial products of mainstream culture.[1]

Elsewhere, Jancovich argues that such distinction also exists within fan groups or cultures, stating that they 'often reserve their most direct and vitriolic attacks for the tastes of other fans – fans who are often dismissed as inauthentic'.[2] Matt Hills refers to this process as one of establishing a sense of 'connoisseurship'.[3] It is these drives within horror fans that tend to privilege the versions of the Blind Dead quartet that contain the most sexual content and that offer the most violent images. However, these more extreme versions were not the ones that would have been released in Spain. This factor challenges the idea that there might be some kind of more 'authentic' version of the sort that Jancovich suggests horror fans prize, as the less violent versions that exist might also be seen as equally authentic as they were the ones released in Spain, and de Ossario and his producers would have been quite aware of the constraints that they were working within in that context. In this way, connoisseurship may be based upon the acknowledgement of various versions rather than simply a championing of the most violent cuts available. It is perhaps better then to simply acknowledge that such films exist in multiple versions with none being particularly more authentic than the others. Whilst these multiple incarnations do make reading the films challenging, as I am attempting to read the quartet in the context of Spain in the 1970s I intend to use the versions that are as close as possible to those prepared for their Spanish release during that decade for my analysis. I believe that it is these that reveal how de Ossario and his producers negotiated state censorship and best support my political reading of the films. So, whilst there may be versions of the films available that contain more violence and sex, these cuts of the films do little to enhance a reading based on the historical and cultural contexts within which they were made and domestically released.

Amando de Ossario, the Blind Dead and the Revival of the Horror Film in Spain

After something of a career false start, due in no small way to the fact that his anti-capital punishment film, *La bandera negra/The Black Flag* (1956), had been supressed by the censors in Spain,[4] Amando de Ossario had established himself as a reliable director of commercial low budget fare such as the westerns *La tumba del pistolero/Grave of the Gunfighter* (1963) and *Rebeldes en Canadá/Canadian Wilderness* (1965). This work led to him being hired to direct the comedy and horror tinged *Malenka: la sobrina del vampiro/Fangs of the Living Dead*

(1969), which was shot in English in Spain and starred Anita Ekberg and which, despite the reference to vampires in its title, was more of a psychological thriller than out and out horror film. By the time de Ossario returned to the horror genre, it had undergone something of a revival in Spain. Indeed, the film made an important contribution to the initial new wave of horror film production in Spain in the early 1970s alongside Narcisco Ibáñez Serrador's *La residencia/The House that Screamed* (1969) and León Klimovsky's *La noche de Walpurgis/The Werewolf Shadow* (1971), all of which proved relatively successful at the domestic box office. This upsurge in horror film production was, according to Joan Hawkins, a response to a particular changing production context:

> When the government tightened restrictions on cheap co-productions, the Spanish film industry needed to find films they could make cheaply and export ... Horror seemed the perfect choice. These films were popular and they sold well. Drawing on the formulae already established by England, Italy and the U.S., the Spanish film industry churned out a large number of Hammer take-offs, psycho killer flicks and gothic supernatural thrillers. Most of the films were European and Euro-American co-productions. Some were filmed outside Spain.[5]

However, the Blind Dead quartet reveal that, in terms of creativity at least, this cycle of Spanish horror production should be considered as much more than simply a collection of knock-offs of other international film industries' successes. As noted earlier, even at their most mundane, they are works that reveal much about the anxieties that were emerging in Spain as the country braced itself for the death of General Franco.

Whilst Spanish cinema did not have a history of horror film production until the late 1960s, the horror genre and Spain may be seen to have a special connection due to the country's long and deep Catholic tradition. This in turn suggests that in order to fully understand the horror films produced at this historical moment in Spain, one must place them firmly in their historical and social contexts whilst still acknowledging their more general generic qualities. A similar argument has been put forward by Peter Hutchings who suggests that the products of British horror film producers such as Hammer Films need to be approached as part of a *national* film culture, that is, one which addresses specifically national issues and concerns. He goes on to argue that, while there may be generic codes and conventions that are reproduced across national boundaries, horror cinema produced *within* particular national contexts will differ in significant ways. For Hutchings, some critical work on the genre abstracts this work from these contexts as it searches for the essential elements of the horror genre. He argues that,

> Attempts that have been made, particularly in their insistence on the genre having either a fixed function or a central core of meaning ... have necessarily lifted films out of the national contexts within which they were produced, thereby evacuating them of much of their socio-historical significance.[6]

In his view, whatever the wider generic codes and conventions are, their actual manifestation at a particular historical moment, within particular national, political and social contexts, can usefully inform any interpretation and understanding of the potential meanings of horror films. With this argument in mind, it would seem vital that in reading the religiously themed horror films produced in a Spain that was heavily under the influence of the ideology of 'National Catholicism', one takes into account the contexts within which such films were made and distributed. With their central figures of the Knights Templar, this would certainly seem the case with the Blind Dead films. Whilst across the films de Ossario posits slightly different myths of origin for the Blind Templars, they are all linked to their partaking in satanic rituals which ultimately lead to their excommunication from the Catholic Church. This fact makes a subversive reading of the films more difficult as they are clearly not anti-clerical as no modern day representative of the Church is presented alongside them.

After having had to convince his producers, who had wanted an already familiar, recognisable and therefore more easily marketable monster such as a vampire or werewolf, that the resurrected Knights Templar would make a suitably frightening focus for a horror film, writer and director de Ossario introduced the Blind Dead to the world in *La noche del terror ciego* (1972). A low-budget production, the film proved successful enough at the domestic box office and found enough audiences internationally for de Ossario to follow it with three

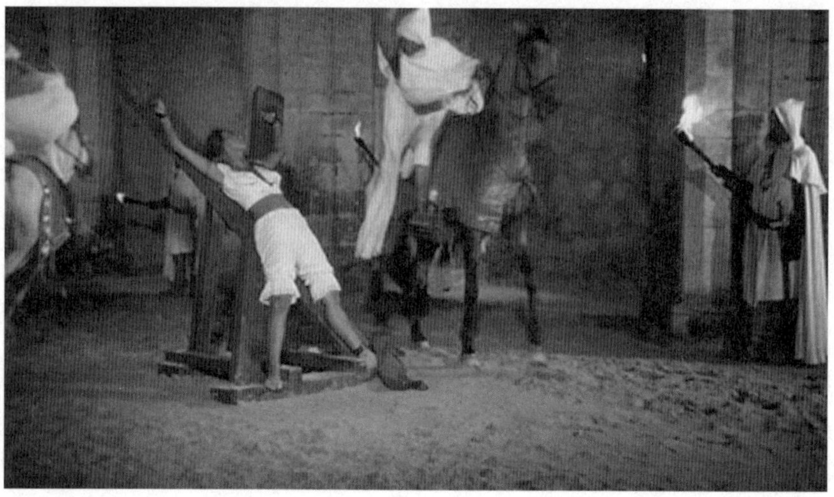

32. Satanic rituals and the Knights Templar – *Tombs of the Blind Dead.*

further works that all featured the Blind Templars: *El ataque de los muertos sin ojos* (1973), *El buque maldito* (1974) and *La noche de las gaviotas* (1975). Across this quartet, de Ossario would revisit his legend of the Blind Dead, often rewriting the mythology of their origins, and creating, in their shambling combination of elements of the mummy and the zombie, one of the most striking contributions the Spanish film industry has made to the international horror genre. Jamie Russell has described them as, 'with their skeletal frames, mildewed cowls, tufts of beard and eyeless faces' being 'distant relatives of the four horsemen of the apocalypse, the ferryman of the Styx, or even death itself'.[7] These Blind Templar Knights are another example of the cinematic undead, coming alive at night and seeking out the blood and flesh of the living and challenging new, modern and liberal ideas and values with their ancient beliefs.

In *La noche del terror ciego*, a group of disgraced Knights Templar, who in medieval times had been killed and left hanging for the crows to pluck out their eyes for taking part in satanic rituals and drinking the blood of sacrificial virgins, return from the grave to terrorise and ultimately devour anyone who stumbles into their derelict village or abbey and stays beyond sundown. This is what happens to Virginia, a young woman who, whilst heading for a vacation weekend in Portugal with her friend Roger and old school friend Bet, leaves a tourist

33. Horsemen of the apocalypse: the 'Blind Dead' in *Night of the Seagulls.*

train in the middle of nowhere when she is reminded of a lesbian affair she had whilst at boarding school. Alone, she comes across the disused abbey and decides to stay the night only to find she is the victim of the risen Templars who, once night falls, rise up from their graves and ride their phantom horses once more. In *El ataque de los muertos sin ojos*, a pre-credit sequence set in the Middle Ages shows the Templar Knights having their eyes burnt out by villagers who had discovered their practice of blood sacrifices. In this contribution to the cycle, the Blind Dead return from the grave in order to take their revenge on the local population who are celebrating their original destruction at a Templar themed fiesta. The modern day villagers end up hiding in their church before one by one they are killed by the Knights until morning arrives and the sunlight unconvincingly destroys them. In *El buque maldito*, the Templars inhabit coffins stored on a mysterious ghost ship that appears in the fog. How they got to the ship remains unexplained, but when a pair of scantily clad models accidently discover it, they become their latest victims, as do those who subsequently set out to find them. In *La noche de las gaviotas*, the Knights' graves are once again to be found in a castle, this time near the sea. In another pre-credit historical sequence the Knights are once more shown undertaking human sacrifices but this time they offer them up to a statue of a frog-like sea monster deity. In the modern era, the inhabitants of a nearby fishing village must sacrifice a virgin each night for seven nights once a year to placate the Blind Templars and keep the village safe. When a new doctor arrives in the community, his do-gooding actions lead to the sacrifices stopping and the Knights attacking the village.

As well as being an original contribution to the horror genre, the figures of the Blind Dead and the films they appear in are also very particular responses to a specific set of circumstances, not least in their engagement with the world of religion. As Spain was a strongly Catholic country, the filmmakers needed to be wary of including any open criticism of the current institutions of the Church within their work. To this end, the Blind Dead are always presented as rogue elements and often referred to across the quartet as the 'Knights from the East', suggesting that maybe they had been under the influence of very un-Catholic forces. So why did the filmmakers go to such lengths to ensure that the films' evil characters could not easily be read as representatives of a Catholic past and the ideas and beliefs of the contemporary Church? The close relationship between the establishment, the Church and the Franco regime begins to suggest answers.

The Catholic Church in Spain

According to Stanley Payne,

> The history and culture of no other people in the world are more totally identified with Roman Catholicism than those of the people of Spain. This special identity stems not so much from the early centuries of Christian experience in the peninsula as from the great historical watershed of the Christian Reconquest.[8]

Following the nationalist victory in the Spanish Civil War, this fervent belief became one of the main ideological weapons of the new Franco regime. Throughout the period of its rule, many of the Church's hierarchy were supporters of the regime and saw its maintenance as something that went hand in hand with their own influence on society. Together the Church and state promoted an ideology that became known as 'National Catholicism'. Payne has argued that this produced 'the most remarkable traditionalist restoration in religion and culture witnessed in any twentieth-century European country'.[9]

As early as the 1940s, the Catholic Church had become hugely influential and General Franco had sought to draw its hierarchy closer to government to consolidate the ideological influence of 'National Catholicism'. The dictator stated this clearly on 14 May 1946, telling parliament that, 'The perfect state is for us the Catholic state. It does not suffice for us that a people be Christian in order to fulfil the moral precepts of this order: laws are necessary to maintain its principles and correct abuses.'[10] By 1953 that had developed to such a level that a concordat was signed between the Vatican and the Spanish state. Payne argues that as the years advanced, the close association between the state and the Vatican also worked to blunt any liberalising tendencies displayed by clergymen. He states that, 'The neo-Catholic tactic adopted in 1945 had produced a bountiful harvest, while the moderating and liberalising changes that the new Catholic ministers had hoped to introduce into the regime had for the most part never taken place.'[11] It was against this backdrop that de Ossario worked on the scripts for the Blind Dead quartet. However, censorship did not only operate on the level of the state; the Church also influenced the aggressive state censorship that existed in Spain during this period.

State censorship of all forms of the arts and media was an important and repressive way for the Franco regime and its allies in the Catholic Church to enforce its ideas. As Núria Triana Toribio has noted,

> Francoism envisaged a nation that was *una*, *grande y libre* (one, great and free) and Roman Catholic, a vision that tolerated neither plurality of ideas nor any negative depiction of the victors. The regime's censorship placed obstacles in the way of national and foreign films that questioned, even slightly, the benefits of this concept of the nation … Censorship was designed to muffle any dissent from the political 'other', through preventing the articulation of alternative ideas or principles in film, television and printed media.[12]

The very particular position of the Church in relation to the state in Spain meant that that any films that focused on religion or religious characters would come under very close scrutiny. The representation of the Church, clergy and religious beliefs were therefore potentially very controversial topics and open to severe censorship. They were also key components in the Blind Dead quartet. De Ossario's creations are variously referred to as practising satanic rituals, eating human flesh and being from 'the East', each designed to clearly explain that they are not representative of the Catholic Church in Spain. The filmmakers also set the first two films of the cycle across the border in Portugal, ensuring that any troubles with the censor they might have experienced could be explained by the non-Spanish location.

Ancient versus Modern: Sexual and Cultural Politics in the Quartet

Across the Blind Dead quartet there are a number of violent scenes and many of these are to be found in the historical sequences that feature the Templars' satanic rituals and human sacrifices. For example, both *La noche del terror ciego* and *El ataque de los muertos sin ojos* contain close-up shots of flesh being slashed and cut before the Knights drink the victims' blood. The latter also includes a shot of a heart being extracted followed by another shot of it being eaten. Marsha Kinder has argued that violent images in Spanish cinema of this period carried the potential to be subversive. She states that,

> Within the Spanish context, the graphic depiction of violence is primarily associated with the anti-Francoist perspective, which may surprise foreign spectators ... During the Francoist era, the depiction of violence was repressed, as was the depiction of sex, sacrilege and politics; this repression helps explain why eroticized violence could be used so effectively by the anti-Francoist opposition to speak a political discourse, that is, to expose the legacy of brutality and torture that lay hidden behind the surface beauty of the Fascist and neo-catholic aesthetics.[13]

It might therefore be argued that the violence in the Blind Dead films brings with it the potential to operate subversively, flying, as it did, in the face of the Francoist censors who wanted wholesome representations of Spanish life to be the norm. However, as noted earlier, the violence of the Blind Dead films is so clearly sourced within the actions of the Templars,